Unmasking Project Management

Unmasking Project Management

The Business Perspective of Information Systems Success

Cassandra Moraveck

UNMASKING PROJECT MANAGEMENT
Copyright © Cassandra Moraveck, 2013.

First published in 2013 by
PALGRAVE MACMILLAN®
in the United States—a division of St. Martin's Press LLC,
175 Fifth Avenue, New York, NY 10010.

Where this book is distributed in the UK, Europe and the rest of the world,
this is by Palgrave Macmillan, a division of Macmillan Publishers Limited,
registered in England, company number 785998, of Houndmills,
Basingstoke, Hampshire RG21 6XS.

Palgrave Macmillan is the global academic imprint of the above companies
and has companies and representatives throughout the world.

Palgrave® and Macmillan® are registered trademarks in the United States,
the United Kingdom, Europe and other countries.

ISBN: 978–1–137–36095–3

Library of Congress Cataloging-in-Publication Data

Moraveck, Cassandra.
    Unmasking project management : the business perspective of
information systems success / by Cassandra Moraveck.
        pages cm
    Includes bibliographical references.
    ISBN 978–1–137–36095–3 (alk. paper)
        1. Information technology—Management. 2. Information technology
projects—Management. 3. Project management. I. Title.

HD30.2.M664 2013
658.4′038011—dc23   2013024480

A catalogue record of the book is available from the British Library.

Design by Newgen Knowledge Works (P) Ltd., Chennai, India.

First edition: November 2013

10 9 8 7 6 5 4 3 2 1

Contents

Figures and Tables

Figures

Tables

PREFACE

AN ADDRESS TO STUDENTS, BUSINESS MANAGERS, INFORMATION TECHNOLOGY MANAGERS, AND PROJECT MANAGERS

Politicians and candidates in government and public sector organizations receive much attention and news report coverage; however, little is known about those managers who work behind the scenes to help in the smooth running of the organization. Information technology (IT) is important to all organizations and little is known about the challenges of project managers. More and more work is being accomplished through the use of computers and information systems (IS).

This book was written because of the various problems that can surface in the management of IS projects and the barriers and challenges that many project managers encounter in their jobs. In response to these concerns, the objective of this book is to provide a broader foundation for business decision makers on IS project management because successful projects span beyond the traditional approaches followed by most MIS departments.

Articles and research literature on how many computer IS projects fail or do not come in within the project budget are easy to find. In some cases, the projects are not considered failures because the systems are actually implemented; however, they do not provide the expected benefits to the organizations and the end users. Often the computer IS are completed and operational but are very time consuming or cumbersome to use, and provide no additional benefits to the organizations over the old systems. In some cases, the initial investment, annual maintenance, and support costs of the IS exceed the benefits; and the organization has to divert resources and management from its core business.

The second problem is that even though there are many articles and books on IS project management, they often miss focusing on the few essentials that all managers should know. Project management consists of core principles that are essential for managing successful projects, but this book offers broader conceptual tools and IS models that will assist those working within the IS environment in public sector organizations.

Public sector organizations are often misunderstood; especially by managers who strive to manage them in the same manner as private sector organizations. Sometimes, personal agendas of top-level managers and the political environment consisting of elected officials create an environment in which many different departments and agencies have authority within its own domain and can present various challenges.

Information technology and business professionals at all levels within the organization need to have some general understanding of IS projects, because technology can impact the entire organization. Good decisions or poor decisions made at the top level of the organization can affect you as a manager, supervisor, and even as a worker. Major decisions about IS need to be a business strategy and need to be supported by the organizational strategy.

This book takes an interdisciplinary approach by unmasking enablers and barriers to IS projects and communicating different ways of working within the environment. Essential IS methods and conceptual tools in this book applies different approaches to project management. The field of IS is dynamic and always changing. Therefore, classroom curriculum needs to evolve to include important concepts to help project managers be successful. This book is for an expanded audience consisting of those majoring in management, such as doctoral students in PhD, DBA, DM, DPA, and DSc programs; graduate students working on a master's degree in an MBA, MIS, MPA, and MS program; advance undergraduates who play a major role in IS key decision making in government and public sector organizations; and IT and business professionals as practitioners.

The fact that project managers encounter problems is not entirely their fault. Though many students obtain college degrees, complete graduate programs, or complete technical or professional development programs, they may not be aware of the real-world problems that exist in IS project management in the public sector and may not understand some important project management principles essential for success. In some situations, there is information overload and students find it difficult to retain the most important concepts of IS project management.

Professional project management practices tend to be lacking in some organizations because managers are assigned to projects because they either have the technical expertise or have an understanding of the business operations but may not have received the appropriate project management education or training. What is even more disturbing is an individual who is unfamiliar with various tasks and activities of software engineering or development and implementation is working as an IS project director or project manager. Accurate knowledge of the kind of problems that exist in organizations is important and then you can work on looking at solutions. Without this knowledge, you are totally unaware of the different situations you may encounter. By unmasking middle space where there is no shared vision there is no pretense of what really happens in public sector organizations.

Central Message

The whole point of this book is to assist you as students or managers at all level in the organization involved in IS decision making and as project management practitioners. To accomplish this, we will examine some core principles of working with IS and introduce some supplemental concepts and ideas that are significant to working within the environment of government and public sector organizations. Chapters 2 through 11 include chapter summaries, review concepts, and discussion questions.

ACKNOWLEDGMENTS

To George, Damond, Sharmaine, Shanta, and Chandra and to those individuals who provided me their own personal experiences in organizations and in managing projects. I am grateful for the experiences I received over the years working in the field of information technology, which provided me a wealth of information that I can pass on to others.

CHAPTER ONE
INTRODUCTION

Technology using computer hardware and software consisting of computer information system programs, databases, networks, and the Internet is essential for providing support to government business operations, public service organizations, and private sector organizations for different kinds of services. Computer information systems assist organizations strategically in how employees accomplish their work, which is important for organizational success. Information systems are important when you consider that the US government provides various types of services to more than 315 million people in 50 states, 3,031 counties, 19,522 municipalities, and 16,364 towns or townships ("Federal, State, and Local Governments," 2012). In 2002, US counties spent 183.2 billion dollars on service delivery (Benton et al., 2007). Governments in many countries are just as reliant on technology for supporting their business strategies.

Are business managers really concerned about information systems projects? Not everyone is concerned with the results of an information systems project implementation unless it directly affects their department or affects how they accomplish their work activities. Some people are concerned when there are problems and they cannot get the reports or the information they need from the information systems. Managers are concerned when they receive complaints from their staff about the information systems not working properly or taking too long to process the information. Many employees are concerned when there are complaints from the public or clients about not being able to have access to government or about when there are complaints about the organizational information systems being too slow when processing transactions for payment of fees. Citizens are concerned when they cannot access online government services.

Other people are concerned when they see their information technology (IT) budgets getting larger and larger with no identifiable benefits. However, most business and project managers are concerned when a project runs over and exceeds the budget amount for the organization or the department, the project implementation is not within the estimated target date, or the newly implemented information system does not provide the perceived benefits and does not increase organizational performance. In addition to these various concerns, project managers need to know how to get the proper level of support and encouragement.

Who exactly is a project manager? And what is a computer information system? For those of you who work as project managers, these are familiar definitions. For other managers, let me answer these questions by describing the definitions in the following section.

Definitions

A project manager is responsible for ensuring that the project is completed on time, within budget, and delivers the functional benefits intended as a result of the project implementation. The project manager manages all of the resources for the project including the team members, ensures that the project plans are developed, and assigns resources for accomplishing the project tasks (Dennis & Wixom, 2003, p. 20).

What is an information systems project? An information systems project is described as "a set of activities with a starting point and an ending point" with the goal of creating a system that brings value to the business (Dennis & Wixom, 2003, p. 30). The value and benefits of the information system should improve an organization's performance.

Many articles do not distinguish between information technology (IT) and information systems (IS). Information technology is defined as "all forms of technology used to create, store, exchange, and use information" (Pearlson & Saunders, 2006, p. 14). Most IT directors and senior IT managers manage all forms of technology in business including hardware, information systems software, operating systems software, utility software, database management systems, the telecommunications network, personal digital assistant (PDA) devices, and the technical staff with many different kinds of specialized skills. In fact, computer system software is a very broad term and can be divided into several different categories.

Information systems are defined as a combination of technology, people, and processes that organizations use to produce and manage the information (Pearlson & Saunders, 2006). Information systems (IS) project managers focus on developing, implementing, and updating information systems (software) often referred to as business application programs, which includes managing the project team and other project resources. An example of an information system is a financial system or an inventory system. Each IS project has specific goals, a start date, an ending date, resources (hardware, software, and personnel), specific tasks, and activities needed to achieve its desired results. Although this book covers many IT management concepts, the main focus is on IS project management in a business environment.

Information Systems Project Management

Another question that needs to be asked is, why write about information systems project management? There are several good reasons and some are economics. Successful IS projects are a good use of taxpayer funds for providing services to the public. Another reason is that all projects have risks. In the many years I have worked in the information technology field in both the private sector and government organizations, I have observed several projects that were successful, as well as managers at various levels of the organizations working together to assist the chief information officer (CIO), the business managers, department IT directors, and the project managers get top-level management support for their projects.

I have read about and seen other projects that have failed miserably, and some that were not considered total failures because they were implemented but did not provide the expected benefits to the organization or improve organizational performance. The ironic thing about this problem is that it keeps happening again and again in all kinds of organizations in both the private and the public sector. Over the years, I have seen some really good project managers put forth their best efforts and face major barriers to their projects. Despite your best efforts, you may have experienced some of your own challenges working within the political environment.

Some people say that you do not really know as much as you think you know about project management until you have actually worked as a project manager. So when planning for this book I use as a starting point looking at some of the challenges that several people have experienced including myself when managing IS projects. My approach is to provide you with a practical book and not overwhelm you with a lot of project management principles, theories, and research models. To accomplish this we will first examine the organization and look at several essential project management principles in Chapters Two and Three. Second, the subsequent chapters cover the nuts and bolts of some important IS models and concepts that will help you to understand some of the enablers to successful IS projects.

The very nature of the political environment in which various departments have authority can pose many kinds of challenges for you as a project manager and even as a business manager. In many cases, few organizations evaluate the success of their IS projects after they have been implemented by surveying those in the organization that are using the system.

Government organizations have elected officials at the central, administrative level of the organization and in various departments throughout the organization. The counterparts to the CEO and top-level executives of private sector organizations in US state government are the elected officials in the state legislatures, legislative committees, and governors (Dufner, Holley, & Reed, 2002). Many US county governments, depending on their size and structure, have an elected board of supervisors. In some county governments, there is a chief administrative officer (CAO) or a chief executive officer (CEO) in the central organization who usually serves in an appointed or elected position. In many organizations, there is a chief information officer (CIO) who reports to the CEO; and the CIO usually manages the organization's central information technology department. In fact, county structures and authority can vary for some states and some county equivalents are parishes (Benton et al., 2007). Many city governments have adopted the council-manager form of government with an elected mayor and city council.

Within many government organizations there are different departments and agencies, each with its own top-level executive who is a department head. Some of them are elected officials voted into office by the citizens and others are nonelected officials appointed to their positions. Another aspect of government is that some departments and agencies can have their own IT director or senior IT manager and technology staff.

Over the years, I was fortunate enough to have the opportunity to manage many different kinds of projects that were successful and worked with many different departments and agencies. I found that some of these projects were very challenging because of conflicting agendas. Perhaps you've had some of these same experiences. I have worked for several different top-level executives, department heads, and elected officials who are department heads and have spent a lot of time observing those working in government organizations.

I find it disturbing in my discussions with IT directors and business managers that many are frustrated while trying to accomplish what they want for their departments or business divisions because they are constantly faced with opposing views from the organization's central information technology department, the CIO, or even from other departments. Therefore, some compelling questions have surfaced from my discussions with other managers over the past few years.

Why do some government and public sector organizations with a CIO at the top level of the organization and a central information technology department work together to support the department heads and their IT directors, and their projects? Why do other organizations with a CIO and a central technology department often appear to be nonsupportive and actually seem to introduce barriers to the department heads and their projects? If you read this book, you will find some of the answers to these questions in the following chapters.

Fundamental Question

To answer the previous questions, this book presents the fundamental question: How do you implement successful information systems and manage the various kinds of challenges you encounter as an IS project manager?

The objective of the information introduced is to describe various approaches to identifying the environment you are working within; identifying enablers and barriers to project success, recognizing and taking charge of things within your control; using conceptual tools and IS research models to help you succeed; and empowering yourself to take charge of your own education, professional development, and growth.

We will examine middle space where there are conflicting agendas and no shared vision. This book describes how you as a business manager, project manager, or IT manager can look at the organization and see things differently. Some people can look outside through a window and see the vast blue sky, the variety of shrubbery with different shades of light and dark green leaves and trees surrounded with smooth, colorful river rocks, and the leaves gently blowing in the cool breeze. They see all types of colorful flowers with butterflies on them being gently sprayed by the sprinklers with crystal-clear water and the wet river rocks glistening in the sunshine.

Other people can look outside through the same window and see the blue sky, see shrubbery and trees badly in need of being cut and trimmed, and see many kinds of insects on the flowers. They see the sprinkler system that is in need of being fixed or adjusted and see river rocks that need to be filled in with more rocks. The latter individuals focus on fixing things rather than viewing the environment in a different way.

The Organization of This Book

This book is organized as follows. Chapter 1 provides a general introduction to IS project management and the importance of IS and its relationship to organizational performance. It discusses the importance of recognizing barriers and enablers to project success within the environment.

Chapter 2 examines project risks, why projects fail or lack functional benefits; describes the concerns of an IT manager, how some citizens of the general public view government organizations; and examines the internal and external forces that can drive changes within the business operations and the IS that support the business. It introduces the importance of the information systems strategic triangle (ISST) that aligns the business strategy, organizational strategy, and information systems strategy. There is a detailed description of the different types of business initiatives such as legislative mandates; the value chain identifying primary and support activities; the different kinds of government programs, products, and services; aging computer systems; and the evolving technology.

Chapter 3 describes the forces of change, how can some visions within the organizations become project missions, the importance of project management and the role of the project manager, software engineering in the business environment, the characteristics of projects; managing IS project priorities, request for proposals, contractual agreements, and the different types of IS.

Chapter 4 describes some common problems in project management. It examines the importance of a collaborative approach to developing and updating information technology standards and policies, project planning, the importance of change control procedures, giving achievement awards, establishing the criteria for excellence, and celebrating and communicating accomplishments. It includes a list of resources and Internet sites for managers to facilitate further the study of IS project management.

Chapter 5 examines the organization and describes real work experiences of IS project managers—the stakeholders in government projects; the concept of centralization versus decentralization, the information technology governance model (ITGM) on decision rights and who has authority over IT decisions, the importance of the economies of scope, and breadth of diversification. It examines the role of the chief information officer (CIO) and the importance of organizational IT standards and policies.

Chapter 6 examines the organizational system concept of middle space when there are conflicting agendas and no shared vision and describes the experiences of those working in middle space. It examines the organization in various aspects of people as tops, middles, belows, and the clients and general citizens. It identifies some barriers and enablers to project success, the choices you can make, mood regulation, distancing strategies, the importance of leadership style, and the influence of politics.

Chapter 7 describes the experiences and choices of others, your educational and professional development, observations of the work environment, and the horizontal and vertical career paths, and women in top leadership positions. Chapter 8 discusses the skills and characteristics of the project manager along with the impact of the organization on IS project management, such as political influences, sense of urgency, resources, the organizational history, the different types of leadership styles, and the importance of being a transformational leader. Chapter 9 describes in detail the ten critical success factors (CSFs) important to project success based on research studies. Chapter 10 describes a quantitative research study of county governments within the United States and reports the results of a successful e-government project. It examines the barriers and enablers to project success especially in governments. Several implications are included as a result of the study, including how department-level executives and their project managers are involved in strong peer relationships and support.

Chapter 11 summarizes the essentials of good IS project management practices introduced throughout the book by reviewing the conceptual tools, research models, and the importance of putting together your own career plans.

CHAPTER TWO

ORGANIZATION AND FORCES OF INFORMATION SYSTEMS CHANGE

There are various forces that drive changes within government and public sector organizations, which impact the business operations and its information systems. There are external and internal forces of change. The drivers of change affect how governments and public sector organizations conduct their business. Changes in the business operations may require changes in how technology is being used to support the business. These may be minor or major changes to the existing information systems or may need to implement new systems.

This chapter explores the forces of change and the relationship to information systems by discussing how people work in an organization, project planning, the organization itself, mainframe computer information systems, business strategy as the basis for successful projects, primary activities and support activities, and the various business initiatives that drive changes. As a project or a business manager, understanding your work environment will help you in making better information systems (IS) decisions for your organization.

Project Risks

Ke and Wei (2006) found that government projects have their own risk exposure and require project management to improve project success. Risks are due to the political environment in which each department has authority within its own domain and may have different agendas from other departments. There may be a lack of interagency cooperation, issues with funding projects, the need to consider citizens' concerns, and the regulatory and legal issues that arise when new projects change how current services are being delivered. Pinto and Kharbanda (1996) report that project failure can be a result of failing to conduct a feasibility study, pushing new technology too quickly, not conducting a risk analysis, ignoring the project environment, and not considering the individuals (project stakeholders) who are impacted by the project.

In some organizations, the information systems (IS) project manager may report to the information technology (IT) director or even a top-level manager or a department head. In other situations, the project manager's position is a temporary assignment. In some cases, the IT manager may be temporarily assigned as a project manager. I have observed some projects that were completed and implemented but did not deliver the expected benefits to the organization. There was no improvement in organizational performance. As a result of the project's lack of success, the IT director, to whom the project manager reported, abruptly left the organization; and there was no further discussion about this person's departure. In some situations, a problem project can actually result in an individual leaving the organization entirely and not by choice. There are similar stories in other organizations in both the private and the public sector. Someone is identified as the captain of the ship and if the ship is wrecked or something disastrous happens, then the captain is usually held responsible.

If you are on the outside looking in at a problem project, you do not know all the problems that surface during the planning and execution stages. Top-level managers do not like surprises when projects are experiencing major problems. Raising the red flag early on in the process is important and keeps the management informed so that other options can be considered immediately to get the project back on track. Yates and Arne (2004) reported in their study that every organization needs to have a risk assessment team and describe the guiding principles for managing IT risks. Sometimes, project managers have trouble with changing the direction on troubled projects because of budgeting and sunken costs (Lee, Keil, & Kasi, 2012).

Sometimes, people have the tendency to focus on why projects fail. Lessons can be learned from reviewing failures. In fact, Pinto and Kharbanda (1996) provide a useful list for students on how to ensure a project's failure. Rather than spending a lot of time focusing on the negatives of what makes projects fail, this book focuses on real experiences and the positive factors that contribute to successful projects and the human factors of project management. You want to have a good understanding of the things you can do to help make a project successful by recognizing the important factors in project management that are not included in many project management books rather than spending your time wondering what went wrong after the project has been completed.

Success and Doing What Works

For some people, the information in this book may or may not be useful. Maybe you are aware of the many challenges involved with managing information system projects through your own experiences. Everyone has a story to tell, and many personal experiences may be relevant to information systems and project management. However, one's own personal experience by itself is not always approached from a detached and unbiased perspective. Suggestions from other managers may be hard to accept when they do not fit your own personal understanding of the problem.

I had a discussion with a top-level manager who said that, in his opinion, research is just a lot of theory and that most researchers lack knowledge about the real work environment. Unfortunately, I have heard this statement many times from different managers while working in government offices. In the discussion, the manager implied that researchers are just theorist and the conclusions are not true to life experiences. A doctorate in Business Administration (DBA) focusing on information systems or other similar doctorates apply research and theories to actual business problems; and those with a PhD focus on original research that is aimed at developing new theories.

Both degrees have their advantages in the academic world and in the work environment because some problems and solutions are not based totally on an individual's own views of "how things should be" for a particular subject or in a given situation, which can be biased. Experience along with education and research in information systems can provide both IT managers and business managers with deeper insight into what works because the approach attempts to give an unbiased, objective, and analytical perspective of information systems project management. Progress can be made in the management and success of IS projects when those with narrow thinking become more open and receptive to others.

Project Management Principles

A good place to start is to discuss the importance of project management and project managers. There are several textbooks that provide information about planning the information systems project and identifying the work breakdown structure within the project plan. Most books I have used in teaching project management courses include the essential principles of project planning, budgeting, putting together the project schedule, allocating the project resources, and controlling and monitoring the progress being made on the project. These core principles are essential to project management but this book provides additional conceptual tools based on research and experiences of those working in the field of information systems. This book takes an interdisciplinary approach to making business decisions involving technology and supplements your knowledge on project management education and training.

Often your education and work experiences enable you to understand the work environment and to understand how to interact with others. Over the years, after learning what works and what does not when managing projects, I wrote the information down in my journal. When I started work on a new project, I was able to apply what I had learned from core principles of project management and my experiences with previous projects; instead of being what is referred to as a should-of, could-of, would-of manager. Observations provide another alternative to interviews because you observe and record the decisions and behavior of other individuals in the business environment. Even when things went poorly in the entire organization as a whole, I would observe and document what happened and continued to review my textbooks on management and organizational behavior. I was able to record a lot of information in my journals. I had the opportunity to observe hundreds of people over the years and could see some of the same problems occurring again and again. There are many experiences that managers will not openly discuss about public sector organizations. However, these experiences are learning experiences and will assist others in managing projects; so my objective is to include them in this book.

As a novice project manager working in government, you can at times have very difficult learning experiences. However, you can gain a better understanding and the others' perspective about management and computer information systems through your own experiences, talking to others, and through your formal education. You can become an expert in your field of work, manage others in achieving the organizational goals and objects, implement successful projects, invest time in yourself, and take advantage of the opportunities that may come your way. You can do this by taking responsibility for your own learning and education.

The technical field is constantly changing and evolving. Staying current with technology, attending classes, professional development courses, or obtaining certifications in specific skills will give you deeper insight and a better understanding of managing IT projects, provide you the ability to make better decisions, solve problems, and give you different perspectives of situations or events.

Let me take a few minutes to discuss the importance of developing your skills. If you are working in the field of technology, continuously learning new skills and working on your own professional development will help you in doing a better job and will prepare you for future promotions. When I was a student, a professor once told me that anyone can take away your job title or even take away your job but nobody will be able to take away your degree, your knowledge, and the positive experiences and relationships with others that you build in life. This information may not be comforting when you do not have a job, but the point he was making is that these are things that last a lifetime. The job market has been tough in the past few years and earning a college degree can be very expensive and is not for everyone; especially if you do not have the financial resources. However, there are other options like getting technical and professional certifications or completing professional training and development pro-grams, and attending training boot camps for learning new skills. The goal is for you to be able to learn new skills so that you can be successful.

Why Projects Fail or Lack Functional Benefits

Now let's examine why some projects fail. Many people have their opinions on why projects fail or why they do not provide functional benefits to an organization to enhance organizational performance. In fact, there seems to be some debate on this subject in literature and people have many dif-ferent answers to this question. You probably your own opinions based on your involvement with different projects. There is no single reason why projects fail or lack the functional benefits. There can be many different reasons such as:

- the business strategy,
- the project sponsors,
- the technology,
- the users of the system,
- project management and leadership style, and/or
- the availability of resources.

Often, failed systems do not suffer failures from one single problem but from a combination of multiple problems or failures. You as an IT manager or project manager need to recognize that computer information systems can introduce changes in how people work, and these kinds of changes can be incremental or can be major. There are many factors that promote project success and knowing what is important helps to reduce the risks of unsuccessful projects.

A project manager is responsible for managing all of the resources of a project in order to implement a successful computer information system and must be aware of all the factors including learning experiences that can promote success. That is why in many college courses you may hear that the professor or lecturer brings real-world experiences into the classroom.

About the IT Manager

This section has a lot to say about the environment that managers work within when managing information systems projects. I had an interesting discussion with Lee, an information technology manager, who is responsible for an IT division within a medium-sized government department. Lee is a novice IT manager who has been in his current management position for approximately seven months. He was asked by the assistant department head to provide him estimates for a new project. The information about the project was discussed in a one-on-one meeting.

Lee is responsible for assigning small to large-sized projects to his technical staff along with project management assignments. If the project is determined to be very large in scope exceeding 12 months, then he will assign resources to the project, and in some situations assume the role of a project manager and make recommendations to top-level managers within the department for the additional project resources and team members, if required.

Lee was asked to provide the project estimates within six weeks so that the top-level management had an idea of the effort in terms of project costs and personnel hours. He was told that the department was under time constraints because of the annual budget cycle and that the estimated project costs have to be included in the upcoming fiscal year's proposed budget estimates for the department.

Although he is familiar with the computer information system that the department plans to replace, Lee feels that there is a lack of detailed information on the business initiative that is driving the change. He is concerned about the project mission that was just generally defined. He wonders how the other business managers normally involved in the information systems decisions in the department feel about the changes in the system and what the department will be able to do differently after the project is completed. He questions what benefits the information system will provide to the department as a whole after the system is implemented, but he received only general information that was not very specific.

Lee knows that he has to meet with his technical staff to develop the estimates and is concerned about their response to the request. If he did provide the project estimates based on the information provided to him, he feels that he will be held responsible for the project estimates and target dates for completing the various tasks even if the scope of the project turns out to be much larger than estimated. A larger scope in the project will require that the project hours to be revised, which could possibly increase the project cost and impact the completion date.

Lee gave a serious thought to his options and was wondering what he should do if the project turns out not be a good fit for the department. He knows that if the project is not successful he will be held responsible by the top-level management. He is also concerned about the list of projects that were previously prioritized in the meetings he attended two weeks ago with the assistant department head. He questioned how this new project will impact his leadership in getting his technology staff to complete all the other projects on the list if he has to pull some of these same people from the current project assignments to be on the new project team for the large project. In addition to these concerns, Lee periodically faces challenges from the organization's central IT department and the CIO and his assistant, the CTO, on IT standards and policies that seems to create barriers to some of his department's projects.

You are probably thinking why discuss the concerns of this IT manager. The reason is that there is something inherently wrong with this project management approach. Often novice managers do not recognize the environment that contributes to successful projects. Lee is working in what is referred to as *middle space* and does not even know it. This is a space that pulls a person between others and he, obviously, should be concerned with the request from the assistant department head.

Lee needs to be empowered to do the things he needs to do as an IT manager or as a project manager. He should have a better understanding of the environment he is working within and how to find solutions to some of the challenges that arise. Taking all of this into consideration, an important question that needs to be asked is, What information systems management principles and concepts are missing that need to be understood and implemented, which can contribute to Lee being successful as a manager?

Lee told me that he has other concerns about the organization itself. He feels there is no clear career path for employees to be promoted to the first-level and even the top-level IT management positions. He said that sometimes he feels frustrated with the organization as a whole. Another question that needs to be asked is, Is there a career path for being promoted into first-level and top-level management positions within the organization?

Now that several questions have been asked, this book will help you in identifying the many important factors and conceptual tools and research models in project management; give you additional information to help you succeed as a project manager and even as a business manager, help you to manage working in what is called middle space, give you insight into available options and choices, and help you in developing your own personal learning, career development, and growth.

The Importance of How People Work

Let's first start by looking at the organization. A topic that often managers have the tendency of overlooking is the importance of how people perform their work in organizations. An understanding of how people perform their work activities is important when designing information systems. As a student in college, one of the courses that I considered most valuable was about organizations as information processing systems. The professor's goal was to get students to think about the organization where they work as information processing systems even "before" technology, computers, and information systems are developed and implemented within an organization.

Many manual business processes exist in government organizations within the departments and agencies and their divisions and business units long before technology was acquired and implemented to the support business. In fact, "every organization is composed of subsystems" and these "subsystems contribute to the common purpose of the organization" as a whole (Ahituv, Neumann, & Riley, 1994, p. 78). An understanding of the organization and its business procedures and business strategy is important for implementing new information systems. This understanding gives a manager deeper insight on how technology can be used to support many activities and tasks within the organization, which will help others perform their jobs and provide the necessary services.

In the field of technology, computer systems analysts examine how people work and examine the kind of activities they perform. The same approach is taken while designing the information system that will assist them in accomplishing their work. Using technology to find different approaches to accomplish specific tasks and activities is supposed to help those using the system in doing things better in different ways and can result in incremental changes or in the major redesigning of how people work.

Do information systems make people more productive? To generalize and say that all information systems makes people more productive can result in many debates; mainly because productivity is mostly measured by inputs and increased outputs. There is still some debate on the value of IT on organizational performance (Melville, Kraemer, & Gurbaxani, 2004; Wang & Berman, 2001). Many people feel that you must weigh the benefits of IT vis-a-vis the costs associated with the technology investments. Determining the benefits means you need look at the use of technology in an alternative way. In many cases, information systems may make people more productive through the use of technology and increase organizational performance because of the different types of benefits resulting from an information system's implementation.

As a manager, you want to be able to recognize that benefits can mean many different things to different groups. Benefits can mean eliminating errors and providing more accuracy, improving quality, reducing time spent on certain activities, being able to have one or two reports to read that contain all the required information you need instead of reading seven or more reports, reducing the cost of doing business, reducing the handling of large volumes of paper and documents, increasing productivity, conveniently getting access to online information; and a host of other benefits. Enhancing organizational performance involves examining the existing procedures and changing those that are inefficient or time consuming. The IS benefits are best defined by the organization, the departments, and agencies within the organization, and their various business units. The technical benefits are best defined by the technology staff.

How people work in an organization affects the design of computer IS. You want to take an interdisciplinary approach to solving business problems using technology. Even if an organization is considering purchasing a commercial, packaged information system, there is still the need to identify the functions of the information system under consideration and how people work and their activities.

Several commercial, packaged IS software can be purchased for different types of IS but they still need to be customized using software parameters or modified in some way to fit the business strategy of each organization. Commercial, packaged software is advantageous in that that it eliminates the time that systems analysts and computer programmers spend on developing, coding, and testing the information system programs; however, reviewing the functionality of the software is important to supporting the overall business strategy and work activities of the organization.

The Public View

Another topic for you to think about is the citizens and the general public that government or your organization serves. A few individuals who do not work in government commonly tend to view each government organization (i.e., state, county, and city) as a single entity or a single business. In reality, each government organization has many departments and agencies that function as diversified entities with different business goals and objectives and provide different types of services; each department or agency is highly specialized in its business operations. Each individual government organization (i.e., state, county, and city) has its own budget that is controlled and approved by elected officials positioned at the central, top, and administrative level of the organization, and by top-level managers who are department and agency heads in organizations. Each department or agency within the organization puts together its *proposed budget* for the upcoming year and each is expected to operate within the *final budget* that is approved by those in the top-level central administration.

So why do I go in depth about the departments and agencies? Because, as an IT manager, project manager, and even as a business manager, recognize that the departments and agencies can be highly specialized with the programs that they administer and the services they provide to the public. They have authority over their business strategy and their information systems projects and which ones they will fund and work on for each budget year.

My experience with government includes working within an organization consisting of 37 different departments and working with department heads, a few of them are elected officials responsible for departments or agencies. Departments and agencies within the organization have many different work groups. How groups work actually influences the design of the information system software. In addition to group influences, it is important that you consider the politics that influences the relationships between people and groups. Successful project managers never separate the human factors from the technology solutions because how organizations and how people work shape the design and the use of computer information systems.

In fact, workgroup systems often referred to as office productivity systems, such as e-mail, word processing, spreadsheets, presentation software, and individual database applications, facilitate communicating, sharing of information, and integrating of information among various workgroups. Some of these systems like individual database management systems (i.e., Microsoft Access) are developed by end users to meet the needs of the individual or small work groups in contrast to information systems developed by IS professionals for the organizations (Doke & Barrier, 1994). Technology software can offer organizational benefits in *how it is used* as long as the end users of the software system do not become overwhelmed with the volume of communication and sharing of information that it overshadows the other important activities of the organization. Often, organizational behavior has a strong role on system design and use.

I realized that if the end users find that a computer information system helps them in some way in getting their job, tasks, and activities done effectively and efficiently and you integrate the system tasks with the procedural processes within the organization, many would support the technology decisions that help change how they work using computer technology.

As a project manager, you must acknowledge and recognize that the business strategy is the main driving force for implementing information systems and it should be supported by both the organizational strategy and information systems strategy with the goal of making the business activities more beneficial and efficient. The functions and features of the system need to benefit the organization. In fact, technology is everywhere. The use of technology and information systems should help to improve overall organizational performance. A useful approach is to consider the managers working in private sector companies with a goal of profits maximization. They think in terms of the business strategy, which is their primary business function, and is supported by their organizational and information systems strategies. This relationship exists with successful IS projects. As an IS project manager in government, balancing these three strategies in the organization would be the most important approach.

Project Manager Assignments

Research by Rosacker (2005) on state government reported that states have chief information officers (CIOs), but the projects are normally organized around functional units or departments that provide a particular type of service. Project managers may be temporarily or permanently assigned to business units or departments and the "IT managers are often selected once and only once to manage such an endeavor" Rosacker (2005, p. 66). As a result, some project managers may have limited project management experience; therefore, factors important to project success are useful to both experienced and inexperienced managers. Many government organizations determine the project managers' assignments based on their IT governance model similarly, which is the distribution of IT decision-making authority within the organization (Weill & Ross, 2005). Chapter 5 discusses information technology governance in greater detail.

Several years ago, while working on my first computer job, I spent the first three years on IS in the private sector as a programmer analyst for a company that worked on federal government contract projects. There was an IT manager who worked for the company that was very successful with his projects. I often talked to this individual and observed this person's management style. This individual eventually became my mentor. It is always good to see one who is successful and find a mentor who can support you in your career. I eventually left the corporation and accepted a position in county government and worked as a computer programmer and was subsequently promoted to a computer systems analyst.

Much of my time was spent in interviewing and meeting with clients who were users of information systems and writing system design specifications for the programmers to code the application programs. Little did I realize, at the time, that government organizations, including states, counties, and cities, are continuously faced with external and internal forces of change, which can have a major or minor impact on how organizations work and their daily business operations. To be an effective manager, you want to be aware of both the political and public influences on project decisions.

Novice Managers

If you are a novice project manager without a lot of on-the-job experience, you probably have the idea as I did that everything should work just like the textbook approach to projects using systems analysis and design methods and the project management information you learned in your college courses or training programs. You will be able to use the core principles from project management courses but will soon find out that although the information you learned are very valuable to you not everything is neatly done as outlined in the textbooks. You may already have had these kinds of experiences as a project manager and as a manager.

There are a few things missing in textbooks and I call these human factors in project management that affect organizational change supported by the use of technology. Many novice managers are not aware of the dynamic environment of government and public sector organizations. Organizations are dynamic, that is, they are always changing. The following sections examine some of these changes.

Forces of Change

Let's start by looking at the organization differently. A good approach is to look at the organization where you work and consider the forces that impact the environment. Some of these forces such as aging computer systems, evolving technology, changing business requirements, and legislation can impact how people work and the information systems that support the organization. Legislative changes require government organizations to change their business procedures to be aligned with the legislative mandates and thus can impact the information systems. Many changes become business initiatives that affect the business operations and the information systems.

Another factor that impacts change is the growth in population in some US regions over the past ten years; and federal and state budget cuts have forced the government organizations to find more cost-effective approaches to providing programs and services to the general public. In fact, the population growth in some counties and states creates the demand for more governmental programs and services from many of the large, medium, and small departments and agencies within government. The external forces of change, in addition to federal and state budget cuts, compel many government organizations to look at continuous changes. Some of these changes can be incremental and others can be major.

Mainframe Computer Information Systems

Prior to the use of desktop computers for personal computing needs, high-capacity mainframe computers were used for various information systems consisting of application programs and was common to many government organizations in the early days of computing. At one time in government organizations, the information systems were highly centralized and an organization's central IT department hosted and supported the business systems for many of the departments and agencies in its central IT data center. Many were the large departments within government and that used mainframe computers because of its input and output capacities and its large auxiliary storage (Ahituv et al., 1994). Early mainframe systems presented challenges because their database systems lacked the ability to access, share data, and integrate with web-based systems. These systems required major customization efforts, expenses, and legacy systems could not share essential data (Nelson & Gentry, 2005). Newer systems that use relational database management systems are more flexible and can be economical to customize or make changes.

Technology keeps evolving over time with the proliferation of personal computers, laptop computers, tablets, smartphones, physically smaller computers originally referred to as mid-range computers with higher capacity and capabilities, application servers, database servers, database management systems and commercial, packaged computer software. This evolution of hardware and software provides an option for many departments to move their computer application systems off the central mainframe computers located in the organization's central IT department into their own departments close to the business divisions using more cost-effective hardware and software with the ability to prioritize their own projects and use technology differently for solving business problems.

In addition to the decentralization of the computer information systems, more and more workers over time are given computers to accomplish their work. There is no need to go to the office clerical support staff to have reports, memorandums, correspondence, and documents typed on their word processors. As a result of decentralization within some government organizations, some departments such as the department of public social services (DPSS) at the county level moved to a state system as a consortium with other counties sharing the information system hosted by one of the several different counties. Other county departments moved their information systems off the central mainframe computers to share in the use of state or other county systems.

The central, organizational IT department in many government organizations must try to make the technology solutions cost-effective for the remaining departments to continue using their data center hosting services and they must evaluate their own strategy. The changing environment and federal and state budget cuts can have an impact not only on state departments but also on counties and cities, and there may be no additional funds to cover the higher cost of doing business.

The Business Strategy

Internal and external forces actually drive changes in government and public sector organizations, such as implementing new information systems or making major changes to the existing information systems. The business strategy is important to an organization's project success.

Next let's take a few minutes to examine the importance of strategy. Strategy is defined as planning and directing of whatever you are trying to accomplish, such as projects, events, or operations. Accordingly, your strategy needs to be planned, tactical, and well thought out or calculated. One of the major reasons that projects run into problems or do not provide the functional benefits to the organization is because they are not driven by the business strategy. In fact, business managers at all levels of the organization who rely solely on the CIO, IT directors, and IT managers to make information system decisions and to make changes to the business strategy are actually giving up their authority over business decisions (Pearlson & Saunders, 2006). Business managers who are involved with IT planning can have a positive impact on resources for the project, quality of the project plan, and IT organizational performance (Kearns, 2007). In fact, the project sponsors are normally the business managers and not technical managers.

Pearlson and Saunders (2006), in their study on technology and management, described the importance of the *information systems strategic triangle* (ISST) as a framework where the "decisions regarding applications, hardware, and other IS components are all driven by the firm's business objectives, strategies, and tactics" (p. 20). Vague or unclear reasons for working on a new project and the lack of key project sponsors outside of the IT department are warning signs and need to be recognized and acted upon. The business strategy is a vision and roadmap of where a business wants to go and how the business expects to get there in fulfilling the vision.

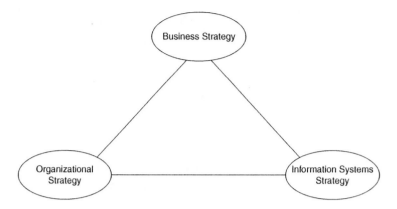

Figure 2.1   The information systems strategic triangle (ISST).
Source: Adapted from Pearlson and Saunders, 2006.

There are three key points in the ISST: the business strategy, organizational strategy, and information systems strategy. The *business strategy* is located at the top of the triangle (see Figure 2.1).

Business and technical managers need to recognize that "successful firms have an overriding business strategy that drives both organizational strategy and IS strategy" and firms are driven by the "business objectives, strategies, and its tactics" (Pearlson & Saunders, 2006, p. 20). The organizational strategy is the *general direction* in which the organization chooses to move to achieve its goals and objectives. The information systems strategy is a support strategy. Successful organizations are successful because there is a balance among the three different strategies.

Business Initiatives

The results of internal and external forces of change create business initiatives within the organization, which can drive changes and can have an impact not only on the business but also on the information systems that support the business operations. Think about the organization and these different kinds of business initiatives. There are several business models that apply mainly to private sector organizations such as (1) Porter's five forces model, (2) value chain, (3) supply chain management, (4) customer relationship management, (5) business intelligence, and (6) integrated collaboration (Haag, Cummings, & Phillips, 2007).

However, only some of these models apply to public sector organizations that are not-for-profit. In what way do they differ? Government organizations differ from the private sector because business initiatives can be driven by other forces such as legislative mandates, that is, changes in laws, the value chain, changes in the business requirements, the need to update or replace aging systems, and evolving technology. To improve managing the information systems environment, you want to be aware of the many different forces of change within an organization and its impact on the business operations and the information systems. The following sections examine some of the different business initiatives.

The Value Chain

Several studies discuss Porter's *value chain*. The value chain model supports the type of activities that "create, deliver, and support a company's products and services" by dividing the work activities into two categories (Pearlson & Saunders, 2006): (1) primary and (2) support.

Primary activities are the organization's core business activities and are the reasons why the organization exists. Support activities within an organization are technology, human resource management including employee recruitment and training and monitoring performance; the general administration activities often referred to as overhead functions of accounting and finance; and the groupware applications and activities. Every organization has these types of general administration and overhead activities and functions. The value chain is a way to view the organization as a series of processes, and each of the processes adds value to the organizations products and services and is a way to identify information technology opportunities. The value chain in the private sector for-profit organizations can be used as an approach to increase or maximize profits. Both primary and support activities can add value and if the total cost of added value is less than what the customer pays, there is profit. The value chain enables an organization to analyze where the managers can add value to its products and services and where to reduce costs (Haag et al., 2007).

You are probably wondering what kind of relationship the value chain has with government and public sector organizations. How does the value chain apply to public sector organizations whose goals are not focused on profit? The value chain applies to its products and services and to the programs that the organization administers.

Government Programs, Products, and Services

The *value chain* in government and nonprofit organizations can be useful in identifying opportunities for the organizational programs, products, and services for the general public and clients the organization serves. You want to have a clear sense of the people you serve. State, county, and city government agencies are required to provide various kinds of services such as hospital and health care programs, mental health services, law enforcement and police protection, fire services, libraries, voter registration, assessment and collection of property taxes, court administration, public welfare and social services programs, parks and recreation, planning and zoning, and many other types of services that interface with the public. The focus is not on profitability. These public sector information systems support the daily operations of the organization and its many departments.

Although there is a need for government supplies and services, human resource management, technology, and administration, the main goal is to fulfill legislative mandates and to provide services to the public. Many of these other types of public services are mandated by federal and state legislation (Benton et al., 2007). In fact, most people do not think about government in relationship to its products. Many products that government departments and agencies produce are the results of the different types of programs and services they provide the citizens and general public. For example, in US county government, there can be various kinds of products such as birth certificates, marriage licenses, death certificates, tax bills, many different kinds of permits, many types of licenses, recorded deeds, parcel maps, and thousands of other types of documents and reports. There are a host of specialized services from state, county, and city governments. Another important fact is that government and public organizations have no control over the growing number of citizens they must serve and provide various products and services. Population growth and movement of people between geographical (states, counties, and cities) areas can create increasing demands on government services.

In the value chain, the sum of each process provides a total value greater than each individual process. Managers can identify the processes that add value to the organization, which results in high-quality products, reduces process times, and increases client and public services. Once the value-added services have been identified, processes that reduce value need to be identified in order to correct deficiencies. Organizations can choose from a variety of technology solutions ranging from computer hardware, operating systems and application system software, mobile devices such as phones and PDAs, and various uses of the Internet and company networks that add value (Haag et al., 2007).

In government, the primary activities of the value chain can be different programs, products, and services offered by many departments and agencies and they are supported by unique information systems such as the sheriff's system, the district attorney's system, the county recorder's systems, the hospital's system, the department of public social services' system, the treasurer-tax collector's system, and many other departments. Most of these departments have their own *unique* business goals and objectives because they largely operate as unique businesses.

Managers need to identify the value-added processes that benefit the organization and the individual departments (Pearlson & Saunders, 2006). A good example of how the value chain benefits an organization is electronic data interchange (EDI) system for purchasing or procurement purposes. Government integration originally started with interorganizational systems and EDI systems. Project managers of EDI systems projects provided a clear definition of functional success in terms of business value and a vision of the organization after the project had been completed. Ngai and Gunasekaran (2004) identified quick response and access to information, reducing data reentry, reducing paper work, improving customer service, fewer errors, flowing of information between partners, reducing manpower, reducing administrative costs, and improving customer relationship as the perceived benefits of EDIs.

Several studies express the need to establish a clear vision of what the organization should look like after the information system has been implemented. Lam (2005) reported the importance of shared goals and objectives when e-government projects involve multiple government agencies. EDI is able to link separate companies and organizations together for processing purchasing information. Many EDI studies identify top management support and project planning along with perceived organizational benefits as critical success factors to implementing EDI (Ngai & Gunasekaran, 2004). The emergence of the Internet, networks, information systems, and other technologies provides added value through business process reengineering (BPR); governments provide different approaches to service delivery (Ahadi, 2004) at a cost lower than the original EDI systems.

Legislative Mandates

A few may be surprised that both business managers and project managers do not always have a choice in determining the estimated completion date for mandated legislative projects because legislation can mandate what changes to bring about and the date on which these changes must be implemented, and this can affect how an organization conducts its business because of the changes in the law.

Legislators introduce bills into government affecting how government organizations handle their business operations and activities. The changes can be minor or major to the business operations and, subsequently, impact the computer information systems that support the business. For some of these projects, additional project team resources must be assigned to the projects for timely completion. Mandated changes due to legislation are business initiatives that may or may not add value to the organization. Because of legislation, governments operate in a dynamic environment, which means there are frequent changes. These types of mandated projects can result in huge penalties and fines to the organizations and to the departments or agencies if not implemented by the mandated due date. Legislative mandated projects often take priority over other types of projects and the appropriate amount of funding and project resources including the technical staff that should be assigned for timely completion.

The Need for Change

The need to embrace continuous change in government organizations and their departments, and many other public sector organizations, can be influenced by population growth within a state, county, and city. Earlier I said that population growth, immigration, and suburbanization can create the demand for more governmental programs, products, and services and can impact the operations in different ways. Information systems can assists organizations in providing services to more people. Another example is the requirement to expand various street names and address sizes to longer street names, which can require changes to the information systems and the databases. These requirements can be because of new residential buildings and streets. The requests from the end users of the system may require expanding the zip code size from five digits to nine digits or expanding other field sizes in the programs and databases to support the business needs of the organization. These types of changes become business requirements and the changes must be made to support the business operations.

Aging Computer Systems

Aging computer information systems can drive changes, which may or may not result in added value to an organization. However, the changes will keep the organization's information systems up and running in order to support the daily business operations of the organization.

A good example is the Y2K problem. Before Y2K, many computer programs were not able to handle a four-digit year. Then, computer programs and databases storing information were originally designed with a two-digit year; therefore, the programs were originally developed with the logic of assuming that the two-digit year of "99" was actually 1999. If the year was not expanded to four digits, the Y2K would appear in the computer information systems as "00" and would be handled as "1900" in the computer programs and in the databases. Some people tend to think that the year Y2K problem was exaggerated and many did not know what was taking place behind the scenes to avoid system failures. The reason why there were few disasters is that there was a lot of planning within organizations. There were numerous newspaper articles on the importance of the computer information systems being modified to handle the change of the century.

The Y2K information systems project was not a major undertaking for some organizations, but for others the project was a major work effort, mainly because of the design of some of the older computer system programs. The older systems were not designed to separate the computer program logic from the database logic (for retrieving and storing the information) and from the client (user) interface logic. In addition, the older databases were not designed as relational databases (tables and rows), which were easier to change a two-digit year to a four-digit year.

As a result of Y2K, many computer programs and computer databases could not be easily expanded from two digits to four digits without significant costs to many organizations. Many organizations were able to change their computer system programs before the year 2000 to avoid any problems. Other organizations opted to install new systems called enterprise resource planning (ERP) systems.

The Y2K technical problems contributed to the radical design of business processes using enterprise resource planning (ERP) software. Some businesses had disparate systems in different locations, divisions, and departments and wanted an integrated solution. Many private sector businesses and organizations did not have the support from top-level management to plan and fund their Y2K projects within a reasonable time frame so they had no other alternative.

In some cases, the modification for Y2K was very costly and provided no additional benefits. However, given the choice of either staying or not staying in business some managers felt there were no other choices available to them for resolving the problem. The ERP vendors sold their products as a quick Y2K solution promising many benefits to businesses and organizations by having standardized modules and centralized databases. However, many IT managers did not realize the ERP systems drive the business strategy rather than support the organization's business strategy, which can result in major changes to an organization's business procedures and can increase project risks. Since ERP was so popular, other IT managers thought that the information systems software would provide greater benefits to businesses that did not have the ERP software systems (Pearlson & Saunders, 2006).

In some situations, popularity of the software drove the decision to implement ERP software. Orfali, Harkey, and Edwards (1999) report that ERP systems provide approximately 80 percent solution and the balance

20 percent must be implemented to fit your business strategy, which can cost more than what was spent on the entire ERP system. In fact, ERP systems originally evolved from materials requirement planning (MRP) software in the 1970s that focused on "internal production planning, calculating time requirements components, procurement, and materials planning" (Haag et al., 2007, p. 323). Often, an ERP software system is a costly alternative and requires a radical change to the business processes. There is some debate in literature over the benefits of ERP because some studies report that 50 percent of ERP projects fail (Morris & Venkatesh, 2010; Sonde, 2008). However, other organizations found that ERP systems add value to the organization and its business operations (Bajaj & Bajaj, 2010). Some organizations can benefit from ERP systems because the software system supports their business strategy by supporting their business goals and objectives.

Evolving Technology

Another significant factor is that technology evolves over time with the proliferation of newer designed personal computers, laptops, iPads, application and database servers, the Internet, and commercial software, cell phones, and numerous kinds of personal digital assistant (PDA) devices. This evolution of hardware and software provides a means for the departments to do business differently and bring the technology closer to the business operations. As standards were completed in 1996 by the World Wide Web consortium, Internet use continually grew. Over the past 15 years, many changes have taken place with the convergence of the telecommunications industry and internet technology that essentially removed barriers to communications.

Telephone services, information technology, and cable television services are no longer seen as separate industries. The boundaries of telecommunications, media, and information technology have dissolved because existing technology and the Internet have evolved to a point that supports all of this technology. In comparison to the technology years ago, the Internet can carry telephone, data, and cable television, which are contributing to the disappearance of boundaries. Changes in regulatory restrictions have also supported convergence (Housel & Skopec, 2001).

Telecommunications is defined as being able to connect to information using networks and information systems. For many organizations, telecommunications creates networks to support business systems by connecting these systems to users, other businesses and agencies, and to customers (Housel & Skopec, 2001). The network infrastructure is important to both private sector and public sector organizations because the network creates a path for communication and information sharing between the various computer systems and the end users. The essential components of a network consist of a variety of media that facilitate transferring voice and data and are comparable to either a residential two-lane street or multiple lanes on a highway. Digital technology enables the transmission of text, images, photos, music, and voice. The Internet is structurally a network of networks (Housel & Skopec, 2001).

Today, computer network transmission speeds have dramatically increased over existing telecommunication lines and wireless communication devices for high-speed services. Use of the Internet has expanded significantly since the mid-1990s starting with the private sector and its use of electronic commerce and subsequently by federal, state, and municipal (county and city) governments. External factors are forces of change within organizations. As people become more proficient with using cell phones and computers through social networks such as Twitter, Facebook, Google+, and many other social media platforms and professional networks such as LinkedIn they expect to have access to various Internet and phone services, including more access to government and private sector organizations and services.

Technology is always changing and can drive incremental or major changes in how people do their work in the business environment. There was a time when everyone had typewriters and carbon paper for making multiple copies of typed documents. Then came along the copier machines, and there was no longer a need to go through the laborious tasks of using carbon paper. Then the development of the personal computers and word processing software eliminated the need for using typewriters. Pay telephones and pagers were replaced with cell phones.

Technology can offer different approaches for doing business and for providing services to the citizens and the general public. The introduction of off-the-shelf, commercial software on the market made word processing, spreadsheet software, and presentation software such as Word, Excel, and PowerPoint available to anyone who wished to purchase. More and more information systems software is becoming available on the commercial market so that many organizations do not have to develop all of their own computer programs to support their business operations. When he was speaking to business leaders, W. Edwards Deming said "We do not have to change, because staying in business is not compulsory" (Jick & Peiperl, 2003, p. xv).

Some may think that government organizations do not have to worry about staying in business because they do not go out of business. That may be true in most cases but they can be faced with huge, shrinking budgets and limited resources including personnel. More importantly, the citizens expect elected-officials and managers at all levels within the organizations to manage government well by making good decisions on how to spend the taxpayers' money. How government organizations react to and manage change determines whether they will be left behind operating under the old status quo way of doing things or change using technology. Technology can support their business strategy to do things differently and better, reduce operating costs, and improve organizational performance in different ways. However, the forces that drive change must be carefully considered.

Summary

How people work within an organization affects how government and public sector organizations manage their programs and how they deliver their products and services. There are two types of work activities: (1) primary and (2) support. The programs, products, and services provided to the public are the core competencies and primary activities of the various departments and agencies within a public sector organization. Support activities include technology; human resources management including employee recruitment and training and monitoring performance; the general administration activities such as the overhead functions of accounting and finance; and the groupware applications and activities. Government is a dynamic, political environment and technology plays a central role in supporting the business strategy.

Many different internal and external forces of change become different business initiatives that impact the business work processes with the organization. As a result, information systems may require minor or major changes in the use of technology or the implementation of new information systems projects. Technology and project management are important for lowering risks and for the success of information systems project.

Review Concepts

- Government project risks and the political environment
- Reasons why projects fail or do not deliver functional benefits
- Planning the project
- The IT and project manager
- Understanding the organization and how people work
- Importance of real-world experiences
- Forces of change
- The information systems strategic triangle framework:
  Business strategy
  Organizational strategy
  Information systems strategy

- Business initiatives:
  The value chain
  Programs, products, and services
  Legislative mandates
  The need for change
  Aging computer information systems
  Evolving technology

Discussion Questions

2.1. Why is information systems project management important to an organization?

2.2. In what ways do government or public organizations differ from private sector organizations?

2.3. Discuss the statement: Organizations are information processing systems before technology solutions are implemented.

2.4. Do you agree with the statement: There is no single reason why projects fail or do not provide the functional benefits? Discuss your response.

2.5. When reviewing the value chain, what is the meaning of primary activities and support activities?

2.6. Explain the concept of the information systems strategic triangle framework. Why is it important that the business strategy is the driver of information systems projects and there needs to be a balance between organizational strategy and information systems strategy?

2.7. Discuss some of the business initiatives that can affect the business operations and its information systems.

2.8. Why do legislative mandated projects take a priority over other types of projects?

CHAPTER THREE
FROM VISIONS TO INFORMATION SYSTEMS PROJECTS

The previous chapter describes the forces of change, business strategy, and different types of business initiatives and how they can influence changes within the organization. When computer information systems need changes or new systems need to be implemented within an organization, those in the organization have a vision. Visions are the big pictures and are essential to changes. This chapter describes how visions need defining so that what develops from the vision is the project mission. In fact, the starting point of many information technology projects is the vision, the project mission, and from this point are the information systems work requests for changes using technology. In some situations, top-level management meetings are initiated for coordination of ideas for new information systems.

I had several discussions on various topics with my students when I was teaching one of my computer systems courses. Some of my students said that I provided them with a lot of information but they wanted me to review what I considered the most important concepts about information systems prior to presenting more advanced topics. As a result of the discussion, this chapter includes some essential concepts about information systems.

Visions create the opportunity for people within an organization to look at things differently by using technology to respond to the needs of the organization, the general public, and the clients the organization serves who use the programs, products, and services. First, we will start by reviewing some fundamentals of managing information systems projects by examining what it means to manage a project, knowing the goals of a project, examining portfolio management, project priorities and selection methods, and the role of the project manager.

Second, we will examine information technology (IT) and project management in public sector organizations, the vision of a project through its completion, and define the project life cycle. Third, we will examine software engineering by looking at the variations of the systems development life cycle (SDLC) phases, the software project management methodology, the integrated approach to managing information systems (IS) projects, and the characteristics of information systems projects. Next, we will look at the Project Management Institute (PMI) method. Finally, we will examine commercial, packaged information systems software, the request for proposal (RFP), contractual agreements, managing systems work requests in a government agency, the IT management structure, the functional project structure, and the different types of public sector information systems.

Project Management

Since there are all kinds of projects in organizations that need managing, let's talk first about project management in general. What is project management? Kerzner (2003, p. 4) defines project management as "planning, organizing, directing, and controlling of company resources" in order to complete the specific goals and objectives of the project. The Project Management Institute's PMBOK Guide (PMI, 2013) defines project management as "the application of knowledge, skills, tools, and techniques to project activities to meet the project requirements" (p. 5). Projects can have many tasks that are divided into subtasks and activities depending on the size and scope of the project. The Project Management Institute was established in 1969 and developed global guidelines and standards for managing projects. It provides information on key concepts of project management and publishes the *Project Management Journal* and the *PM Network* magazine, which provides valuable information to experienced managers and students and has members worldwide.

If an organization does not have a project management method, it runs the risks of the project not being completed on time, within budget, and may not achieve the desired results. Project managers in government organizations can experience different kinds of challenges because they have to manage several different project stakeholders who can make many kinds of demands on project managers. Working in a political environment means that you can be working with multiple departments, elected officials, and may even experience the impact of public interest groups external to the organization.

All projects regardless of their type have three main goals. These need to be completed on time, be within the costs, and meet the project specifications. When an IS project is completed, the system should meet the functional specifications of the organization and the systems' end users (Belout & Gauvreau, 2004; Rosacker & Olson, 2008). Routine tasks for supporting the daily business operations of the organization are not considered IS projects. Computer operations or production support problems and help desks problems initiated by the end users of the information systems need to be worked on and corrected but are not considered projects.

What about project risks? Managers need to recognize that all projects have risks. An information systems project can have operational (technical) risks and the project can fail when it is implemented or the information system may not function properly or meet the needs of the users of the information systems (Huff & Prybutok, 2008). As an IT or a project manager, you should be able to determine the risks for the project by identifying what could go wrong and carry out further research and analysis on the proposed software and hardware. Are there any hardware and functional problems that you can identify at this time? Trying to anticipate the problems and identifying them ahead of time will help the planning go smoother for you. More details on this topic can be found in most project management books (Mantel, Meredith, Shafer, & Sutton, 2005, 2010; Meredith & Mantel, 1995, 2011) and in Chapter 11 of the PMBOK Guide. Project managers in government can encounter many unique challenges, including ambiguous goal definitions and influences by politicians. Some of these challenges include legal and regulatory issues, politics, planning, and human resources who lack the technical skills.

Portfolio Management

Another important topic is portfolio management. Most courses in project planning emphasize the importance of prioritizing projects. Why? Because normally organizations have many different kinds of projects that need to be worked on, funding source to pay for the project costs, and the necessary resources to work on them. In fact, Jeffery and Leliveld (2004) report that IT expenditures in 2002 were $780 billion in the United States and it is estimated that $100 billion of US IT projects have failed.

When the government organizations are involved with selecting project priorities, Wen and Stephen (2006) found that most organizations use the Delphi survey on a group of experts for use of new technologies and a collective opinion is formed versus a formal scoring method for prioritizing projects. Managing the portfolio involves planning for approving and evaluating the IT investments. A project request can come from multiple sources within an organization such as the CEO, the elected officials in public sector organizations, the department heads, business managers, and from other stakeholders in the project.

Organizations can have many different types of computer projects, including those for maintaining the software and the hardware. This is another reason why IT portfolio management is important. It is a method of identifying IT projects that are organization-wide projects and those that are for specific departments and agencies and prioritizing them. Often, organization-wide projects need prioritization and approval from the top-level central managers in central administration. A resource to assist you is the study by Ward (2006), which provides a comparison of the different kinds of information technologies and their ranking in both public sector and private sector organizations.

Organization-wide information systems projects in the public sector, often referred to as enterprise systems in the private sector, are those that affect all of the departments and agencies within the organization as opposed to projects that affect one, two, or a few other individual departments. Projects that are subsystems of the organization need prioritization and approval from top-level department heads or managers at the department or agency level in government. Although the scope of some projects can impact the entire organization compared with projects that are subsystems (i.e., department or agency) of the organization, the scope of a project does not diminish its importance.

In government, organization-wide projects are normally managed by a central organizational, business committee, the CIO, and a project manager and are aligned with both the business and the organizational strategies by obtaining inputs from various departments and agencies. For department and agency projects, most department-level executives as department heads have a committee of top-level business managers and an IT director or senior IT manager within their own departments and agencies to review their IT projects and align them with their business strategy and departmental goals and objectives.

Several studies emphasize the importance of establishing a plan for managing the IT portfolio of projects, the business initiatives, and the need to determine the funding source for the various projects (Pearlson & Saunders, 2006). This is important because many organizations can invest millions of dollars in technology that includes computer hardware, computer software, technology staff, the telecommunications network infrastructure, and maintenance and support of the various computer systems.

Portfolio management is important in managing the workload and the availability and assignment of resources. PMBOK refers to it as "the central management of one or more portfolios to achieve strategic objectives" (PMI, 2013, p. 10). Some projects may involve upgrading the computer system hardware, software, databases, and the network. Other projects can require minor or major changes by enhancing existing information systems or implementation of new information systems by designing and coding new programs or by installing commercial, packaged information systems software.

In some medium-size to large departments, the technical staff is highly specialized with several individuals working in various technical positions as computer support technicians, database administrators, network administrators, computer programmers, systems analysts, system administrators under the direction of an IT director. In smaller-size departments, the network administrator or technical support specialist may perform the several duties such as a network administrator, technical support specialist, and database administrator. The computer programmers may perform the tasks of project leader, programmer, and systems analysts all working under the direction of an IT manager.

Just out of curiosity, I did an Internet search just to see what kind of results would come from using the key words *IT portfolio management*. The results of the search listed the State of Texas (www.dir.texas.gov) portal. Under the topic of project management practices, there is information on their project management approach based on classifying its projects as small, medium, and large with additional categories and requirements. The portfolio includes the characteristics of each project, such as the estimated cost, the project team size, departments involved, time to deliver, impact on agency, impact on outside agency, technology, supplier involvement, and system complexity. This state government developed a plan for identifying the IT projects and determined what information is needed to established their priorities. A narrative with a general description and an overview of the project needs to be included in the portfolio for each project. Every government organization and the departments within an organization need to have an IT portfolio management methodology.

In addition to the project portfolio, I kept an inventory of the systems within the departments I was responsible for directing and managing. Under my direction, my technical staff kept the description of the hardware, software, and users of the systems and other statistical information. I used this information for my own benefit and I would give the information to new technical personnel who were hired as part of their orientation into the IT division. This information gives them an overview of the systems they will be involved with supporting and maintaining within the organization. You may find this information very advantageous to keep and update periodically when there are changes.

Project Priorities and Selection Methods

Next, let's talk about the selection methods for your projects. You can find much literature on different types of project selection methods and principles. Some are numeric and others are nonnumeric selection methods. Since this book does not cover everything about project management but supplements what you have already learned in your undergraduate education or training, there is a list of some project management resources for you in Chapter 4 of this book. In a government environment, legislative mandated information systems projects normally take priority over most others with the exception of operations support because the impact of not completing these projects can cause major disruptions to the business processes. In some cases, not completing legislative projects on time can result in fines, penalties, and even lawsuits if the information systems project is not implemented by the legal deadline.

My own observations of project priority decisions at the department and agency level within government organizations are based on mixed methods that are similar to the Jury of Expert Opinion and the Delphi method, which is discussed in Chapter 7. Top-level managers in central administration and department heads within the departments and agencies take into consideration their budget, project resources, and availability of funding.

Organization-wide project selections are normally made at the central, top administrative level of the government organizations with input and feedback from the various senior executives and managers in the departments that utilize the computer information systems or the technology. Examples of organization-wide systems are financial systems and human resource systems such as a payroll system and personnel systems. These systems are often referred to as enterprise-wide systems in the private sector, for-profit organizations.

The Role of the Project Manager

What is the role of the project manager? The role of an IS project manager includes the responsibility of ensuring that the project is delivered on time, within budget, and delivers all the functional benefits intended for the project. An IS project has many tasks and activities with a starting point and an ending point with the goal of creating a system that brings value to the organization (Dennis & Wixom, 2003). The project manager is responsible for managing the resources for the project including the team members and for ensuring that the project plans are developed; the tasks and subtasks are defined; schedules are established; and resources are assigned for accomplishing the project tasks and activities. It is important for the project manager to focus on the business strategy of the project and to align the project with both the organizational strategy and the information systems strategy so that there is a balance (Booth & Philip, 2005; Pearlson & Saunders, 2006). For example, if the project requires specific computer hardware such as printers, scanners, personal computers, database management systems, and network servers for the project should adhere to the organization's IT standards on manufacturers and hardware and software purchases.

By following a software systems engineering methodology, you as a project manager will find it beneficial to have two assistant managers or leaders for large projects. An assistant project manager or leader responsible for the functional analysis should be knowledgeable about the business operations of the specific department or agency and works closely with systems analysts and the project stakeholders (end users). The other assistant project manager or leader should be responsible for the technical tasks manages the programmers, database administrators, network specialist, and other technical team members. A contract administrator will be able to assist in keeping track of the project's paperwork, change control requests, costs, project plan updates, and handle questions on billing. A project controller or accounting specialist will be able to keep track of the labor charges, project supplies, equipment and software purchases, and other project documents (Christensen & Thayer, 2001; Meredith & Mantel, 1995). The project manager and team members are ultimately responsible for the *project deliverables* such as the project plans and schedules, status reports, system and functional design requirements, specifications, computer programs, system and end user documentation, training manuals, and other types of deliverables. The team members need to have the required skills and their roles and responsibilities clearly defined. For commercial, packaged software, the vendor's chief liaison normally works in a partnership relationship with the project manager but reports to the project manager. The end users or stakeholders of the information systems are involved during various stages of the project for communicating the user requirements and for acceptance testing.

IT Project Management in Public Sector Organizations

Strategic planning in private sector organizations is based on the goal of achieving competitive advantage. Many articles on private sector organizations show the CEO at the top of the organization, and the CIO normally reports directly to the CEO and is involved with strategic planning (Pearlson & Saunders, 2006). In most organizations, the top-level heads of the functional departments are subordinate to the CEO. In addition to understanding the structure of project management in an organization, you need to identify the stakeholders in a project. Although the pure project organization and the functional alignment of projects appear frequently in books and review articles, this book does not cover them in depth. Pure project organization and functional project organization can be found in project management books.

In contrast to private sector organizations, Dufner, Holley, and Reed (2002) provide an extensive analysis of stakeholder involvement for IT strategic planning in US state government involving elected and non-elected officials. Their study identifies several project stakeholders in state government such as the state legislatures, state legislative committees, the governor, the executive committee, state agencies along with the CIO and the central IT office and system end users. The results from a survey of participants from 48 states indicate that even though there are fragmented authority structures, strategic planning is mostly performed at the state agency level, the CIO, and the central IT level of state government organizations. Their study found that it is not uncommon for departments and agencies to receive federal and state funding, which can contribute to the distribution of authority (Dufner et al., 2002).

When examining county government, Benton (2002) describes the structure of some counties as noncharter and charter counties with either a board of county commissioners and an elected executive administrator or an appointed executive administrator. The expectation is that a charter "is expected to grant a county a greater degree of self-rule" (p. 474). Some counties are governed by a board of commissioners with no executive leadership. This study evaluated the linkage between the type of structure and spending on all types of county government services.

The county IT management structure shown in Figure 3.1 consists of those in central administration who are elected officials (e.g., board of supervisors), the chief executive officer (CEO) who is appointed, and the chief information officer (CIO) who reports directly to the CEO. The central IT department is under direction of the CIO, and the chief technology officer (CTO) is an assistant to the CIO.

The elected and nonelected officials who are department and agency heads and their department IT directors or IT managers are normally involved with strategic planning and establishing technical project priorities within their departments and agencies. There are 37 different departments and agencies within this particular organization. Approval of departmental/agency budgets and budgetary spending involves the elected officials in the organization's central, top administration level for general administration and budgetary control.

Several large departments may have IT directors responsible for their technical divisions and some of the medium-size departments may have IT managers. Many of the small departments do not have IT managers but have technical specialists or are supported by the organization's central IT department. In fact, some departments, regardless of their size, may choose to have their information systems managed by the central IT department and the decisions are based on the organization's IT governance agreement,

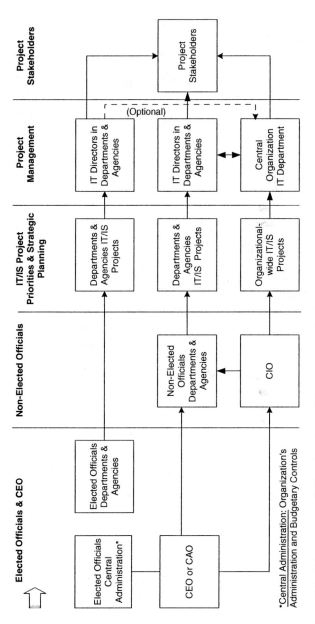

Figure 3.1 Management of IT projects in a public-sector organization.

which will be discussed in detail in Chapter 5. Some departments and agencies in county government may receive federal and state funding that contributes to the distribution of authority.

Let's take a few minutes to examine project planning. Information systems project planning and development can be compared to building a home. First, you have a vision and then there are meetings and discussions about a new home. You examine the feasibility of building a new home, buying an existing home, or remodeling your home. Second, you define your vision and the preliminary plans and there is the development of the project plan and blueprints before the construction begins. There may be several iterations of these plans until it meets your final approval and the estimated costs are defined. You start with general information and work your way through the detailed information.

Third, there are many phases to the construction of a home. During the building phases, there are many inspections to make sure everything meets building codes. Finally, when the building is complete, there is a final inspection to make sure everything has been completed as specified in the project plan. Then you are scheduled for a residential walk-through to inspect everything by making sure that things work properly in accordance with the project plan. The home was built based on the project plans and everything within the home works (performs) based on your expectations. The end results are how the house is structured, how the house looks, and how the lights, water, heating and air conditioning, fireplace, windows, doors, and other items function in meeting your expectations.

You are probably wondering how building a home relates to implementing an information systems project. Let me explain this in a different way by sharing with you in the following section one of my own experiences with a major project in government that started with a vision from the department head, who is an elected official.

From Vision to Completion

A few years ago, an elected official wanted to improve on the business functions in one of his departments within the agency he has authority over as a department head. He envisioned providing more efficient services and faster turnaround of documents from the public and the external business market by eliminating the need to physically move thousands of pages of paper documents through each of the various business units in his department for processing. At the time, his department was processing thousands of document pages per day. He heard about technology that would allow an organization to automate the internal tasks and activities and eliminate handling paper documents by scanning the documents at the front-end of the business process. The documents would then be released after they had been examined using the computer screen and they would then flow through an online workflow process.

This department head as the project sponsor envisioned his staff performing the tasks and activities by viewing the documents online on the computers. The work activities would flow through different business units for calculating the fees, collecting the revenue, verifying that specific information on each document is correct, and entering information into the information system without touching a piece of paper. This department head was hoping that his vision could be turned into something tangible.

The first step was to identify a funding source for the project. Without funds to pay for the project costs, planning would be useless. After meeting with the department head and his assistant, the funding source for the project was identified and the assistant department head submitted a *systems work request* to the technology division to do some additional research for this project as follows:

The first phase of the project involved establishing a working committee of business managers, technical managers, and those familiar with the business operations to assist in making sure there was a clear vision and to define the project's mission. The committee members were to work on the *preliminary analysis* phase, which is fact finding, information gathering, and analysis of both the internal and external environment. I served on the committee as the project manager along with an assistant functional design manager. The project stakeholders were identified, including those who were external to the organization. This was the time for everyone on the committee to start learning more about the project. Don't be surprised if you learn something new, which is good, because this approach will help you make informed decisions about the project.

The scope of the research was to look at several different organizations to see who was using this workflow approach to their business strategy for handling their high-volume day-to-day business activities. There was a broad search for other software in the commercial market. The approach taken was to narrow down the packaged solutions to a few alternatives. The committee members spent a lot of time on telephone calls, in conferences, meetings, and interviews. There were many site visits to other organizations within the state and outside that had workflow systems. The objective was to see how the systems operate for handling the different business strategies.

The committee members could see how these systems were actually functioning within the different operational environments in other organizations and were able to ask some of the following questions about the different functions of the software. What can the software system do and cannot do? What was the total cost of the project to each organization? How much was spent on software customization? What were some of the problems encountered? Detailed information was gathered on the different commercially developed, software systems being utilized at these sites, the project costs, the computer hardware, and the network infrastructure requirements.

Several months were spent on information gathering and attending working session meetings. The approach taken was to avoid being disruptive to the day-to-day activities of the department and its operations and to avoid overburdening the department's human resources. The committee felt that the information gathered during these working sessions would assist them in identifying the software system's functionality and getting an understanding of what may be required of the software vendors to customize their system to the department's business strategy, if required. This time was well spent taken that the organization had the potential of spending millions of dollars on the project. On gathering information, a formal report was submitted to the department head followed by a presentation and meeting with the department head, his assistant, and other business managers. Consequently, the department head decided to give the approval to move forward with the next phase in the process.

The second phase of the project was to determine if this project should be worked on. Is the project really feasible? This phase is referred to as the *feasibility study*. What would happen if you do nothing? What are the shortcomings of the current system? Is there any commercial software in the business market that appears to be capable of meeting the business strategy of this department? Would it be more feasible to have the software system custom built by a vendor company? Are there any legislative or legal requirements that must be considered in the project strategy? Are the technology and hardware reliable for high-volume workloads and data storage? What are the project risks? The committee members worked on gathering the information for answering these questions. They did not want to mimic other organizations using packaged software without considering what is fundamentally different about their business operations. More time was spent on the feasibility of the project, which involved additional personnel including different project stakeholders and information systems specialists. Included in the feasibility study were a project risk assessment and a contingency plan.

After the feasibility study was completed, another formal report was submitted to the department head, followed by several meetings. The department head and his assistant decided to give the approval to move forward to the next phase in the process. To do this, approval was obtained from the department head and information about the project was submitted to the top-level elected officials in central administration (in charge of administration and budgetary control) identifying the funding source so that work could start on the project planning. In this case, the project did not impact the total net county cost. The project costs would be funded from a special fund established and approved by the state just for technology projects for departments like this one in county government.

The third phase of the project meant that it was time to work on the *information analysis* phase for developing the request for proposal (RFP) to purchase the software, hardware, and professional services; and a project plan with timelines. The project team was established and more information was gathered for the RFP. The RFP needed to include information about the existing system and the new information system's *functional requirements* or *concepts of operations* for supporting the department's business strategy from the *users' perspective.* Do not confuse this with the technical design or specifications for developing the programs. The system's functional requirements determine what functions are required to achieve the business objectives of the department, agency, or the organization for organization-wide projects and needs to be completed prior to the decision to purchase a software system.

This work was accomplished by building on the information from the preliminary analysis, the feasibility study, and the business and technical knowledge of those in-house by identifying the requirements for the project. The information was needed to develop the request for proposal (RFP) to purchase the commercial, information system software. For some of the business tasks, the working committee members determined that it will be necessary to change some of the department's current business procedures. Another important point to be aware of is that it was decided by the committee members from the start of the project that an external consultant would be used as a technical advisor but not as a chief project planner. The organization had ownership of the project and felt this approach would improve project success and lower the overall project risks.

Even though the department was considering purchasing a commercially, developed packaged software system and the required hardware, the vendor companies responding to the RFP would be asked to identify any gaps in their software systems and they would have to include this information in the overall project plan for customization of the software along with the associated costs. Sometimes, vendor software can meet the broad functional requirements but not the unique functional business requirements. The working committee members decided that some gaps are acceptable for customization but too many gaps in the system's functional design means the vendor's software system does not have all the functionality required to be aligned with the department's business strategy and could significantly increase the overall project timelines and costs if discovered after the software is purchased.

The RFP was developed and then reviewed by the working committee, the project team, the stakeholders, the organization's legal counsel (attorney), and the department head and his assistant. The RFP went through the normal process of being reviewed by the top-level central administration for financial justification and the purchasing department; and the bid was opened up at the organization's purchasing department's website to all interested commercial, software vendor companies. It was important that the RFP respondents and their companies meet specific criteria including the information systems software's ability to support the department's business strategy. The respondent companies must be financially stable, have the required expertise and personnel to work on the software installation and any software customizations, and have previous experience with this type of project with other government organizations. These requirements would help to minimize the project risks.

The respondents of the RFP were required to include in each of their responses a more comprehensive project plan, the costs of the project including all software and hardware costs, network infrastructure requirements, any required new programming and customization costs, implementation costs, and personnel costs. This information was stated in the RFP. It is important to note that the total costs of the project is determined by including all of the costs to the organization, including the in-house project manager, team members, facilities, internal network infrastructure upgrades, and any additional project management hardware and software costs.

Finally, after the RFP responses (in binders) were received from the vendor companies, each response was reviewed by the committee members during many working level meetings. Three top vendor companies were invited to give presentations on their RFP responses and each of their approaches for implementing the information system. Subsequently, the top vendor company was eventually selected based on the predefined selection criteria. On selection, the next approach was to design the contractual agreement as a result of the RFP and to include a project plan based on the business strategy and the known requirements for the project. The contractual agreement, as a standard practice, went through several administrative reviewers (legal counsel, purchasing department, and CIO) before being submitted to the executive office for budgetary approval by the board of supervisors in central administration. The project plan would be refined by the department's project manager to contain more specific project plan tasks details when the software company's project liaison was on site. The subsequent phases would follow a software system design and implementation approach, which is discussed in more detail in the following sections.

Earlier, I compared an information systems implementation approach to building a home where there is a vision and meetings are held to discuss the vision. From the vision comes multiple meetings, information gathering, and a feasibility study, conceptual design requirements, and the project plan is developed. There were several phases in the process using a systems approach in which the project phases are divided into many subtasks and activities.

In the end, the information system was implemented successfully by the project team. The entire process started with identifying the funding source and going through the various planning phases and activities for implementing the information system. The entire process, from the working committee to the completion of the project, took two and one-half years. The project was on time, within budget, and it met the functional expectations of the organization and the users of the system.

The Project Life Cycle and Software Engineering

All projects, regardless of their size and the type of project, have a start date and ending date. This means any project including information systems projects progresses through four phases of a project's life cycle: (1) conception (start), (2) planning, (3) execution, and (4) termination. However, the software systems approach to developing and implementing an information systems project expands these phases even further, which is discussed in the following sections.

Implementing a new system or customizing information systems software requires highly skilled technical staff trained in software engineering and uses a system approach to development and implementing computer information systems. The systems development life cycle (SDLC) approach is a systems analysis and design strategy for gathering the necessary business requirements and information from the organization and end users in order to design the functionality needed to accomplish the organizational activities and tasks for implementing a computer system (Hoffer, George, & Valacich, 2008).

What is a requirement? "A requirement is simply a statement of what the system must do or what characteristics it needs to have" (Dennis & Wixom, 2003, p. 101) and is often referred to as the business needs. Information systems projects have many business requirements. This information is used during the systems analysis and design phases because the system specifications are written from the perspective of the business by focusing on what the system should be able to do. Requirements are necessary for turning high-level business needs into more detailed information and specifications that can be used for software engineering.

Even if an organization is considering purchasing commercial software, there is a need to use a systems methodology. Systems design and development techniques are rooted in software engineering; and IT managers and IS project managers need to be knowledgeable about this approach (Ahituv, Neumann, & Riley, 1994). The tasks are divided into phases called the systems development life cycle (SDLC) with various tasks and activities within each phase.

There are several different strategies used by information systems professionals to support systems analysis and design that will assist in implementing successful system implementation projects. These strategies include but are not limited to adopting the appropriate systems development methodology; adopting a project management methodology and software tools (e.g., Microsoft Project) for tracking projects; and selecting computer-aided systems engineering (CASE) tools used for obtaining using requirements, design, and implementation. It includes strategies for adopting procedures for evaluating and selecting commercial, packaged software; selecting appropriate database formats and database management systems; and purchasing computer hardware.

The primary goal of systems analysis and design is to create computer information systems that add value to the organization, maximize profits for the private sector organizations, reduce operating costs, and increase organizational performance (Dennis & Wixom, 2003). The system's methodology needs to be able to support the project's goals and objectives. Some approaches are better than others when gathering information for the systems development. There are several different systems development methodologies but the SDLC methodology has been used for several years, is reliable, and is a way of ensuring that business needs are met using a phased approach when implementing new information systems. Activities within each of the phases can vary depending on the type of the information system.

Variations of the SDLC Phases

Hoffer, George, and Valacich, (2008) refer to five phases of the SDLC for development, implementing, and maintaining information systems projects:

1. Conception (start)
2. Planning
3. Analysis and design
4. Implementation
5. Maintenance

The important point to keep in mind is that there are several other variations of the SDLC phases. Some SDLC methodologies identify from five to ten different phases or more but still basically incorporate the starting phase of the project, which is the conception phase, and the different phases with the tasks and activities for planning, analysis and design, implementation, and maintenance.

Ahituv, Neumann, and Riley (1994) identify ten SDLC phases (see Table 3.1). I have found the ten-phased approach to be very successful with my projects. The various software engineering tasks, activities, and project deliverables within these phases can vary depending on the project and are identified within each of the phases: (1) preliminary analysis, (2) feasibility study, (3) information analysis, (4) system design, (5) programming and/or packaged software installation, (6) procedure development, (7) conversion, (8) operations and maintenance, (9) postaudit review, and (10) termination.

The *preliminary analysis* and the *feasibility study* phases are the *prelaunch* stages of a project. These two phases answer questions about the project in addition to whether it is technically, economically, and organizationally feasible. Research and fact finding take place at this point before decisions are made to move forward with project planning. It is important to investigate what is going in the external and internal environment and identify the technology trends that are pertinent to both the vision and mission of the project (Kemp, Funk, & Eadie, 1993). Novice project managers sometimes fall short of completing these two phases or spending sufficient time to obtain the required information. Another important point to remember is that after the information system has been implemented, the *postaudit* phase is an evaluation of the system's performance to find whether it meets the project's objectives. This is the phase in which lessons learned are recorded for historical references.

As you can see from the ten-phased SDLC approach, there can be several variations of the SDLC phases in literature, but most include some form of the five SDLC phases previously identified by Hoffer, George, and Valacich (2008). Regardless of how many phases are in your software engineering approach and the SDLC, project management identifying the appropriate tasks and activities is important to the implementation success and is discussed in detail in the next section. The important point to remember is that information systems project management uses a system development approach to implement projects (Ahituv et al., 1994).

Another important strategy for systems analysis and design is the ability to obtain accurate end-user information using software tools. The CASE approach for developing user requirements using visual representation for software engineering is another strategy that can provide overall

Table 3.1 Information systems development life cycle with ten phases, tasks, and activities

Activity	Content	Deliverables
1. Preliminary analysis	Information requirements. Input sources. System boundaries. System location.	Preliminary conceptual report.
2. Feasibility study	Economic. Technical. Organizational.	Feasibility report.
3. Information analysis	System specifications. Project plan. Resources required. Project budget.	Systems analysis documents.
4. System design	Specifications for programs, files and databases, and conversion. Review of economic feasibility. Specifications for procedure development. System test plan. Hardware/software selection schedule.	Specifications for programs. Specifications for procedures. Conversion plan.
5. Programming	Coding of programs and/or installation of a commercial, packaged application system; and parameter changes. Program modifications. Program testing and documentation. System testing.	Programs. Operators and input entry manuals.
6. Procedure development	Instructions for users, input/output clerks, control personnel, and operating personnel. Conversion procedures.	Procedures manuals. Training manuals.
7. Conversion	Training. Creation of new files and data bases. Parallel run. Tune-up of changes. Acceptance testing.	Conversion log.
8. Operations and Maintenance	Operations of System. Modifications and/or enhancements.	Modified programs. Maintenance logs.
9. Postaudit	Review of objectives and costs/benefits of system. Evaluation of system operational characteristics.	Postaudit report.
10. Termination	Evaluation of system postaudit report. Review whether system is effectively and efficiently meeting management's objectives.	Report justifying termination of the system.

Source: Adapted from Ahituv, Neumann, and Riley, 1994.

benefits of gathering information system requirements. User requirements are obtained from the end users to capture how software systems are to perform in relation to business tasks and functions. Text documents for obtaining this information have been used for many years. However, a newer approach is being used to visually show the user requirements using objects that show the relationships of how parties interact with the objects in order to achieve the desired software functional goals. The CASE approach is being used in many industries because it enables the project team members to use diagrams to show the functionality of the system (Dennis & Wixom, 2003; Hoffer et al., 2008). Due to the emergence of the CASE tools, the Use CASE approach is becoming a more widely used practice for capturing user and functional software requirements (Lundell & Lings, 2004).

There was a time when information systems managers had no other option than to develop customized information systems internally using systems analysts and computer programmers to develop the programs. Today, there are several different options available to organizations. Commercial, packaged information systems software offers some organizations the option of purchasing software rather than the organization dedicating time and resources to designing and developing the application programs for the software. Look broadly at the packaged software on the market. If you do not have the time to do the research, hire a consultant with the technical expertise and knowledge in the business operations of your department to accomplish this task.

Many organizations purchase packaged software systems when the business functions are not unique such as those functions found in human resources, payroll, financial accounting packages, and other commonly used software systems (Dennis & Wixom, 2003). These systems do not have to be custom-built by developing them within the organization but they are not turnkey systems. You cannot install the software and expect everything to be functionally complete (Pearlson & Saunders, 2006). Most of the package systems, such as enterprise resource planning (ERP) systems, give you about 80 percent of what you need and the balance 20 percent must be customized to fit your organization. However, the 20 percent you need to implement may cost you millions of dollars (Orfali, Harkey, & Edwards, 1999). The SDLC phase that normally consists of developing and coding the software programs is replaced with the tasks of installation of the commercial software. Commercial information systems software may require modifications to programs or changes to program parameters giving customized functions.

Another option for organizations is the application service providers (ASPs). The major advantage of the ASP model is economies of scale

(Pearlson & Saunders, 2006; Walsh, 2003). Users from one or many locations access the hosted application system through a virtual private wide-area network or the Internet. The applications or computer information system, hardware platform, and operating system software are maintained by the ASP provider in one location.

Regardless of whether you plan on buying a package software system or are considering having it custom-built there are various phases of the information SDLC that can lead to successful project implementation. It is important for you as a project manager to give serious consideration to the methodology and to the SDLC approach by integrating factors to ensure the success of the project's implementation.

Software Project Management Methodology

Now let's discuss the details of a software project management approach. An information systems project management methodology is an approach that provides a framework for managing the project resources, tracking the tasks and activities, and costs of information systems projects. Project tracking is necessary to determine whether a project is on time, is within the project's estimated costs, and has the appropriate project team resources and other kinds of resources. It provides a channel for identifying problem areas so that the project manager can respond with appropriate decisions to reduce the overall project risks. However, a good project management methodology alone does not always guarantee project success because there are several key critical success factors that influence the project outcomes, which are discussed in detail in the following sections.

Studies by Pinto (1986) and Pinto and Slevin (1987) identified four project phases, meaning that all projects have a starting phase (conception) and an ending phase (termination), and between these two phases are planning and implementation. These are called the project life cycle phases. The phases of a project are listed as follows:

1. Conceptualization phase (start),
2. Planning phase,
3. Execution phase, and
4. Termination

These four phases are identified for all projects regardless of whether they may or may not be information systems projects (see Figure 3.2).

Pinto developed a survey questionnaire in 1986 that identifies factors contributing to project success. Several other studies identify these ten

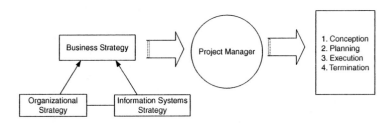

Figure 3.2 Business strategy and project-life cycle phases.

factors that contribute to project success (Pinto & Prescott, 1990; Pinto & Slevin, 1987, 1988). The results listed the ten critical success factors (CSFs) as follows:

1. Project mission,
2. Top management support,
3. Project plans and schedules,
4. Client consultations,
5. Personnel,
6. Technical tasks,
7. Monitoring and feedback,
8. Client acceptance,
9. Communication, and
10. Trouble shooting.

Integrated Approach

The project management methodology using the ten critical success factors is integrated with the SDLC methodology for software engineering. Software engineering consists of the SDLC phases with its tasks and activities. This approach uses both the *project management methodology* for tracking and managing the project and the *software engineering SDLC methodology* for developing and implementing information system.

Regardless of whether the system acquired is a commercial, packaged software system or custom-developed by in-house systems analysts and programmers or contractors, a project management approach and the SDLC methodology are important to successful projects for working on the project tasks and activities, monitoring the progress of the project, and tracking the project timelines, resources, and cost. In other words, you are using project management for tracking the progress of the project, its costs, and other resources, reducing project risks, and a systems development

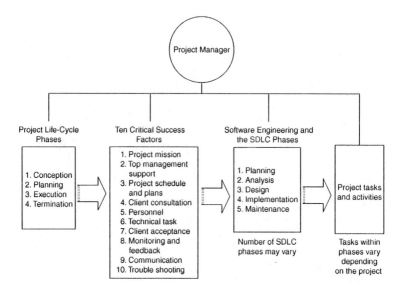

Figure 3.3 Project management integrated with CSFs and SDLC phases.

methodology using the various SDLC phases for designing the systems software or installing the packaged software, and for customizing the information system, see Figure 3.3.

Bryde (2003) provides a useful list of the project life cycle activities in addition to planning for time, costs, and the scope of work such as monitoring and controlling the project and change management. The study identifies the need for defining the benefits and goals, managing risks, contract management, quality management, configuration management, and a host of other areas.

Management of project stakeholders is important to information systems project success as well. Who are project stakeholders? The project stakeholders are those who have an interest in the project, are the primary beneficiaries, and can impact the project outcome. Public sector organizations can have numerous stakeholders including top and middle-level managers and the end users of the systems.

We live in a world that demands immediate and visible results. It is much easier for stakeholders of a project to see its progress when they can see something like a building and a bridge or something else that is tangible because they can clearly see the progress made and the results of the effort. They know it is there because they can see it and they can touch it. This is not the case with software engineering for developing information systems.

Information systems software projects involve processes in which the results of the tasks and activities, if done correctly, will be an information system that is within budget, on schedule, and provides the functional benefits to the organization. The project stakeholders with the exception of project team members cannot see the immediate results of the phases of software development and implementation. Why? Software is not something tangible that they can see and touch, but, in the end, when they turn on their computers and access the information system using the user interface screens, they can understand its true value. The programs function as planned and produce output in the form of meaningful information using transformational processes within the information system, updating databases, producing documents, reports, and the ability to access online information, and a host of other benefits. For this reason, communication with stakeholders and project status reporting on a regular schedule is very important for these projects.

Characteristics of Information Systems Projects

The focus of information systems projects is on software development, installation, customization, and implementation. For commercial, packaged software systems, installation of the software is a major component of the project plan but may require parameter changes and some customization. Amescua and others (2004) published an approach of viewing project management as a software life cycle process. The approach is a set of clearly defined processes and procedures consisting of two different components:

1. Software project planning, and
2. Project tracking and oversight.

Since information systems projects involve tasks and activities within the SDLC process, the study's goal was to development a traditional Software Project Management (SPM) Framework, see Figure 1 in the study article (Amescua et al. 2004) Although, the goal of the study was to refine the framework even further using domain analysis, the traditional SPM Framework shows how software project management is driven by process. Many different professionals and students participated in designing the SPM Framework over a two-year period.

The main elements of the traditional SPM Framework are project, process, artifact (resource and product), component, role, and agent (person).

Amescua et al. (2004) described a software development project as consisting of *processes*. Within those processes are activities that are further divided into subtasks that use *resources* that result in *products*. The *resources* are the software and hardware technologies, abstract concepts; and the *products* are the results of the *resources* such as coded computer programs, documents, results of verification and validation testing, and so on. A *component* is the percentage of time required to produce the *products*. There are persons who perform in different *roles*. A person (project manager, team member, business experts, etc.) is referred to as an *agent* who is ultimately responsible for the execution of the tasks.

After saying all of this in the previous paragraphs about information systems project management, you should be able to see why project management is integrated and merged with the ten phases of the SDLC (Christensen & Thayer, 2001), as shown in Figure 3.4.

You would want to start with the general and gradually progress to the specifics within the SDLC phases. If you are thorough in spending the time on researching, collecting the information, and performing the analysis within the first few phases of a project life cycle approach, it will help reduce the risks of functional design flaws within the information system. Even if you are purchasing a commercial, packaged software system, you need to go through the same process in the first few phases of the SDLC for obtaining the concepts of operations or functional requirements so that

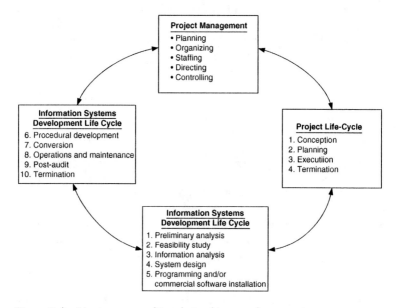

Figure 3.4 Management and its relationships to software projects.
Source: Adapted from Christensen & Thayer, 2001.

you can make the right choices in software that is available on the market that will meet the organization's business strategy. Some commercial, packaged software may require a limited amount of customization and/or parameter changes by the vendor company.

The Project Management Institute (PMI) Method

Now let's examine the Project Management Institute's method; mainly because the Project Management Institute (PMI) has established standards for project management by putting together the professional knowledge from many of its members who work as project managers. Generally accepted standards means the knowledge and practices can be applied to most projects and the practices have had a significant impact on project success but should not always be applied to all projects because some projects can be very different. The project manager and team members must determine the appropriate practice for a specific project. The PMI published its first Project Management Body of Knowledge Guide in 2001 and by 2012 PMI had more than 700,000 members, volunteers, and certificate holders worldwide in 185 countries ("About us," 2013, para.1) and is a global not-for-profit organization and offers six different professional certifications. The PMI method is process based, in which the processes actually overlap and interact throughout a project. The PMI's framework actually divides the processes into five distinct groups of initiating, planning, executing, controlling, and closing within each phase of the SDLC for software projects. The processes are defined as follows:

1. Inputs (document plans, design requirements, specification, etc.)
2. Tools and techniques (mechanisms applied to inputs)
3. Outputs as deliverables (coded programs, documents, products, databases, reports, etc.)

The PMBOK Guide identifies several knowledge areas, such as integration management, scope management, time management, quality management, human resources management, communications management, risk management, and procurement management. Another area just recently added to the Guide is Chapter 13 on project stakeholder management (PMI, 2013). Within these areas, the PMBOK Guide provides information on the role of the project manager, the organization, the project team, and stakeholders. The chapters in the Guide identify project planning, budgeting the project, costs estimating, and risk management. There is information about allocating resources, monitoring and controlling the project, and evaluating and terminating the project.

Project managers in government may encounter many different kinds of challenges because of the political environment. Sarantis, Smithson, Charalabidis, and Askounis (2010) report from their research of literature that goal-driven, e-government projects demand flexibility and the ability to address change; and that several project management approaches for e-government need to be flexible. Although some government information systems project management approaches may differ in comparison to private sector organizations, the PMBOK Guide provides some valuable information for project managers. It is important for you to recognize that government is a dynamic environment in which newly elected officials serve in top-level management positions. Some leave the organization due to term limits or from not being reelected. In addition to the turnover in top-level management, the departments and agencies are highly specialized and diverse, with top-level managers who have authority over their own budgets, domain, and project priorities. Project stakeholder management can present unique challenges to public sector project managers. Awareness of the environment you are working within and having an understanding of project management standards and practices can assist you in improving information systems project success.

Commercial, Packaged Information Systems Software

Another important topic to consider is that for many years information system managers had no other option than to develop in-house information system software using their systems analysts and computer programming staff. Today there are several different options available to organizations. Commercial, packaged software offers some organizations the option of purchasing information systems software rather than the organization dedicating time and resources to designing and developing the software. Dennis and Wixom (2003) report that many organizations buy packaged software systems when the business functions are not unique, such as those functions found in payroll, financial accounting packages, and other commonly used software information systems.

The ability to purchase commercial, packaged computer software has provided organizations with more options. The trend of packaged software in the 1980s rose for manufacturing organizations followed by ERP systems in the 1990s (Keil & Tiwana, 2005). Software purchases of commercial-of-the-shelf-system (COTS) packages represent 70 percent of the corporate business software totaling almost $200 billion worldwide. However, according to the study, buying can be risky because not all packaged software supports the business needs of organizations. The research lists the following criteria for evaluating COTS software: functionality, reliability, cost, ease of use, vendor reputation, ease of customization, and ease of implementation.

Software vendor companies have to compete in a competitive business market so it is expected that they will make the software solutions attractive in order to obtain new customers. Many vendor companies are very good at analyzing the specific business requirements of the customers in addition to the broad business requirements (Bajaj & Bajaj, 2010). The organization's business and technical managers need to determine if the product offers the functionality needed to support the organization's business strategy before purchasing the software. As organizations become more dependent on commercial software, there is a need to carefully evaluate the software products before buying them. A formal process for evaluating COTS software products is essential to ensure that the product will support the business (Lawlis, Mark, Thomas, & Courtheyn, 2001). If uncertainty about the software worries you, make a list of questions that need to be asked.

More and more software packages are appearing on the business market. You want to critically assess the software highlighting the main strengths and weaknesses. You want to "to be able to see the forest as well as the trees." Pay attention to unanswered questions and write down your observations. Some individuals organize their thoughts and ask questions about the software system. These same people need evidence and do not believe everything the vendor has to say and others want to believe and find the evidence they need. This is the reason why a software engineering approach is so important. You do not hire a lawyer to build a bridge. You hire an experienced civil engineer. You do not get someone who knows nothing about software design and development to implement a new information system. You get an experienced software engineer who understands the business and uses an SDLC approach.

You want to develop the system's functional requirements, often referred to as the *concept of operations* for the new systems, and include it as part of the RFP package. If you are going to replace a current system, include the description of the current system and the reasons why you want a new system. The functional requirements determine the characteristics of the new system from the end-users' perspective. This can be accomplished by an end-user working committee (stakeholders) with support and guidance from the project manager and the project team or you can use an impartial third party representing the end users with experience developing the functional requirements. Christensen and Thayer (2001) describe the importance of this approach in chapter 2 of their book on best practices for software engineering. You may find it advantageous to include a consultant and/or contractors familiar with the new technology and your business operations. Avoid diluting the SDLC phases and tasks.

Do not take the *Potemkin village* approach to evaluating information software just because the packaged software system looks good. There is a story about Catherine the Great who ruled Russia from 1762 to 1796 and the ambitious Calvary officer name Potemkin who tried to win her attention and made a showplace of Catherine's empire by putting up façades of villages with no actual functional buildings. The structures were just realistic, pasteboard façades. When Catherine passed by the villages and was greeted by the villagers, it was an impressive display of her empire because everything looked really good but the buildings had no functional benefits.

Request for Proposal (RFP)

Before a government department or agency can move forward with purchasing computer hardware and/or software, the department is required to go out to bid. A bid proposal gives all companies and vendors an equal opportunity to respond to the bid requirements and provide the costs associated with the proposal. A *request for proposal* to purchase hardware, software, and professional services commonly referred to as an RFP is a detailed description of the software's functional requirements and hardware requirements for a given department or government agency along with the detailed description of the functionality required that meet the business strategy for computer information software and hardware usability (Austin & Boxerman, 1998). RFPs are used in a formal vendor selection process (See Appendix A, RFP Table of Contents).

The following is an example of the sequence of events for an RFP; that is, requesting services for a computer information system and moving it to a hosting site with operational support: The focus of this project was on relocating the information system to a different data center facility:

1. Develop request for proposal (RFP),
2. Review of proposal responses and costs,
3. On-site presentations from three finalists,
4. Recommendation of company selected from the finalists,
5. Recommendation presented to the top-level management,
6. Development of a contractual agreement,
7. Obtain approval from board of supervisors,
8. Start work on a detailed transition plan,
9. Begin parallel testing, and
10. Implementation.

In some situations, a department or agency may develop a *request for information* (RFI) with the system requirements to see what products or commercial software systems are on the market before putting together a formal RFP. Companies responding to a formal government RFP must meet specific requirements of financial stability and financial capital, provide information on the experience and qualifications of management and technical personnel resources, provide the company history, have applicable licensing, and provide a list of clients to who they have provided their products and services to currently and in the past, and the primary contact person. The PMBOK Guide (PMI, 2013) provides a lot of information on procurement management in Chapter 12. However, government organizations have their own rules and regulations on procurement, including procedures for purchasing software, hardware, and professional services. Contact your procurement department for this information.

Contractual Agreements

After the bids from the vendors have been received, reviewed, evaluated, and the contract awarded, meaning a vendor has been selected, a contractual agreement between the vendor company and the government agency is developed. This contractual agreement includes all the hardware and software, conditions including warrantees on hardware and/or software, and includes maintenance support extending from one to three years or more, and professional services. My own experiences found that many companies have templates of contractual agreements that they have formalized with previous clients and will provide you a copy of the template. You can request a copy of their contractual agreement as a starting point for developing your government contract. If you are not RFP and contract literate, find someone who is knowledgeable to assist you in developing the RFP and contract.

Often, contracts from the vendor must be revised to meet the specific government's contractual policies and standards. The project director or manager normally works with the legal attorneys and the purchasing department to ensure that they are following the government procedures for developing their contractual agreements. All contractual agreements are normally submitted to top-level executives in the central, administrative organization for approval to spend funds. In the case of many county governments, the contracts are submitted to the county executive office for review and then sent to the board of supervisors for approval after being voted on by the members of the board. See Appendix B, Contractual Agreement Table of Contents.

Your organization's contract should be written in a way to help minimize software and hardware risks. Research by Yates and Arne (2004) can assist you because they provide information on risk management and the legal considerations including the need to write the contract in a way to reduce risks by requiring the disclosure of financial information and any pending lawsuits. You may find this information useful because it provides information on the technical, organizational, and business risks associated with a project.

Managing Systems Works Requests for an Agency

The project manager is essential for managing the work that has to be done on all projects. All projects have a start date, target completion date, their own funding source, and resources that are assigned to the project. After the project ends, the resources go back to what they were doing prior to the project assignment. In government organizations, a *funding source* means identifying where the money is coming from to pay for the project before you can start any planning on it. All projects need a funding source. Some projects may be small or medium-size projects that require modifications to computer information systems due to changes in the business operations or due to some changes in legislation. Others may be large projects consisting of designing new programs or implementing new information systems.

Most organizations establish some formal procedures for assigning the work that has to be done. Many business initiatives are in the form of *systems work requests* from the end users in the departments, divisions, and business units often requesting changes to the existing computer information systems. These requests are normally reviewed and approved by a manager or supervisor before being submitted to the IT manager or project manager. Are these requests viewed as projects? Yes, they are projects but many can be incremental changes or small to medium-size projects. The resources including the technical staff for most work requests are already budgeted within the annual yearly budget cycle for a department or agency. The work has no impact on increasing the annual budget nor does it impact the level of technical staff and other resources available to work on the projects. Often, the project priorities and work performed operate within the fixed total cost of the budget year based on predefined projects and resources in the annual budget. It is a matter of determining the priority of which project's work request will be worked on based on each department's project priority list. That is why project portfolio management is very important for establishing project priorities.

There are other ongoing maintenance support projects such as maintaining the databases to fine tune them to function properly; upgrading the operating systems; and upgrading personal computers, networks, and computer hardware. These types of projects are normally prioritized and budgeted by the technical managers and scheduled within the annual budget year; and the tasks are performed by database administrators, systems administrators, and other technical support professionals.

Often, there are new projects that arise because of business initiatives that do not have a funding source and are not included in the annual budget. A funding source needs to be identified to cover the project costs and other project resources. These kinds of projects need top-level management approval and are often large-scale projects to be completed within one year or very-large-scale projects exceeding one year. There is a need to identify not only a funding source for the project but also the estimated hours, personnel, hardware, software, contractors, consultants, and other project resources. The project manager and the team members are normally temporarily assigned to large projects.

IT Management Structure

To be effective, many IT management literature report that the CIO should report directly to the organization's top-level executive such as the CEO or CAO. This places the CIO at the strategic level in the organization for managing the technologies (Haag, Cummings, & Phillips, 2007; Pearlson & Saunders, 2006). IT directors or senior IT managers within the departments and agencies should report directly to the department or agency head. This establishes the importance, participation, and credibility of the positions being at the top level of the management structure.

The IT management structure can vary in different government organizations. Some departments may be supported totally by the organization's central IT department for various computer support activities, including the management of the wide-area network (WAN), the local area network (LANs), and the information systems. Other departments and agencies may have their own IT director or IT manager along with their own dedicated technical staff. The following is an example of the IT management structure within a large to medium-size departments in one county government organization.

Within each department in government that is large enough to have its own technical staff, the IT director or IT manager is responsible for the technical staff that supports several business divisions and units within the department. Most of the smaller departments have senior IT managers instead of IT directors. Depending on the organizational structure of each department, the IT director or IT manager may report to a department head or to the assistant department head.

The technical staff members normally work in project teams varying in size. Most departments have a systems helpdesk to handle the telephone calls for service-related computer problems and support and also handle e-mail requests for support. Smaller departments often use the organization's central IT department's helpdesk in the central organization.

The Functional Project Structure

Since most departments and agencies within government organizations are highly specialized within their core business, many use the *functional project organization* structure rather than the *pure project organization*. Most departments and agencies have flexibility in how they want to handle their project assignments. An overview of the structure in the following example is of a county government agency, see Figure 3.5.

Within the functional structure, each department and agency is able to budget and prioritize its projects and information technology work requests for the department or agency and obtain the appropriate resources. Projects normally differ in size and complexity. In the particular department in this example, project Team A is assigned to the routine production support, which is handling the operational problems and fixes in the programs that can occur on a day-to-day basis within the computer information systems. The systems *help desk* handles the initial requests from the end users of the information systems, troubleshoots problems, and escalates unresolved problems to project Team A.

The same project Team A does more advanced troubleshooting and makes sure that any production or daily operational problems are corrected so that the computer information systems stay operational and available to a department and end users in accomplishing their daily business activities. In addition to these responsibilities, Team A may work on the small-size projects, which normally consist of minor changes or modifications to the computer information system programs. These types of *systems work requests* often require modifications or enhancements to the existing application programs.

Project Team B is assigned to medium size projects and sometimes to large size projects that can be worked on and completed within the budget year of 12 months. The systems work requests may require changes to the existing computer programs or may require the need to develop or install new computer programs to support the business operations of the end users within the many business divisions and units. Large size projects that exceed the annual budget year of 12 months are normally assigned to project Team C and may require the reassignment of some of the technical staff from other areas of the department and organization including individuals from Team B on a part-time basis and other business specialty resources. Some very large and complex projects may require outside consulting and additional contractor technical support to supplement the team, if necessary.

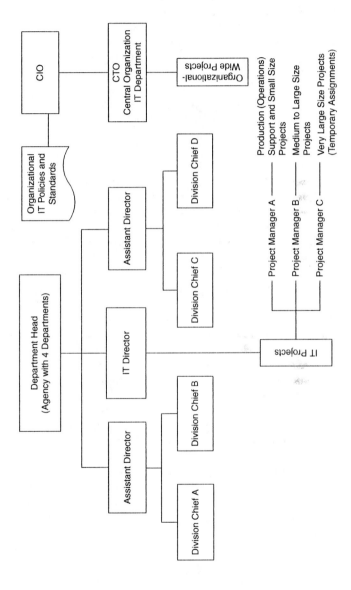

Figure 3.5 Functional project organization of a county government agency.

Many of the professional and technical staff members prefer new development projects; therefore, most of the personnel are rotated based on a predetermined schedule spending a few months working on production or operations support and small projects; and then assigned to Team B or Team C to work on the new work requests projects. By implementing a rotation schedule, many individuals have the opportunity to work in the various areas of technology and it helps technical staff to keep their skills up-to-date in all areas of technology development and support. Very large size projects that normally exceed 12 months may require additional funding and resources, and funding and a budget are assigned by either top-level management or the IT director to an IS project manager in project Team C.

The project team members may be a mix of staff such as an assistant technical manager, and an assistant functional manager, systems analysts, computer programmers, office support staff, database administrators, system programmers, hardware and network specialists, business managers, end users; and whatever other resources are required for a project. For some large projects, the department or agency IT director or IT manager may serve as the project manager on a temporary assignment. This team structure adheres to a software engineering approach.

Several of the medium- to large-size departments and agencies within this particular county government organization are decentralized, meaning that their IT functional divisions for project management are within the departments close to the business units. Some departments or agencies often have their own IT directors or senior IT manager and technical staff to support their computer information systems. Many of the smaller departments were decentralized prior to the move because they did not have their information systems hosted on a mainframe computer in the organization's central IT department.

In contrast to the functional project organization, the *pure project organization* is when one project department or *project management office* manages all of the projects within an organization. For example, in the pure project structure, a project manager is assigned to project A for any one of the many functional departments within the organization; and another project manager is assigned to project B, and so on. After each project is completed, project manager A and the team members return to whatever they were doing before they were assigned to project A and they are eventually assigned another project (Mantel et al., 2005).

Different Types of Information Systems

Computer information systems consist of computer hardware, computer software, operating systems, databases, and the infrastructure network.

There are two main types of computer software: (1) application and (2) system.

Application software consists of programs that are written often in a specific programming language with instructions for solving problems and performing specific tasks. The application software can consist of many programs that work together and they are commonly called computer information systems. Whereas system software is an operating system that controls the application software and manages how the hardware devices work together. There is also utility software that provides additional functionality to the operating systems' anti-virus software, spam blockers, screen savers, and so on (Haag et al., 2007) and other types of security software. Databases and database management systems are used for managing, storing, accessing, and updating the information from the information systems. Computer information systems are more than *data processing* because they can process and store more than textual data. There is the ability to process, store, and update the databases with objects such as images, photos, maps, and music and voice.

A question that you should ask yourself if you are involved with information systems decision making is: How do you prepare yourself for making good business decisions about information systems projects? You start by knowing the different types of information systems used to support overall organizational performance.

Now that you are at this point in your career and education, take a few minutes to think about how you view the information systems within your organization. My own search for understanding an organization and its use of technology lead me to identifying the differences in the types of information systems. Your understanding of the environment will pave the way to helping you make good information systems decisions. Doke and Barrier (1994) reported that many of the information systems described in literature are limited and do not represent the many different types of systems and they developed their own list of information system classifications. The following subsections describe the information systems based on my own research of the business environment.

Transaction Processing (TPS) Systems

The TPS systems support the daily business operations of the organization's agencies, departments, and functional units and capture daily transactions such as payments and fees, and other information. What does an information system do with a transaction? The data are processed and converted into meaningful information and reports are usually generated daily. When transactions are involved, the data go through a processing cycle. The transaction processing cycle consists of: (1) recording and the data collection, (2) conversion and verification, (3) data validation, (4) files and database updating and processing, and (5) generating reports (Ahituv et al., 1994). These systems are considered *mission critical* to the business of government organizations and support the day-to-day operations of various departments or agencies such as the sheriff's department, tax collector's property tax system, auditor-controller's property distribution system, assessor's property appraisal system, county clerk's system, court systems, district attorney, department of public social services, and transportation and land management systems are just a few. Most of the TPS systems were initially designed and developed by the government departments and agencies starting in the early 1970s. Some of these information systems are highly complex and were developed using the COBOL programming language and enhanced over the years, which adds to the complexity of these systems. Others systems have been replaced with newer information systems with added functionality and relational database management systems.

Specialized Transaction Processing Systems

Many software systems are designed and customized by vendor software developers. Information systems such as geographical information systems (GIS), imaging systems, records management systems, and document recording systems are examples of systems not categorized in some studies. Some of these *specialized systems* do not recognize typical transactions but use documents that are recorded as source documents. One example of source documents are bank checks that have magnetic ink character recognition (MICR) encoding, which are read by special devices. Then there is optical character recognition (OCR) that uses special readers that can recognize preprinted characters. Another form of optical recognition is bar coding. In fact, optical scanners can capture the digitized images of the entire source documents (Ahituv et al., 1994). Many of these information systems actually process both the data from the source documents and information from the transaction can be entered into the system by entry operators. Other systems process the information using hypertext markup language (HTML) and extended markup language (XML) technology (Phillips, 2001; Steinfield, Markus, & Wigand, 2005) for capturing transaction data and using workflow technology for processing the data and source documents through the system and the various business units to perform their daily tasks and activities.

Today, several software companies are developing more commercial, packaged software for TPS and specialized systems, which are slowly being seen on the software market. Some of these information systems in the private sector provide a strategic and competitive advantage (Dufner et al., 2002) because the goal for private sector organizations is to maximize profits.

Orfali, Harkey, and Edwards (1999) and Ahituv and others (1994) provided a model of the strategic information systems grid for the private sector organizations based on identifying those systems that give an organization a competitive advantage. Information systems are mainly defined into two categories for strategic planning: (1) strategic information systems and (2) support systems. In contrast to private sector organizations, government organizations focus on strategic planning for delivery of their programs, products, and services; therefore, the strategic grid model has been adapted to public sector organizations (Figure 3.6).

Many government information systems are designed to collect and process revenue from transactions in the form of fees and payments from clients and the general public for products and services and for distribution of funds. An example of transactions can be payments from the property tax bills from residential homeowners who own their homes or other types of real estate property and from payments for different types of licenses, fees (e.g., court fees), and documents fees. The payments are

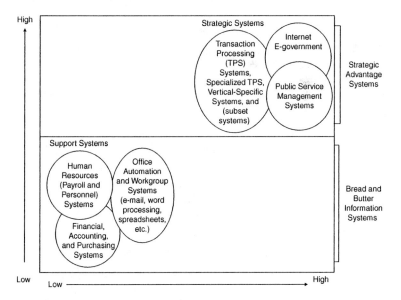

Figure 3.6 Public-sector information systems strategic grid.

Source: Adapted from Forrester Research as cited by Orfali, Harkey, & Edwards, 1999.

transactions that are processed by the computer information system and the information is updated and stored in the organizational databases. The information needed to provide these kinds of services are updated by the various business divisions within the information systems and stored in the databases.

Vertical Information Systems

Software systems that are designed uniquely for a particular industry such as health care, radiology, patient scheduling, and the pharmaceutical industry are referred to as vertical information systems (Haag et al., 2007). Many government organizations can have TPS information systems, specialized systems, and vertical information systems software (e.g., hospitals, public health clinics, and mental health). The information is processed and stored in databases for reporting, inquiries, updating, and retrieving and accessing the information.

Systems for Organizational Use

Other types of systems are data warehouses that collect and gather information from different operational databases and are used to create different systems such as decision support systems (DSS), management information systems (MIS), executive information systems (EIS) to be used by different departments to provide managers' access to information for organizational use (Gray & Watson, 1998). These systems are *subsets* of the other information systems and contain transaction data, client information, and other types of data from various information systems. The information is subsequently stored in databases in some meaningful structure for further reporting purposes to assist decision making. Information is extracted from the many different operational information systems (Doke & Barrier, 1994) and loaded into the MIS, DSS, and EIS systems. Data warehouse systems, DSS, MIS, and EIS systems contain point-in-time information, which means the data are extracted from the operational transactional databases at a specific point in time; whereas transactional databases are *dynamic* and are constantly being updated whenever a transaction takes place.

Public Service Management Systems

Public service management systems are designed to provide information to give the public access to specific information as a way of providing government services. Many of the clients and general public walk into government offices for accessing and using these kinds of systems and services. The information is not available via the Internet because *confidentiality legislation* in some states do not permit government to put this information online accessible to the general public using the Internet.

The general public can physically walk into government offices and use its computers to access the information and gain access to specific government records and information. These systems differ from customer relationship management systems in the private sector. For example, customer relationship management systems are used by banks in the private sector to analyze the transactions by millions of customers at its branches and through ATM machines or online banking for examining customer behaviors for providing new services.

E-government Systems

Government organizations use Internet technology for providing services. Electronic government (e-government) is different from e-commerce, which is used by private sector organizations for buying and selling. The e-government application software programs are designed to utilize the Internet and virtual private networks to provide different types of online services to public employees, the general public, clients, other government agencies, and the business market (Moon, 2002). Many of these systems are custom-built to support each department and agency within government.

Back-Office Support Systems

In addition to the systems previously mentioned, there are back-office systems that handle the administrative support functions and activities within an organization. Back-office information systems consist of financial and accounting systems, personnel and payroll systems, and purchasing systems. These kinds of systems often referred to as *horizontal software systems* are general enough to be used in a variety of organizations and industries (Haag et al., 2007). Back-office systems are essentially those that every organization has and needs to support the internal activities of the organization. Several vendor companies provide commercial, packaged software solutions such as ERP systems that can be purchased but often require modifications or changes to the business processes within an organization.

Back-office information systems support functions such as human resources, personnel, payroll, financial, and accounting systems and important to the organization but do not give you any strategic advantage. These horizontal information systems are often referred to as bread-and-butter systems because every company or organization has them and everyone needs them (Orfali et al., 1999). These types of information systems are important to the organization but are not necessarily highly specialized and many software packages can be purchased from companies that design and develop the computer programs for these information systems. However, generally speaking, some of these systems are better for supporting public sector organizations and others work best for private sector organizations.

There are several different packaged software systems on the market that can be purchased by organizations for these types of systems. Your method of evaluating the commercial, packaged software system in detail is important to see which one best supports the business strategy of the organization and the departments (Keil & Tiwana, 2005). It is not uncommon for organizations to avoid focusing on the business strategy and put their primary focus on the information systems strategy.

If an organization has to totally change how it does its business because of how the commercial, packaged information system is designed, there is a need to determine whether the changes in the business processes really adds value to the organization as a whole, which is discussed in this book on the subject of the value chain and organizational performance. If the packaged, information system under consideration has too many gaps in its business functions and features it is probably a clear indication that the information system software does not fit within the organization's business strategy. If the vendor company you are working with says they can enhance and customize the system to fill the gaps, you need to determine how long it will take and at what costs. If it takes too long and increases your project budget significantly, it is probably an option you may not want to pursue. Be aware that some vendors may provide low project estimates, which can come from underestimating the scope of work that needs to be accomplished.

Workgroup Systems

Office productivity software including *e-mail* is often referred to as workgroup systems that help workers to communicate and collaborate. Workgroup systems consist of commercial off-the-shelf software such as word processing, spreadsheet, individual or small workgroup database software, presentation software, e-mail systems; and the software systems are normally connected to the organizational network infrastructure for accessing and for sharing information. Office productivity systems are used to automate the office activities and support workgroups including video conferencing. Workgroup systems support the activities of office staff, managers, professionals, general workers, and executives (Haag et al., 2007). You buy the software and have permission to install it on your computers and use it because you purchased one of many user licenses (i.e., word processing, spreadsheets, and presentation software). This type of software is considered off-the-shelf, commercial, packaged software. Programmers do not have permission to gain access to or change the code in the software programs.

So why do I make all this fuss about the different types of computer information systems? The reason is because you as a business manager or as a technical manager at all levels in the organization need to recognize that all computer information systems are not created equal, which means that they are designed for different purposes in order to support the different business strategies within both public sector and private sector organizations to improve organizational performance. This is a topic that I found to be blurred in my discussions with some top-level managers who did not take into consideration the differences when they made strategic decisions about organizational project priorities. This is the main reason why the information on the types of information systems included in this book. Managers will benefit from having a better understanding of the different types of information systems and workgroup systems.

Decisions and the Business Strategy

During a top-level management meeting, decisions were being made that did not take into consideration the different types of computer information systems in the organization and how they fit within with the business strategy of the many different departments and agencies within the organization as a whole. More importance and more funding were given to back-office support systems with little importance placed on the other project priorities within the organization.

There was an IT director from one of the departments discussing the importance of a unique mission-critical information system and was explaining the differences in the various systems in the organization. In particular, one information system was in need of being replaced. After all, this type of information system handles the primary business functions of three departments within the organization by collecting millions of dollars in revenue and provides products and services to the citizens and clients. The information system was originally developed in late 1970s. Organizations have difficulty taking advantage of the latest information systems features and functionality on a 1970s computer system foundation or computer system's architectural design. The longer an organization waits, the higher the costs of replacing the computer information system.

Although the mainframe computer hardware, operating systems, and databases had been updated over the years to newer versions of hardware and operating system software, the information system itself was designed using older architecture design for the application programs and the databases. Other design limitations would become problems in the near future because of the design features and the limitation of field sizes within the databases and within the programs and costs associated with making changes.

During the meeting, it seemed that little importance was placed on the business and the organizational strategies, and the types of information systems that would increase organizational performance. Even though the mission-critical system being discussed was old and in needed of replacement, top-level executives were influenced by other priorities. In most situations like this one, the department lacked the political clout and, therefore, this the organization failed to act. There is far more political influence at the central, administrative level of the organization among the CIO, CEO, and the elected board of supervisors. The political environment and the dynamics that take place within government and public sector organizations can either promote change within a short period of time or it can take place anywhere from two to five years. Sometimes, organizations act on the here and now and not on future concerns.

The decision to replace the information system came five years later when it was determined that the system will cost millions of dollars to keep it operational with no new functional benefits to the departments and the end users. Many of the employees with expertise in the business and technical area have either retired from employment or left the organization for jobs elsewhere. In the interim, short-term solutions were identified to keep the information system operational until a new system can be worked on and implemented.

By knowing the different types of systems, most managers at all levels within the organization will have a better understanding of how the information systems support both the business strategy and the organizational strategy and be more objective in making their decisions. This information is important for both technology managers and general business managers. More importantly, the CEO, CIO, and some department heads have a powerful influence on project priorities. Unless there is strong collaboration between these top-level managers, some projects are delayed for future consideration.

The strategic information systems grid previously shown in Figure 3.6 gives you a clear description of how strategic information systems support an organization to support its programs, products, and services. The grid identifies the primary business systems and the support system for the organization. The grid has been adapted to include public sector organizations and their unique information systems and e-government.

Table 3.2 Types of computer information systems

Category	Description
Transaction processing systems (TPS), specialized TPS systems, and vertical information systems	TPS systems are considered mission critical to the business operations and some are specialized systems in government that are normally custom-built systems that support the programs, products, and services of each department or agency. Vertical systems are unique to a specific industry such as healthcare (radiology, patient-scheduling, pharmaceutical systems).
Supply chain systems	For the private sector, supply chain systems tracks inventory and information among business processes and different companies.
E-government systems	Uses enabling technologies of the Internet and online application programs. In government, e-government systems interface the public, employees, business entities, and provide information and services. These systems use the Internet, intranet, and virtual private networks, and integrate with internal information systems.
E-commerce systems	Uses enabling technologies of the Internet and online programs for private sector organizations for the electronic market place and the consumers for buying and selling.
Public service management systems	In government organizations, public service management systems are unique to each department or agency. The future needs of the customers are determined and met by providing the public access to information (e.g., GIS maps, parcel property maps, property homeowner information, and public records). Statistical reports from these systems help in developing future services.
Customer relationship management systems (CRM)	In the private sector, the CRM systems are designed to collect transaction (e.g., ATMs) information on customers and for predicting customer behavior for insight into their needs for developing future services.
Back-office information systems such as financial and accounting systems, human resource systems (e.g., payroll and personnel) including ERP Systems.	In both public and private sector organizations, these information systems support the daily business operations by streamlining or reducing costs on the manner in which the business is being done. Often referred to as *horizontal software systems* because they can be used in many types of organizations and industries.
Manufacturing systems.	In the private sector, back-office systems such as manufacturing systems provide the technology tools, products, services, and people for turning raw materials into manufactured goods.

Continued

Table 3.2 Continued

Category	Description
Data warehouse systems consisting of decision support systems (DSS), management information systems (MIS), and executive information systems (EIS)	In both the public and private sector, these information systems provide information for managing, controlling, and analyzing. They are *subsets* of the other systems. Data are extracted from the transaction processing systems (TPS) and other operational systems and loaded into data warehouses for systems such as DSS, MIS, and EIS.
Office productivity systems and workgroup systems	In the public and private sector organizations, workgroup systems include e-mail systems and software systems that are packaged off-the-shelf software, which can be purchased from commercial, vendor companies for office support functions such as word processing, spreadsheet software, presentation software, desktop publishing, individual or small workgroup database management software, etc.
Network infrastructure systems	In both public and private sector organizations, infrastructure systems are used to connect and share information (telecommunications). They create a path for communication and information sharing, for example, the network (intranet, Internet, portals, virtual private networks).

Although government and public sector organizations and the information systems that support its business operations are not-for-profit, they do provide strategic benefits in relationship to the business operations, the programs they administer, and the products and the services they provide to the clients and the general public from the various government departments and agencies, and can improve overall organizational performance. Table 3.2 identifies these systems and includes some of the private sectors systems as comparisons.

The availability of commercial, packaged information system software on the market to buy or purchase for government organizations can be limited for some transaction processing systems. The solutions for these unique systems at one time were generally custom-built software. Some of these information systems were and still are being developed by the government organizations using systems analysts and computer programmers within the organization. However, more and more information systems software is being developed commercially on the market by vendors for government organizations.

Often commercial, packaged software developed by software companies in one state may not fit the needs of another state. Why? It is because of the differences in states and local legislation that mandates how the organizations and their business divisions must operate and function to adhere to legislation. There can be a wide range of diversification. The functionality may differ greatly in commercial, packaged software developed in different states from different vendor companies. Managers in the organization need to examine the functions and features of the commercial software system carefully. Beware, when there are too many gaps in the functionality of the commercial information system it can be an indication that the information system does not totally support the business operations in your organization. Enhancements to the software by the vendor or the software development company may be required and may take much longer to complete or result in the project being delayed or, in some situations, even cancelled. The customization needs to be included in the project timeline and total project cost.

Awareness of the Differences

Top-level executives and managers who are aware of the differences in the various types of information systems information can make better decisions on prioritizing, purchasing packaged software, developing and implementing custom-built software systems. Successful managers find a balance by using a business strategy that is supported by the organizational strategy and the information systems strategy.

Managers in organizations that identify the business initiative, the project mission, and have a clear vision of what the organization will be like after the project has been implemented. They will have a clear roadmap of the benefits of the project. An awareness of the categories of computer information systems in the organization and how they are aligned to support the business strategy assists top-level managers in making informed decisions.

System Boundaries and the Environment

Now that you are more familiar with the different types of information systems, let's talk briefly about an *information system's boundaries*. What about those individuals who think that one information system can do everything for everybody within the organization and even for other organizations? This can be difficult to achieve because of external constraints such as legislation and federal and state rules and regulations that impact how organizations conducts their business. You need to be aware of the fact that the information system's boundaries are determined by its *goals and purpose*. The information system is designed to accept *inputs, process,* and *transform* the information into *outputs*. The outputs from the information system are used to achieve its purpose. In other words, "The features that define and delineate a system forms it boundaries" (Ahituv et al., 1994, p. 87). The information system is inside the boundaries and the environment is outside of the boundaries. This is something everyone needs to recognize because all information systems have boundaries.

The interaction between an information system at its boundaries is called *interfaces* and can be in the form of inputs and outputs from other computer programs and systems (Ahituv et al., 1994). An example of a *system interface* is an e-government system that uses Internet technology and accepts payments (inputs) in the form of transactions. The e-government system may have various features and functions for providing information to the public using the Internet and also accepts payments and fees from the public and the business market. The e-government system actually interfaces with the organization's internal information system. The organization's internal or in-house information system, subsequently, processes the payment transactions, updates the internal databases, and prints other confirmation documents and reports as outputs. Many of the internal information systems process the appropriate collection information and interface with the organization-wide financial system for processing the final distribution of revenue. The topic of system boundaries would take too much time to discuss in this chapter, but this information provides you with some of the basics on system boundaries and system interfaces. Several IT management books provide information on system boundaries.

Summary

Individuals in organizations have visions, and visions are the starting points for changes to the business operations and services and can affect the information systems that support it. Each information systems project needs to have a clearly defined project mission. Some of the fundamentals of information systems project management are reviewed by examining project management in the public sector organizations, description of a government project, portfolio management, selection methods, and the role of the project manager. This chapter examines project management in a government organization, the project life cycle, software engineering consisting of variations of the systems development life cycle (SDLC), the software project management methodology (approach), ten critical success factors, the PMI method, commercial packaged software systems, the request for proposal (RFP) to purchase software hardware, software, and professional services, and the contractual agreement.

This chapter describes the functional project organization, how systems work requests are handled in one government organization, and the different types of information systems in public sector organizations. The differences between strategic systems that focus on the primary, core business processes that are highly specialized and other systems are considered support systems for administration, financials, human resources, purchasing, and other overhead activities. The chapter emphasizes the importance of recognizing that all systems have boundaries, which is different from system interfaces.

Review Concepts

- The importance of visions and project missions
- Project management
- Portfolio management and project priorities
- Role of the project manager
- The project team
- Variations of the software engineering and systems development life cycle (SDLC)
- Ten critical success factors
- The project management methodology
- The PMI method
- Commercial, packaged systems and in-house developed systems
- The request for proposal (RFP)
- The contractual agreement
- Functional project team versus the pure project organization
- Computer systems work requests
- Different types of information systems
- System boundaries
- System interfaces
- Public sector information systems strategic grid
- Strategic systems and support systems

Discussion Questions

3.1. Discuss why some visions can turn in to computer information systems work requests.

3.2. Describe the different types of computer information systems.

3.3. Why are some information systems considered strategic and others considered support systems?

3.4. Why do you think it is important to establish project priorities?

3.5. Discuss why portfolio management is important to an organization.

3.6. What is the meaning of a project management methodology?

3.7. Discuss the ten critical success factors.

3.8. What is the reason for an RFP?

3.9. What is the importance of a contractual agreement?

CHAPTER FOUR
AVOIDING SOME COMMON PROBLEMS

After you work as a project manager for a while, you will discover that there are some things you can do that will assist you in avoiding some of the common problems in managing information systems projects. Reviewing your project management books, journal articles, and discussions with other project managers will teach you about the different approaches to project management and how to deal with some of the issues in the profession. This chapter examines the importance of a collaborative work environment for reviewing and updating information technology standards and policies, the project plan, and how decisions made at the top level of the organization can impact project planning. It describes the importance of change control procedures; the three areas important to measuring project success and project outcomes; and the need for you to celebrate and communicate accomplishments. There are some web sites and other resources included for both business managers and project managers.

Information Technology Standards and Policies

Most organizations in both the private and public sectors develop information technology policies that establish information technology (IT) use and standards for the organization. Organizational IT policies are important to organizational success and need to be developed in collaboration with the chief information officer (CIO), senior executives, department heads, business managers, and the IT directors within the departments. IT standards and policies are essential because it helps to reduce conflicting agendas. It is important that the policies and standards be reviewed and revised periodically by the organization. Business managers, project managers, and IT managers at all levels in the organization want to be able to communicate with the top-level management and have annual review meetings on organizational standards and policies. The requests for these meetings can be directed to the chief executive officer (CEO) and the CIO. There needs to be a partnership between the CIO and the department and agencies for supporting the objectives of the organization as a whole; and business alignment with IT needs to be an ongoing process (Booth & Philip, 2005).

Technology standards and policies need to be developed and modified through a collaborative effort between the departments and should consider IT governance (decision rights). There needs to be policies on computer hardware, software, computer use, technical training, technical committees, and security practices, employment of contractors and consultants, use of computer manufacturers, packaged software systems, system development methodologies, financial and accounting policies on cost centers and internal service funds, and many other standards. The purchasing department normally establishes policies on the procurement of computer hardware, software, and professional services.

What about collaboration? Collaboration means working together on a common goal and it is very important to organizational success. You want to work on promoting collaborative meetings with the CIO, business managers, and IT/IS managers on both the business strategies and IT strategies. This can be accomplished by participating as member of a steering committee for establishing IT organization-wide standards and policies.

An example of an IT standard established with no collaboration was a case in the mid-1990s when several departments were using Visual Basic programming language for developing some of their new information systems. The central, organizational IT department decided that another programming language would be the standard programming language for the government organization for developing new information systems. It was only after a major system experience of significant problems, which were due to the high volume of nightly processing that could not be completed in a timely manner, that the project was considered a failure and the organization had to reassess its options. Later, the IT standards and policies were updated to be more flexible and included Visual Basic because programming languages serve different purposes.

A collaborative agreement could have prevented many other IT directors and IT managers from being caught in middle space with conflicting agendas. A collaborative approach is important to successful organizations (Vangen & Huxham, 2003).

A lower-risk project is a wiser choice when using a different or a new technology. The best approach is to start with a small pilot project as a test case to see how and if the technology supports the business and information systems strategies. Another approach is to identify other organizations that are using the technology and visit those sites to see a firsthand account on how it supports the business operations. Research consultants are a really good resource for providing the information in this area. Newer technology needs to be tested, proven, and free of programming errors and problems before supporting and investing the funds and resources in a project that may or may not be successful. In addition to these concerns, the technical staff needs time to receive the appropriate training and to develop their skills and expertise. You want to be able to reduce the risks involved with implementing new or different technology.

Decisions on Projects

If the decision is made by top-level managers to go ahead with a major project, the first thing you *do not* want to do is quickly develop the detailed project plan with estimates and costs for the project. Why not? In most cases, you do not have enough information about the project to develop a detailed plan. The first step you can take is start work on identifying what you need to do in order to develop the project plan.

Project Plan

The project plan contains the information on how you are going to do what you want to be able to do in order to start work on the project. Several elements of the project plan can fall within the following categories: the project overview, objectives, general approach, contractual aspects, schedules, resource requirements, personnel, evaluation methods, and potential problems (Mantel, Meredith, Shafer, & Sutton, 2005, 2010). The project plan identifies the funding sources for the project, the resources needed to work on developing the project plan in terms of human resources and hours, software and hardware, facilities, and everything else needed prior to developing the detailed project plan. Projects vary in detail depending on the size and complexity of the project.

The first thing you want to do before replacing or making major modifications and enhancements to an existing system is the preliminary project planning, starting with the general information and working on refining it to get to the details as you progress through your research, information gathering, project meetings, review meetings, and discussions. This approach is taken with the assumption that someone has completed a postaudit review of the existing system deciding that it no longer meets the business strategy of the organization. You want to use the *funnel approach*, starting with the general information and working toward the details and the specifics. Work on identifying the individual activities that you, the others, and the group have to perform in your project plan and present it to the management.

Preliminary project plans are uniquely different for each project, see Figure 4.1 (this is relatively a simple example). Of course, not all projects need all the elements identified in the preliminary plan because it normally applies to medium to large projects. This approach does not apply to what is considered smaller size projects. However, all projects, regardless of their size, need to have their project tasks and activities defined along with the schedules, hardware and software resources, and the personnel.

Department ABC's Project

	Task Name	Duration	Start	Finish
1.	Orientation meetings with assistant department head, business managers, IT director, and IS project manager (PM) on the project's business initiative	1 wk	11/7/11	11/11/11
2.	Identify committee members to interpret impact of legislation on business	1 wk	11/14/11	11/18/11
3.	Schedule meetings with legislative review committee	1 wk	11/21/11	11/25/11
4.	Committee and PM review impact of legislation on business operations and develop project mission, objectives, and proposed changes to the business operations (business strategy)	2 wks	11/28/11	12/9/11
5.	Identify personnel needed to review the existing information system	1 wk	12/12/11	12/16/11
6.	Project manager orientation meeting with end users and technical staff	1 wk	12/19/11	12/23/11
7.	Review current information system to determine which programs need modifications and/or new development	2 wks	12/26/11	1/6/12
8.	PM schedule follow-up meeting with end users on information gathering for system requirements	1 wk	1/9/12	1/13/12
9.	PM schedule meeting with managers on the general approach, feedback, and discussion of business strategy	1 wk	1/16/12	1/20/12
10.	Review project mission and identify resources for the project team	2 wks	1/23/12	2/3/12
11.	Work on the detailed project plan	2 wks	2/6/12	2/17/12

Figure 4.1   Project planning.

There are some system projects that do not come within the project costs and budget because too little time is spent on preliminary project planning and identifying the various detailed project tasks and activities. If the project manager is not given enough time to spend on this issue, it is because the top-level executives or managers are requesting estimates based on their own timeframe and the *sense of urgency* without considering the importance of planning (Pinto, 1986).

Some of the details for the information system project may surface during the project development phase and impact the project's target date, which could have been identified in the project plan. Large projects can be very complex, and it is important to ensure that all aspects of the project are identified and discussed so that all of those involved have some understanding of the scope and size of the project.

A good approach is to reflect on the things you know about the requirements that should be in the project plan and think about other things as you organize your thoughts on what needs to be included in the plan. Be flexible about altering it as you put it together.

If you do not know the source of funding for the proposed project, you will not be able to develop a project budget based on your estimated costs. For example, if you were going to work on a major project for your home, you want to know where the funds are coming from to pay for the project. It might come from your own savings account or it may come from a home loan. You want to be able to identify the source of funding for the project before you even start any work on your project plan. In government, a top-level manager will provide you with information on the funding source for the project before you even start your information gathering or feasibility study and project planning for obtaining project cost estimates.

In some situations, top-level executives or department heads may ask for project estimates without giving the project manager enough time to work on the planning to find out what is really required to identify what needs to be done. In some cases, the project is a legislative mandate, meaning the law changes how the organization or the department does business. The project target date is mandated by legislation. There may be a need to meet with the appropriate individuals to interpret the legislation before it can determine what has to change in the computer information system or if new computer programs have to be developed. It is also necessary to develop the project mission that everyone can agree upon, and you want to be able to get additional technical resources, if required.

The more time you spend upfront on planning can mean less time spent on things that surface later during the development phases of the project. Project planning will provide you the information for understanding the general scope of the project and is a way of sorting out the project. Chapter 5 of the PMBOK Guide (PMI, 2013) provides more information on project scope management. This approach allows you the time to identify the source of funding, the resources, tasks, and activities you feel are required before you actually start the actual detailed planning phases of the project. The plan should clearly define the project mission and the goals and objectives so there is agreement from all those involved (stakeholders), who have interest in the information systems project. You want to have time to identify all of the project stakeholders, including public interest groups, that could impact the project. After you and your technical staff are able to identify the tasks and activities by working with others, you can then start working on more detailed project plan with tasks, activities, and their estimated costs, see Figure 4.2.

What about using consultants to help with the planning? Consultants can bring valuable expertise to the project team and can augment your team resources. Managers with experience and graduate degrees working as employees within the organization may be valuable to you as internal consultants. Consulting with internal and external consultants and with experts is healthy and can point you to the right direction. Often in government and public sector organizations, you need approval before you can hire external consultants and contractors. Remember, if you do use consultants and contractors you are still ultimately responsible for the project. The project manager who is internal to the organization should be leading

	O	Task Name	Duration	Start	Finish	Predecessors
1		⊟ PLANNING	21 hrs	Mon 2/20/12	Wed 2/22/12	
2	▦	Review project mission and vision with technical team and end-users	4 hrs	Mon 2/20/12	Mon 2/20/12	
3		Meetings on overview of business processes and programs affected by legislation and details	8 hrs	Mon 2/20/12	Tue 2/21/12	2
4		Overview of proposed project plan	9 hrs	Tue 2/21/12	Wed 2/22/12	3
5		⊟ PRELIMINARY ANALYSIS	192 hrs	Wed 2/22/12	Tue 3/27/12	1
6		Review current system programs and subsystems	80 hrs	Wed 2/22/12	Wed 3/7/12	
7		Obtain user requirements	56 hrs	Wed 3/7/12	Fri 3/16/12	6
8		Develop proposed project work plan with hours and cost estimates	21 hrs	Fri 3/16/12	Wed 3/21/12	7
9		Meeting with feedback to task force on revised project plan proposal	3 hrs	Wed 3/21/12	Wed 3/21/12	8
10		Project plan proposal submitted to executive management for approval	32 hrs	Wed 3/21/12	Tue 3/27/12	9
11		⊟ ANALYSIS & DESIGN	240 hrs	Tue 3/27/12	Tue 5/8/12	5
12	▦	Interviews with end-users	40 hrs	Tue 3/27/12	Tue 4/3/12	
13	▦	Develop requirements, report requirements, and screen changes	56 hrs	Tue 4/3/12	Thu 4/12/12	12
14		Develop work plan detailed tasks	18 hrs	Thu 4/12/12	Mon 4/16/12	13
15		Write program specifications and database modifications	126 hrs	Mon 4/16/12	Tue 5/8/12	14
16		⊟ DEVELOPMENT	195 hrs	Tue 5/8/12	Mon 6/11/12	11
17		Make program modifications and write code for new programs	195 hrs	Tue 5/8/12	Mon 6/11/12	
18		⊟ TESTING AND DEBUGGING	207 hrs	Tue 6/12/12	Tue 7/17/12	16
19		Test individual programs	80 hrs	Tue 6/12/12	Mon 6/25/12	
20		Test system with all program processes	68 hrs	Tue 6/26/12	Fri 7/6/12	19
21		Obtain end-users' review and approvals	19 hrs	Fri 7/6/12	Tue 7/10/12	20
22		Implement system and perform troubleshooting	40 hrs	Tue 7/10/12	Tue 7/17/12	21
23		⊟ DOCUMENTATION	39 hrs	Tue 7/17/12	Tue 7/24/12	18
24		Complete end-user documentation	18 hrs	Tue 7/17/12	Fri 7/20/12	
25		Complete system documentation	12 hrs	Fri 7/20/12	Mon 7/23/12	24

Figure 4.2 Detailed project plan.

the project because it is important to have someone who understands the business strategy, the organizational strategy, and the information systems strategy, and has the prior working relationships with the business managers, the end users, and the technical staff from within the organization.

A. H. Weiler once said, "Nothing is impossible for the man who doesn't have to do it himself" (Byrne, 1996, para. 540). The consultant should not have any conflict of interest in the commercial software being considered for the project and should not be influenced by biased interested commercial, software vendors and stakeholders. You want to choose consultants carefully and review the consultants' credentials and background for experience on project accomplishments and professional references. The consultants should be knowledgeable in the technology and software being considered for the project.

It is a well known that several information system projects fail and some projects are cancelled. In other cases, the computer information system is implemented, and it meets the expected target date and budgeted costs but it does not deliver the expected benefits to the organization and the end users of the information system. There are many studies in literature on why systems fail and the subject is an entire book in itself. Many studies attribute failure to the lack of experience of the project manager, lack of skills of the project team members, lack of top management support, purchasing an information system that does not fit the business functionality of the organization, problems with the technical infrastructure, and a host of other reasons.

Eman and Koru (2008), in their study, replicated the international survey by the Standish Group. The study examined cancelled projects, including those that did not deliver usable functionality and those that did not meet project budget and target dates. Results from 232 respondents in 2005 reported that 15.5 percent of projects were cancelled and 50 percent rated the ability to meet project budget and target dates as either fair or poor. Results from 156 respondents in 2007 reported that 11.5 percent of the projects were cancelled and 47 percent rated the ability to meet project budget and schedule targets as fair or poor.

The largest number of respondents came from the United States, resulting in 37 percent in 2005 and 38 percent in 2007. The combined rate for projects cancelled and those completed but unsuccessful in 2005 was 34 percent and for 2007 was 26 percent. The respondents reported that lack of top management support, lack of management skills, and misalignment of IT with the business as reasons for project failure (Eman & Koru, 2008). In some situations, even top-level managers and IT managers unfamiliar with the business strategy can misalign IT with the business. When things do go terribly wrong with the project, the organization will start pointing fingers at someone who they think is the problem.

Change Control

How do you handle requests for changes when the project plan has been completed and work is being performed by the project team members? You want to have some formal procedures of handling system change requests. It is important as a project manager that you control change requests from end users of the new system after work starts on a project because too many changes can slow down the progress of a project and impact the project costs and target completion date. Sometimes you may receive many requests for enhancements or changes to the system such as adding different types of reports and changing the online input screen for entering information. If you start receiving too many requests for changes in the information system, there is a good chance that some major areas were missed in the analysis phase of the project. This can become a real issue if you do not respond to these concerns early on in the project.

The request procedures should be defined by your department or organization along with change control procedures and a project methodology defined. The change control methodology defines how you are going to handle the requests for changes to the information systems being worked on and implemented. It should be a formal procedure the end users must follow when submitting requested changes to the information system. The change requests are normally reviewed and approved by the managers or supervisors in the business divisions prior to being sent to the project manager. A change control request form should be completed by the requestors and reviewed by a change control IS committee and the project manager for approval. These forms are most often available online, see Figure 4.3

Decisions can be made to make the changes or to put the change requests on hold until after the computer system has been implemented. I have observed several projects not meeting the estimated target completion date because of too many change requests.

Raising the Warning Flag

What do you do when you feel the project is experiencing major problems? If the project is not going according to the project plan and the schedules are not being met, it is one of the major warnings signs that there are problems. The project needs to be examined to determine what needs to be done. When there are delays in one phase of the project, it can put the entire project behind schedule.

Holistic View

When a project is in trouble, you want a holistic and unbiased view of the problem and take the appropriate action to try to resolve the problem.

(Please complete the fields on the form)

Requestor's Name: _____ Date: _____ Telephone: _____ E-mail: _____ (Send Change Control Request via e-mail to: ghi.workrequest.desk.gov)
Project/Computer System's Name:
From Department/Division/Business Unit:
Reason for the change:
Impact on the project:
Impact of not making the change:
(Below for IT Department/Division Use Only): Estimated hours to implement change: _____ Systems Analyst: _____ Programmer: _____
Actual Total Hours _____ Project Name: _____ Systems Analyst: _____ Programmer: _____
Estimated Project Completion Date: _____
Actual Project Completion Date with Change: _____
[   ] Approved for immediate implementation Initials: _____ End User's Initials: _____ [   ] Delay Until _____ _____ _____ _____ Project Director / Manager: _____ Date: _____ (Signature)

Figure 4.3 Change control request form.

Sometimes a project manager feels that he or she can resolve the problems all by himself. In other situations, the project manager can go into denial because he does not want to stop the work and reassess the project so the project gets further and further behind schedule and then experiences multiple problems.

The best approach you can take for a troubled project is to have someone who is not a stakeholder in the project to reassess the project so that there can be an unbiased assessment. The reassessment can even be performed by a project evaluation committee or team. The reassessment will require evaluating the skills of the team and any issues of hardware and information system software. Consider several reasons why there are problems. The committee may feel it is necessary to redefine the project goals and determine whether the essential goals can be accomplished. Risk analysis of the project needs to be done by identifying the major risks and method of minimizing them. The results of reassessing the project may require revising the project plan and will require getting final approval from the project sponsors and stakeholders. Whatever the circumstances are with a project, the committee performing an assessment should be objective and unbiased. Even during the feasibility phase of a project, there may be a need to evaluate the various options.

There was a case in which the project manager (middle) reported to a central steering committee (tops). The project was in the planning phase. There were three options presented by the project manager to the steering committee along with his recommendation of which option was in the best interest of the organization. The steering committee was going to vote on the options when one member of the steering committee suggested that the three options be studied further by a subcommittee (belows). As a result of this suggestion, a subcommittee of three representatives from various departments was appointed by the steering committee. The subcommittee was to make its recommendations to the steering committee.

Unknown to the IS project manager and to some of the steering committee members, the subcommittee's chairperson (below) had previously applied for the position held by the IS project manager who was in charge of the project and this same subcommittee chairperson was not selected for the position. It is important that a subcommittee or an evaluation committee be impartial.

As a result of the subcommittee's evaluation, the option recommended was not the one proposed by the project manager. When the steering committee members did vote on selecting one of the three options, the majority voted on the option recommended by the subcommittee. A short time later, the subcommittee chairperson eventually left government employment. Unfortunately, one person can influence decisions on a project, which may not be in the best interest of the organization as a whole. This same subcommittee individual left behind the results of his or her influence on project decisions that impacts the organization.

The project manager felt that there were conflicting agendas among the steering committee members and that establishing the subcommittee was just another approach to influence the steering committee members not to support the option that the project manager recommended. The question to be considered in this type of situation is: What are the consequences and challenges for managers within the organization long after the subcommittee chairperson who influenced the decision has departed from the organization?

In this particular case, the project was implemented successfully by the project manager and team members because all three options were viable options. However, the organization did not take advantage of a lower-cost project, and many features of a newer architectural information systems design that would have included a relational database management system in which the database logic is separate from the application system programming logic instead of implementing the information system on a mainframe computer. Shortly after the project was implemented, the project manager decided to move on to other opportunities and accepted another position. Sometimes you just have to move on when you feel you are not getting the level of support that you need in a position.

Expert Opinion in Business

The preliminary analysis for gathering important information and the feasibility study are important before making a decision to move forward with a new information systems project. Not all organizations do a thorough job of conducting these two phases of the SDLC approach, which should involve the key business managers before making a decision to implement a new information system. I find it disturbing in some situations that great care is not taken in making decisions on implementing new information systems projects.

Experienced managers take great care in getting all the information before moving forward with change. A good example of relevancy is consumer market surveys, which use what is called a *grass-roots approach* for sales forecasting. The approach is to survey customers and future customers regarding their plans and purchases. Information is gathered on how they would respond to new products, product features, or improvements. This method can be used with a combination of other judgment forecasting methods such as jury of executive opinion that involves a group of high-level managers to collectively make the forecast (Hillier & Hillier, 2003).

See Table 4.1. The management science method has five main judgmental forecasting methods as follows:

1. Manager's opinion
2. Jury of executive opinion
3. Sales force composite
4. Consumer market survey
5. Delphi method

Why is it that in some organizations a decision is made to replace or acquire a new computer information system but the same amount of detail and extensive research and analysis and planning is not done or even considered by top-level management?

It is interesting to see how much detail and involvement of other managers go into the marketing forecasting methods. By looking at information

Table 4.1   Types of judgmental forecasting methods

Method	Description
Manager's opinion	This is a method that involves a single manager's best judgment to make the forecast. In some cases, some data may be available but the emphasis is on the manager using his experience and knowledge to make the judgment.
Jury of executive opinion	This method involves a small group of high-level managers who make the decision. The decision is based on their knowledge and experience. This method is used for critical forecasts.
Sales force composite	This method uses a bottom-up approach for sales forecasting wherein the estimate for sales in a region is provided by the person responsible for this region. The estimates are provided to various levels of upper-level management for review and for sales forecasting.
Consumer market survey	This method uses what is called a *grass-roots approach* for sales forecasting. The approach is to survey customers and future customers regarding their plans for purchases. Information is gathered on how they would respond to new products, product features, or improvements.
Delphi method	This method uses a panel of experts. These experts are in different locations. In this approach, they have to fill out questionnaires. The results are provided with the next questionnaire so that each can evaluate the information and have the opportunity to change his or her response. The goals of this method is to narrow the conclusions. The persons responsible for making the decisions will do so by assessing input from a panel of experts to develop the forecast.

systems in another perspective is that when plans begin on acquiring a new information system, many organizations overlook the preliminary analysis and start out with a feasibility study to determine if the project is even feasible and identify the potential benefits or expectations to a department or to the organization as a whole. Even before the preliminary analysis and feasibility study, the organization needs to determine

1. the business initiatives promoting change;
2. the vision and project mission;
3. the measurable outcomes; and
4. identify internal experts through internal networks.

Project managers should work toward making the project mission and expectations of measurable outcomes a joint effort by identifying the expectations of both the department or agency and the organization; and it needs to include more than just the financial expectations and performance. A good approach is to perform some up-front research. If you are considering vendor software, research the packaged systems available in the software market and examine their use in other similar organizations to see which ones could potentially be considered for the organization.

Is there a one-size-fits-all approach to decision making for new information system projects? The answer is "no," because it depends on the scope and complexity of the information system. Some organizations may use several of the five judgmental methods listed previously in a marketing situation. The reason the different judgmental methods are shown is to communicate to you how detailed the process is before actually making a decision to move forward with a project. It is true that an information systems strategy is not the same as in a marketing strategy; however, it is just as important that thorough investigation and analysis is done when an organization plans for major changes or acquiring a new information system. After all, many organizations invest millions of dollars in their computer systems.

Top-level executives and managers can move too quickly in making plans for acquiring a new computer system without the organization taking the time to define the project mission, the business strategy, and the impact on the departments or agencies that the information systems is to support. One person's expert opinion is not enough. Organizations should identify experts both in the business areas and in the technical areas of the organization and survey managers in the departments or organization that will be affected by the change. A thorough approach helps to avoid narrowly focused projects that are not in the best interest of the organization as a whole.

There may be people who have the information and knowledge of the business and the technical areas. Identifying the right people will help achieve the information systems strategy that is aligned with both the business and organizational strategies. If the systems project is organization wide and affects many departments, then feedback from the departments is important. Studies report that information systems that are solely initiated by one person or by a top-level executive place the organization at a disadvantage because it is not a collaborative effort driven by the business strategy.

Internal Experts

Top-level management in many organizations rely on internal experts to evaluate what is going on inside and outside of the boundaries of the organization. Evaluating the options may mean site visits to other facilities or organizations that are using the various commercial information systems to see the advantages and/or the disadvantages to the organizations. A thorough investigation will assist you in finding out who has been successful and who has not and finding out what are some of the problems they encountered with the new information system. How do other organizational business strategies differ from your organization or from your department?

The Three Areas of Measuring Project Success

The first question to be asked in managing and implementing information systems is how to meet the needs of both the information system users and the organization. Pinto (1986) conducted a study involving 457 project managers to determine how they measure the value of the project. The survey measurements were later refined in two more recent studies by Belout and Gauvreau (2004) and by Rosacker (2005) to more accurately measure schedules and budgets. I used the same survey to measure project success in county government. The results of the implementation should improve organizational performance. My research used the three items from the adapted questionnaire by Rosacker (2005) and seven items from PIP questionnaire (Pinto, 1986), resulting in a total of ten items to measure success. Project success is measured on the basis of three areas:

1. The project plans and schedules are met,
2. Costs are within the original budget, and
3. The solution implemented achieves the functional goals (the system provides the functionality as expected by the departments and/or organization and the end users.

The functional benefits means the system will directly benefit the end users through increasing employee efficiency and effectiveness, lead to

Figure 4.4   Three areas of measuring project success.

improved or effective decision making or performance for the clients, and the overall project is considered a success. You want to work toward making the expectations of the functional benefits a joint effort because you want to fulfill the needs of the department or agency, the end users of the information system, and the organization, see Figure 4.4.

All the items were rated on five-point Likert scale ranging from 1 (strongly disagree) to 5 (strongly agree). See Appendix A. It is important that knowledgeable IT directors and managers understand the significance of all three areas. Figure 4.5 lists the items in the survey questionnaire used to measure the variable project success.

After developing the project plan with the appropriate timelines, the project manager can draw up the detailed project plan with the various tasks, subtasks, and activities. There are several academic books on how to develop the project plan. Some books contain hundreds of pages and can be somewhat overwhelming and some others are condensed and focus on the essentials.

Visit Amazon.com and you will find many project management books, including those containing references at the end of each chapter or at the back of the book. These types of books include information from other research articles and information technology sources.

What about issues that can arise that you don't know about and are unexpected? When working on the project plan, it is important for the project manager to add in hours for the *unexpected* or for the unplanned issues that might cause some additional time to be spent on the project tasks and could subsequently impact the total project hours and costs. Some project team members may need sick leave time off from their work assignments or there may be delays in delivery of hardware and software products and other unforeseen events. Taking into consideration the unexpected is necessary because government projects are normally budgeted within the annual budget cycle, so all costs need to be included. Managers who do not include the unexpected issue that can arise run the risks of going over the total project costs that has been budgeted. Going over the budget can create a whole new set of problems for the organization.

The first set of questions relate to your evaluation of the ultimate performance of the information systems project in which you were involved. Please indicate by selecting the appropriate number of the **extent** to which you agree or disagree with the following statements as they relate to the outcome of the project.

	Strongly Agree	Agree	Neutral	Disagree	Strongly Disagree
1. The project has/will come in on time.	5	4	3	2	1
2. Project schedules are being adhered to.	5	4	3	2	1
3. This project did/will come in on budget.	5	4	3	2	1
4. The project costs objectives have been/will be met.	5	4	3	2	1
5. The project is/will be used by its intended clients.	5	4	3	2	1
6. This project will directly benefit the intended users: either through increasing efficiency or employee effectiveness.	5	4	3	2	1
7. Use of this project has/will directly lead to improve or more effective decision making or performance for the clients.	5	4	3	2	1
8. The project will/has a positive impact on those who make use of it.	5	4	3	2	1
9. The results of this project represent a definite improvement in performance over the way clients used to perform these activities.	5	4	3	2	1
10. All things considered, this project was/will be a success.	5	4	3	2	1

Figure 4.5 Project success outcomes.

Source: Adapted from Pinto, 1986.

Learn to Celebrate

How do you celebrate yours and your team members' accomplishments? So far, the discussion has been on management and the project managers. So let's focus on the project manager's relationship with the team members. Skilled and competent project team members are valuable assets not only to the project manager but also to the organization as a whole. When things go well for the project manager and the team members, they go well for the organization. Team members need to believe that you value their efforts for completing important tasks. Even you as a project manager need to feel valued by your department and organization. A culture of encouragement includes celebrating accomplishments. When you and your project team members and staff are working on a major project, you do not want to forget to celebrate when you accomplish some major milestones or work tasks. Try to make a work environment that brings some kind of recognition to others for their accomplishments.

I bring in snacks for my team members to have during break time, like pretzels, juice, coffee, fresh fruit, and oatmeal cookies. Occasionally during lunch time near holidays, we schedule potlucks during lunchtime following a major work effort and I treat everyone to drinks and dessert. During other times, there are brown bag luncheons where everyone brings their own lunch and I provide the drinks, fruit, and dessert. This time is used as a general discussion session after lunch about what went well and what we need to work on and to celebrate our accomplishments. We learn to celebrate because it helps to build morale and adds social interaction to the team. The meetings may cost me some money from my personal budget but it is money well spent.

If you want to recognize individual team members or others in the organization, you can do this during your project team luncheons or team meetings. You can give out recognition certificates and computer-generated awards for specific accomplishments during the project. Just make sure you recognize the accomplishments of several of your team members for different achievements over time and not just a few individuals.

Recognition Awards

I find it disturbing that some managers do not define the criteria for excellent employee performance. Before you start giving out individual recognition awards for achievement, you and the other managers in your organization or department need to define the criteria for excellent employee performance. If you do not do this, the awards recognition can be based on whomever you or someone else thinks should be getting the award and the awards recognition can become meaningless to your employees. In some cases, it can affect the overall employee morale if mediocre and poor performers are awarded recognition. I have observed this happening in a couple of departments and it really does affect employee morale. In fact, some of my students tell me how upset they feel when someone who is a poor performer at work gets an achievement award. In other words, a poor performer is being rewarded for his poor performance, which does not encourage other workers to strive for excellence.

When you celebrate accomplishments, avoid celebrating after work hours in places just for cocktails and drinks. There was a situation in which a top-level manager did this very same thing. Several people in the team did not drink alcoholic beverages, and others said that after some individuals were there at the celebration and had a few drinks it was quite embarrassing to see their behavior. The same individuals who complained about the after-work celebrations said that they never attended anymore because they felt the only individuals who enjoyed were the drinkers. This approach to celebration is not considered as team building and is not an appropriate approach for celebrating accomplishments.

Learn to celebrate your own accomplishments with your coworkers, family, and friends. Put together your personal plan for your own career path and the decisions you will make along the way. Celebrate when you accomplished a major milestone for a project or completed a major task from your personal plan. For example, you recently passed a final exam, you completed a training session, you finished your course, you completed your class paper, you completed your training certification, or you completed your degree. Learn to celebrate your own achievements. Life can be a lot more fun when you learn to celebrate.

Communicate Accomplishments

Project status reports communicate the progress to those stakeholders directly involved with the project and they should be completed on a regular schedule. A newsletter can be used for communicating information about the information systems project to those who do not receive the status reports. This is a really good approach to keeping everyone informed. Give your newsletter a unique name and a really good design layout with various colors and graphics to make it look professional. When working on major projects, publish a newsletter every three months with information about the project and distribute to the departments that are involved as end users of the information system. You, as a project director or manager, and a few key project team members can write articles about certain aspects of the project.

Many individuals in the organization do not know what your accomplishments are unless you communicate it in some way. The newsletter is a very good approach to communicate with everyone and discus the new functional features of the information system and to announce when you reach major milestones. In addition, you can publish your responses to questions you receive from the end users about the system.

If there are new members in the project team, they can be introduced to everyone using the newsletter and if someone leaves the team because of a reassignment, this too can be communicated in the newsletter. It can be distributed online via e-mail so there is no need to spend time printing copies for distribution. One of my managers and I review each newsletter before it is released for final distribution. You can do the same and publish your newsletter on a schedule that you feel is appropriate for the project.

Avoid saying what a wonderful job you and your project team members are doing in the newsletter. Leave your egos at the front door of the office. After the information system project is completed, the organization and the end users will be the judge of how well the system meets their needs and whether you and your project team did a great job. Focus on the project and the functions and goals of the information system project, not on individuals and egos in your newsletter.

Resources for Project Managers

This section includes several resources for project managers. Some of the web sites and other resources useful for information systems project management can be accessed using the Internet. Your project management textbooks, IT management textbooks, and the PMBOK Guide can provide you further information. Many of these books can be accessed through the book publishers or through Amazon.com:

1. The Project Management Institute (PMI).
   a. www.pmi.org
   b. This site has many resources for project managers, including the *Project Management Journal*. Members have access to their online library of research articles and the institute provides training for various PMI certifications.
   c. *The Project Management Body of Knowledge (PMBOK)*, 5th edition. Published by PMI, this excellent resource for project managers contains standards for project management and includes information on stakeholder management.
2. *Project Management in Practice* (2011) by Mantel, Meredith, Shafer, and Sutton.
   a. This book presents the core essential information for project management for developing the project plan. I have used this book for undergraduates when teaching information systems project management and find that it covers many core project management essentials, including how to use Microsoft Project for developing

your project plan. It comes with a CD or website software download that includes a trial version of Microsoft Project.

3. The Institute of Electrical and Electronics Engineering (IEEE).
   a. www.ieee.org
   b. IEEE is a professional association for the advancement of technology. Membership entitles you to articles, journals, training tutorials, the online ieeexplore library, and many other benefits. The Computer Society provides information on project management and project standards for developing and implementing computer information systems for computer professionals and students.

4. *The Project Manager's Guide to Software Engineering's Best Practices* (2001) by Mark J. Christensen and Richard H. Thayer.
   a. This book contains information on software engineering standards. There are IEEE standard templates for computer systems development and maintenance. I use this book in my information systems analysis and design courses as a supplemental textbook when teaching undergraduate students working on their bachelor's degree.

5. Middle Space.
   a. http://www.executiveforum.com/PDFs/oshry_synopsis.pdf
   b. http://www.powerandsystems.com/resources-a-thought-starters/books.html
   c. These sites have additional information on middle space and provide access to information on the books published by Barry Oshry, PhD.

6. Request for Proposals by state.
   a. http://www.findrfp.com/
   b. You can review the proposals to see how they are written for various government products and services.

7. How to write a proposal.
   a. http://www.findrfp.com/Government_Contracting/How_to_Write_ Proposal.aspx
   b. You can go to most government websites and select the purchasing department and you will find bids for government proposals.

8. US Bureau of Statistics.
   a. http://www.bls.gov/
   b. This website provides statistical information on jobs and the job market along with the job descriptions, qualifications, information on work experience, and the pay rate in various regions of the United States. Select the publications tab and the Occupational Outlook Handbook.

9. Government Census Bureau.
   a. http://www.census.gov/govs/
   b. After selecting the government's main tab, you can find information on the government census, structure of governments, and other pertinent government information.
10. *Computerworld.*
    a. http://www.computerworld.com
    b. This site has information on technology trends in business.
11. CIO Magazine.
    a. www.cio.com
    b. This site provides CIOs and technical leaders with information on technology trends in business.
12. *Public Administration Review.*
    a. This journal is available at the Wiley online library located at http://onlinelibrary.wiley.com/ or http://www.blackwellpublishing.com
    b. This journal provides valuable information on government administration and is a peer-reviewed journal.
    c. The journal can be accessed through most university online libraries.

Summary

Project planning is essential for information system projects and it contains the details of how you are going to be able to do what you need to do in order to start work on the project planning. Change control procedures are really important and assist you in completing major milestones, meeting target dates, and staying with the project costs.

A systems approach means going through the preliminary analysis, feasibility, and the information analysis for major projects before starting work on a project plan. This approach includes identifying the business initiative, the vision and project mission, and defining the measurable outcomes of the project not just in terms of financial performance. Project success is measured based on three items and measuring the outcomes. When a project is in trouble, it is essential for you to raise the warning flag early so the project can be reassessed and the organization can consider the options. If you are a project manager, you want to recognize your achievements and achievements of your team members. You can do this in different ways and learn to celebrate various accomplishments. Several Internet resources are available for project managers, including the website for the Project Management Institute and IEEE.

Review Concepts

- IT standards and policies
- Project planning
- Change control procedures
- Types of judgmental forecasting methods
- Business initiatives, project mission, and measurable outcomes
- Project Success measured by:
  Project plans and schedules met
  Costs are within original budget
  Information system achieves functional goals
- Project Implementation Profile Questionnaire
- Celebrating and communicating accomplishments
- Internet resources for project managers

Discussion Questions

4.1. Why are information technology standards and policies important to an organization?

4.2. Discuss the different reasons for the project plan.

4.3. Why is it important to have change control procedures?

4.4. Why is one person's expert opinion in business not enough to move forward with an information systems project?

4.5. Describe the Delphi method.

4.6. Discuss the three areas to measure project success and the project outcomes (results).

4.7. How would you celebrate your accomplishments? How would you celebrate your team members' accomplishments?

4.8. Discuss some of the resources available for project managers.

CHAPTER FIVE
STAKEHOLDER MANAGEMENT AND IT GOVERNANCE

Many different disciplines are involved with the management of information systems (MIS). The field of information technology requires a wide range of leadership skills. In fact, management science, software engineering, communications, organizational theory, information theory, and several other disciplines in "sociology and behavior sciences have made contributions to the field of information systems" (Ahituv, Neumann, & Riley, 1994, p. 4). Business decision makers must look beyond the traditional approaches of the MIS departments when making decisions on information systems in their organizations. This chapter describes some essentials, principles, suggestions, and concepts that managers need to consider when implementing information system projects.

Real work experiences of others often provide a wealth of information on project management. You learn valuable lessons from your experiences and by staying up-to-date with technology, and constantly working on improving your management style. For this reason, many researchers include case studies so that students and professionals have a broader range of information on situations that can surface in the workplace and obtain insight on how they were managed. This chapter presents some of those human experiences and introduces ideas that can help you to succeed and overcome some of the barriers to your success.

This chapter examines the importance of the organization's information technology standards and policies and collaboration from top-level management that can create shared visions. It describes the importance of identifying the project stakeholders, centralization versus decentralization of IT, economies of scope, breadth of diversification, the IT governance model on decision rights, the role of CIO and other managers within the organization, and elected and nonelected officials as department and agency heads.

Stakeholders in Government Organizations

Let's discuss the stakeholders who are the individuals or groups that benefit from the project and have an interest in it. Stakeholders need to be identified so that you can analyze their expectations for the project and communicate with them on the project status (PMI, 2013). Organizations in the private sector are influenced by stockholders, customers, competitors, unions, general society, and even government. The power of the CEO has a major influence on the organizational cultural and the strategic choices made with the goal of maximizing profits (Byars, 1991).

Chapter 13 of the PMBOK Guide (PMI, 2013) provides information on project stakeholder management and emphasizes the importance of not only identifying the project stakeholders but also being able to manage, communicate, and monitor the relationships. There are multiple classifications of stakeholders and their involvement with the project is important. Some stakeholders can be supportive and others can be leading to ensure project success; and some may be unaware, neutral, and even resistant. Chapter 13 of the PMBOK can guide you in completing the power/interest grid shown on page 397.

In contrast to private sector organizations, public sector organizations are influenced by politicians, legislative mandates, and internal and external stakeholders. Stakeholders in information systems projects can be a variety of different individuals and groups. A clear understanding of who the stakeholders are for a project enables the project manager to work toward ways that will benefit the majority of the project's stakeholders (Flak & Rose, 2005).

A study by Dufner and others (2002) report that when strategic planning takes place in US state organizations. the governors may have limited budget and appointment authority over state agencies. Why? It is because, "Elected officials preside over loosely coupled structure of state government including agencies that may receive independent funding streams from the US federal government" (p.414). In fact, my own experiences in managing software projects in US county government involve a variety of stakeholders both internally and externally, see Figure 5.1.

An example of external stakeholders, their interests, and influences in government are the voters and the e-voting systems for elections used by many states (Moynihan, 2004). In some states, the election systems have been scrutinized by special interest groups and the general citizens because of concerns over the security and accuracy of voting. Some very good information systems have been eliminated because of the powerful influence of special interest groups. Project managers in government must consider external stakeholders and their influences on the software

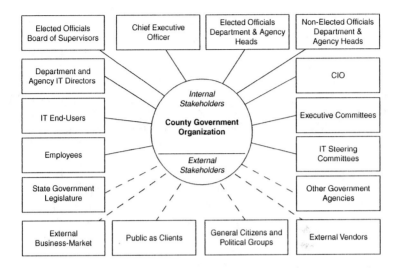

Figure 5.1 Stakeholders in county government.

projects. External stakeholders to the organization are not easily controlled and managed. "One clear message that comes through time after time is the prevailing power of such stakeholder groups in aiding or thwarting a project's successful development" (Pinto & Kharbanda, 1996, p. 47).

Even internal stakeholders who have an interest in a project can raise concerns from other departments and agencies within the organization. Project managers need to recognize the concerns of the stakeholders and "work on understanding their concerns or making necessary adjustment to the project" (Pinto & Kharbanda, 1996, p. 47).

Centralization versus Decentralization

An example of relevancy involving internal stakeholders is centralization versus decentralization projects. Nothing causes more concern and anxiety to department heads, managers, and to the employees within an organization than when a newly elected official or a new CIO starts talking about centralization of IT functions. The topic of whether to centralize or decentralize information systems under the organization's central IT department seems to appear frequently as a topic of discussion whenever a new CIO is hired into the government organizations. In this case, the internal stakeholders are the department heads and their employees from many of the departments and agencies within the organization.

A few years ago, a recently hired CIO within a few months after his arrival started working on a project plan to centralize the organization network support functions and e-mail systems of all 37 departments under the administration of the central IT department. The details remained blurred on centralizing specific IT functions and how this project was going to provide timely and quality support of the business strategies of the individual departments and agencies with the organizational strategy.

One full-time person can fill a technical position that is funded within each department or agency's budget; and in some departments, these positions were budgeted and funded under special programs. A department or agency can have several of these positions. One of the topics that surfaced during the planning on centralization is that within some departments or agencies one-half or one-fourth of a technical employee's work tasks are network support and e-mail support, the balance was dedicated to other IT support tasks specific to each business division or unit. To move the network support positions from the departments and agencies under the control and budget of the central, organizational IT department, it would require many departments to restructure their funded positions within their own departmental budgets. There was no way to move one-half or one-fourth of a person to the central IT department's budget.

Another subject that surfaced during the discussions was that moving IT staff positions under the management and budget of the central, organizational IT department would require involvement with the human resources department, labor unions, labor negotiations for responding to concerns on employee rights and seniority affecting job transfers. These same technical employees were familiar with the business operations of each of their own specialized department and agency. Another concern expressed by the managers in the departments and agencies is who will be responsible for paying for the computer hardware and software costs associated with the centralized project. As a result of all these concerns, the project plan was put on hold for a future feasibility study.

Now, let's look at this project in relation to the organizational system of tops, middles, belows, and the public they serve. The tops for this project are the elected officials in central administration, the CEO, the CIO, and the CTO. The middles are the top-level managers who are department and agency heads; and the belows are the IT directors, IT managers, and the technical staff. For this project, the elected officials who are department and agency heads operate within their own domain and the centralization project was optional for them and their technical staff.

During my many years of experience with government, I have found the decision to centralize IT or decentralize IT functions is a difficult one.

An important fact that is often overlooked for this type of project is that it needs to be driven by the business strategy in collaboration with the decisions by the top-level managers and not solely for cutting operating costs. Since many of the stakeholders are top-level managers and department and agency heads, collaboration is important for achieving organizational efficiency (Janssen & Kuk, 2007) and the project needs to be aligned with the business, organizational, and information systems strategy.

Before discussing this topic any further, it is important to review the history of centralized computer systems. In the early years of computing in the 1970s to the mid-1990s, organizations were highly centralized. Mainframe computers were used in many government organizations. Several of the large departments had their computer information system programs on a central mainframe physically located in the organization's central IT department. Some of the other departments that could afford it had their own information systems within their departments on mini-computers.

As technology evolved over the years, departments were able to purchase personal computers, printers, servers, mini-computers, and various types of software to run on their own computer systems, making it beneficial to bring the technology closer to the business operations. This approach gives the departments the ability to prioritize their own projects and maintain their systems without having to compete for the resources with other departments in a centralized organizational environment. The wide-area network (WAN) for the organization has always been centralized, but many departments started maintaining their own local area networks (LANs).

Second, from another perspective is that the development and growth of the Internet allows further flexibility for the departments and organizations to link their system together and provided different approaches to doing business. The Internet and computer servers provide transparency of locations by using the wide area networks (WANs), local area networks (LANs), virtual private networks (VPNs), the intranet, and the Internet. It provides a way for computers in different locations to be linked together without having to physically centralize the desktop computers, mini-computers, and servers, allowing for further decentralization and communication with others and outside of the organizational boundaries.

Small and mid-range computers have evolved over the years with as much processing power and capacity as mainframes computers. As a result of decentralization, many government organizations with the support of the CIO and the department managers work together to develop IT standards and policies to ensure hardware and software purchases, security, and computer use in the best interest of the organization as a whole.

Economies of Scope

If you are considering centralization or decentralization of IT functions, it is important for you and other managers who are involved with IS decision making to consider the *economies of scope* in relation to the *breadth of diversification*. Research indicates that when firms have diversification in the breadth of their products and services, in many private sector organizations the decision is usually made to decentralize its information technology decisions. Diversification breadth "refers to the degree of product/market relatedness of a multi-business firm" (Sambamurthy & Zmud, 1999, p. 3). Acquisitions and mergers is a good example of diversification.

On diversification, the business units within the departments and agencies have *distinct business strategies* and *requirements* with knowledgeable business and IT workers within those business units in the departments and agencies. For those organizations that have related products, services, expertise, infrastructure, and there are numerous commonalities, the IT decisions are normally centralized (Sambamurthy & Zmud, 1999). There may be commonality in supporting the organization's network infrastructure, but again it may be influenced by how the IT workers functionally work within the departments and business units. Are they totally dedicated to network support or do their jobs require other computer-related tasks and functions specific to the business units?

Many of the business operations and the information systems that support the various departments and agencies within government are unique and highly diversified. For example, law enforcement is diverse from hospital services; public social services is diverse from the county recorder; the district attorney's department is diverse from assessor and tax collector; the register of voter's department is diverse from the transportation and land management department; the clerk of the board is diverse from mental health; and the list goes on and on. The information systems are designed to support the business strategy of each department or agency. Benton (2002) provides a useful list because it identifies hundreds of county services in the article's appendix under the various categories of (1) traditional services, (2) local services, and (3) regional services. Some of these services include finance, police protection, judicial, legal services and prosecution, public health, social services, and transportation.

Economies of scope can benefit an organization because it can *share its resources across multiple departments* or agencies when there is commonality and the IT workers' knowledge and expertise *does not impact the responsiveness, delivery time, and quality of the services*. In other words, it can be beneficial when the firms are able to share the IT expertise, knowledgeable IT workers, and IT investments across multiple firms when there is no diversification in products and services (Sambamurthy & Zmud, 1999). If there is much diversification, then the cost of centralization will most likely exceed the economies of scope.

Examples of centralization of IT decision authority in many firms are the networks and its infrastructure, organization-wide IT standards and policies on computer use and security, organization-wide information systems, other information systems that can be shared by other departments and agencies and even by other governments, and the approval of acquisition of computer hardware and software purchases so they conform to the organizational infrastructure standards.

In fact, some state governments mandate counties to use centralized information systems that are managed and controlled by the state or by other counties. It is not unusual for counties to share IS resources such as Internet portals, networks, and information systems with larger counties (Daniel & Ward, 2006; Haung, 2007) and benefit from the economies of scope.

If a government organization makes the decision to centralize or decentralize specific functions, it should driven by the business strategy and be a collaborative decision between the top-level managers in the organization and supported by the CIO and technical managers and their technical staff. Most decisions are not be solely based on reducing operating costs because these projects often have the tendency to negatively impact organizational performance as there is no driving business strategy. In some cases, narrow-scoped projects can impact the organization's ability to respond quickly to the technical problems and negatively impact the service quality to the business units and the end users. In other cases, a business strategy that is carefully planned and collaborated with top-level managers can result in benefits to the organization and its departments and agencies.

With regard to centralization, it is important for you to understand how people work. Several departments within a government organization process information by entering it into their computer information systems and scan documents locally within their departments. Scanning documents such as document images, photos, and maps can use large amounts of network bandwidth if it is performed centrally using the organizational network rather than locally within each department. Processing large amounts of data and information has the potential of creating other kinds of problems.

Centralizing computer functions of some departments that normally perform their work locally can have a major impact on the transmission performance of the infrastructure networks. In addition to these concerns, security and confidentiality of some documents could pose potential risks for departments such as the sheriff's department, county recorder, courts, hospital, and the district attorney. In some organizations, many computer support functions remain within the various departments or agencies and other functions are managed under the direction of a central, organizational IT department. What is even more important is that there is a collaborative agreement between the CEO, CIO, and all top-level managers in the organization.

Some department heads may see the benefits of centralization of some functions and IT investments and others may see the benefits of staying decentralized. Many organizations in both the public and private sector organizations have a mix of both centralized and decentralized systems. The central IT department in many organizations supports those departments that determine the best business strategy that works for them. Many individuals in the departments feel that decentralization of their computer systems puts them closer to business units and gives each department greater control over establishing their own project priorities. In this type of environment, they do not have to compete with the entire organization for priority to be assigned to their projects and for assigning the technical resources.

Organization History

Let's next examine organization history. It is a well-known fact that those who do not know enough of the history of the organization cannot do a good job in shaping the future. Why? They actually run the risks of making the same mistakes of the past. Organization history is important before deciding to implement new information systems or centralization and decentralization of IT. The history of the information systems projects within an organization or within a department or agency is sometimes overlooked.

I really enjoy watching reruns of the different sports games that I recorded when my favorite team won the games. Even though they did some things that were very disappointing and did not score any points during parts of the game, it really did not matter to me because in the end I knew that they had already won the game. I knew the history of what they did wrong and what things they did right. In the end, I knew they had won. However, I did not watch the reruns of the recorded games that my team lost. Why? I did not want to remember their losses. I believe that some novice project managers do not complete postaudit reviews of their large projects. As a result, the organization does not know the history. They do not know what was done right and what was done incorrectly for their projects because over time the history is lost. Small project failures are easily forgotten, but large project failures and even those projects with major problems that cost millions of dollars can be too painful to even want to remember.

Department heads and managers who are not elected officials may come and go over the years, but most of them have long tenures with the organization. Elected officials are voted into office and some serve out their terms and others are not reelected. The political environment puts new top-level managers at the helm of the organization that do not have the history of past project successes or failures. Cats-Baril and Thompson (1995) examined a case study of a US state project and identified the problem with department heads changing frequently. The commissioners who manage the departments are appointed to two-year terms by the governor. From the start, the project lacked an in-house project manager to manage multiple departments and the project experienced many problems, which added to the problem of the short tenure of department heads.

Every department and agency within an organization needs to have some type of historian to retain the history of major information systems projects that costs millions of dollars. If project managers as a standard practice would complete the evaluation of the system in a *postaudit report*, as identified in the postaudit phase of the SDLC listed in Table 3.1 of Chapter 3, historical information would be available. Postaudit reports need to be completed and evaluated for newly implemented systems or systems that go through major modifications and even project failures with input from the team members, the business managers, and end users of the system. These reports need to be retained by the organization as historical records.

Elected Officials

Be careful not to overlook the organizational environment you are working within as a manager. Do not forget the elected officials who have authority over their agency or department and which IT/IS projects they choose to budget. There is a need to collaborate with both department and agency heads. Those who are at the top central level of the organization have authority over general administration and budgetary controls. Other elected officials who are department heads feel they are responsible to the constituents who elected them to office and they have authority over the decisions, business strategy, and information systems strategy within their own departments.

For example, if you consider county government, there can be an elected board of supervisors overseeing central administration and budgetary controls; and top-level department heads such as the elected county sheriff, district attorney, treasurer-tax collector, auditor-controller, county assessor, county clerk, and the county recorder each responsible for their departments or agencies. Consideration must be given to the fact that elected officials operate within the domain of their own agency or department and even at the top level of the organization.

Nonelected Department Executives

What about nonelected executives who are department or agency heads? Depending on the organization's structure, the department heads who are not elected officials are usually appointed to their positions by the CEO and/or the organization's central administration elected officials. These department heads must consider the impact that any changes and legislative mandates may have on their daily business operations for administering programs and providing the products and services. Being responsible for a department or government agency means department heads are totally accountable for things that go right and for things that can go wrong within their own department or agency and must operate within legislative laws.

Department heads must respond to both the positive and negative issues that can arise. If there are problems, they must deal with public scrutiny, public interest groups, criticism, the press, and news reporters. There can be fines or penalties if there are violations of legislative mandates in the business operations. One department head told me that one of the major indicators that he and his staff are doing a good job is not viewing negative news reports about himself or his staff on the television news reports or in the newspaper.

So far you have been able to examine the importance of the business initiatives driving the changes, centralization versus decentralization of IT, the economies of scope, the history of the organization, and the elected and nonelected officials who manage the central administration and budgetary decisions or those who manage the departments and agencies.

The next section examines who actually has authority over information technology and the information systems projects. You may think this is a strange topic to examine; however, if there is a blurred vision of who is responsible for IT decision rights, it can be the reason for many conflicting agendas and no shared vision on many different types of projects.

Who Is in Charge of Information Technology?

Department heads have the authority to make decisions on their own business operations and their annual budgets. The organization's central administration, with its elected officials and CEO, is in charge of the organization's administration and budgetary approval. The *information technology governance model* on IT decision rights is important to the organization, the CIO, and managers at all levels. What is information technology governance?

Information technology governance is the distribution of IT decision-making authority between the organizational IT and the departments within the organization (Sambamurthy & Zmud, 1999). It identifies who has the authority to make the IT decisions in an organization and at what level. Authority for IT decisions can be made at the organization, department, and the federal levels. The *federal* level means there is mixed or shared responsibility of who makes the decisions on key activities within a specific sphere. In some organizations, there is a blurred vision on who has authority for many of the different kinds of information technology decisions.

In many organizations, the CIO is responsible for managing the IT resources at the central, top level of the organization. The role of the CIO in the decision-making process can be beneficial to attaining value-added business goals or it can cause a lot of controversy within an organization. In most government organizations, the CIO articulates a vision and is instrumental in guiding the organization in establishing information technology standards and policies.

CIOs with technology background having a general understanding of the organizational and business strategies of many departments and agencies contribute to organizational success. The organization may establish subordinate positions such as chief technology officer (CTO) and chief network officer (CNO) to work alongside the CIO to handle other strategic IT areas.

The CIO should adept at communicating with the CEO, the department heads and their business managers, and the technical managers involved in IS decisions (Booth & Philip, 2005). It is well known that top management attitudes can influence the behavior of other managers in an organization (Jick & Peiperl, 2003). If top-level managers do not encourage two-way communication at various levels of the organization, it influences the behavior of other senior managers and embeds in the organizational culture.

In contrast, there are organizations and even some departments and agencies within an organization that do not feel the need for a CIO but opt to have their own IT director or IT manager handle their information systems decisions. Some view the IT director or IT manager within their own department as the strategist and feel that this person has a better understanding of the business strategy because of the working relationships within the department and because they work closely with the business units (Pearlson & Saunders, 2006).

Organizational Culture

Another important topic to consider in relation to decision making is organizational culture. What is organizational culture? There are many definitions, but in general it is a shared belief by a group of people of certain standards and values for evaluating and acting within an organization (Stevens, 2004). The organizational culture established by top-level executives in the manner they behave and act and can influence the behavior of others in the organization. It is seen in work practices within the organization and is something that can actually be seen and observed by the working group of work behaviors; especially of those at the top of the organization (Van den Berg & Wilderom, 2004). As a result of the workers' perception, they will make their own assessment of the organization's culture.

Most tops can be overloaded with their responsibilities and they normally establish the rules of the organization. However, in the government environment, there is also the impact of legislation. These are the statutory laws that set the rules over and above the authority of the tops. Top-level executives must operate within the established laws. Top-level managers must manage their day-to-day business operations within legislative mandates when directing and managing the organization and its departments or agencies.

As a project manager, it is important for you to try identifying the tops, the middles, and the below (specialized workers) groups. Who are the clients and the general public you serve? Communication between the tops, the middles, and the belows is necessary to provide the programs, products, and services to clients and citizens. Communication is important to organizational success, true collaboration, and shared visions. The kinds of words we use with each other do matter and should never be demeaning or intimidating.

CIOs and managers who encourage upward communication recognize that feedback from others within the organization is essential to organizational goals. In another study, executives at one firm said, "They consider employee communication the most important managerial activity in this company" (Jick & Peiperl, 2003, p. 349). This particular organizational culture promoted communication among its employees.

IT Governance Model

Despite the difference in views of the importance and responsibilities of the CIO, the IT governance model can assist top-level management in working together using IT governance to establish project priorities and to identify information technology resources. The role of CIO in the *IT governance model* determines which approaches on decision-making authority will work best in obtaining the governance arrangements that refer to the patterns of authority for key IT activities of an organization or corporation.

Studies identify three distinct spheres or categories of information technology activities:

1. Information technology *infrastructure* management
2. Information technology *use* management
3. *Project* management

Centralized governance means that the central organizational IT has the authority over all IT activities of a specific sphere, see Table 5.1. *Decentralized governance* means the department IT has the authority over

Table 5.1 Information technology governance (decision rights) arrangements

Sphere of Activities	Description	Decision Rights (Authority)	Level
IT infrastructure management	Consists of decisions on the hardware and software platforms, enhancements to these platforms annually, the network and data architectures, organizational standards for procurement, security, and deployment of IT assets.	Organization IT	Centralized
		Department or Agency IT	Decentralized
		Federal (mix)	Centralized and decentralized
IT use management	Involves decisions on the prioritization of information systems and technology, short-term and long-term planning, budgeting, and delivery of the daily operations and services.	Organization IT	Centralized
		Department or Agency IT	Decentralized
		Federal (mix)	Centralized and decentralized
Project management	Involves blending human resources knowledge of infrastructure capabilities and capacities with knowledge associated for the conceptualization, acquisition, development, and implementation of information systems.	Organization IT	Centralized
		Department or Agency IT	Decentralized
		Federal (mix)	Centralized and decentralized

Source. Adapted from Sambamurthy and Zmud (1999).

all IT activities of a specific sphere. The definition of *federal governance* means both the central organizational IT and department IT have authority over key information technology activities within a specific sphere. In other words, they share in the responsibilities.

The previous Table 5.1 is an adapted version of the governance model by Sambamurthy and Zmud (1999) for government as a nonprofit organization in the public sector. Organizational IT replaces corporate IT and department IT replaces divisional IT. The main difference between the corporate and the public sector IT governance models is that government organizations have many different departments and agencies as their primary business functions that are highly specialized and diversified in comparison to private sector organizations, which may only experience diversity in their products and services because of mergers with other firms.

Many departments and agencies within government are highly specialized business operations with knowledgeable IT workers who support the different types of information systems, such as: (1) the mission-critical and specialized transaction processing systems, (2) vertical systems, (3) subsets of the systems for organizational use, (4) e-government systems, and (5) public service management systems. In some organizations, there may be more commonality between departments and agencies in areas such as the network infrastructure, back-office information systems, and office productivity or workgroup systems.

Communication

Communication between the CEO and the CIO has a major impact on the role of information technology in an organization (Johnson & Lederer, 2007). A collaborative approach to IT governance consisting of the CIO, the department heads and their business managers, and technical managers work in the best interest of the organization as a whole and contributes to a shared vision. If there is no balance between the business, the organization, and the information system strategies, the CIO will be working with conflicting agendas, which can have a negative impact on the communications between the CIO and CEO regarding the real problems or issues.

Weill and Ross (2005) report that many problems can arise if IT decisions are not aligned with the organization's strategic objectives. Their study reported that 60 percent to 80 percent of senior executives in top performing companies have a clear understanding of the IT governance for the business. The study found that effective IT governance aligns the IT investments in the business with the business priorities and clearly defines accountability. According to the study, the first step in establishing governance is to agree upon who should be making the decisions. The survey was sent to 256 enterprises in America, Europe, and Asia/Pacific. The enterprises consisted of both for-profit and not-for-profit organizations. The survey questionnaire was developed by MIT Sloan's Center for Information Research and distributed in 2002 by Gartner Inc. The second study was based on 40 interview-case studies at large companies. The results (Weill & Ross, 2005) found that there is no single best IT governance model and it can vary to encourage different behaviors. Most IT governance in the companies that participated in the study had a blend of centralized and decentralized governance. The researchers suggest defining the performance objectives of the business first and then designing the IT governance to obtain those objectives.

Information technology governance identifies what type of decisions are centralized under the authority of central IT department, which ones are decentralized under the authority of the organization's departments and agencies, and what type of decisions are made as a collaborative decision (federal) from both centralization and decentralization. CIOs who practice true collaboration and integrity are important in top-level management and concentrate on the major strengths of those in the organization that will ensure success of the organizational as a whole. You need to consider the stakeholders within the organization.

For IT governance to be effective, it is important that the CIO's focus is not primarily about being positioned vertically to be in control of IT in the organization but is more about collaboration versus control, competency versus authority, and strategic flexibility for sustaining the *business value* of the organization versus just efficiencies alone (Peterson, 2004). This is accomplished by integrating IT decision making across the business departments and agencies within the organization and with the various IT stakeholders. Since rigid controls can negatively impact organizational performance, the focus of IT governance needs to take into consideration that governments are to effectively and efficiently provide the programs, products, and services to the public they serve with the goal of improving organizational performance.

About the CIO

The role of the CIO has grown in importance over the years from being a data processing manager or director to overseeing the entire organization's IT resources (Haag, Cummings, & Phillips, 2007). For the CIO to be effective, the position must be strategically placed at the top level of the organization and report to the top-level CEO (Pearlson & Saunders, 2006). The CIO is a top-level manager who is responsible for managing the IT resources at the central, administrative top level of the organization in both private sector and public sector organizations. What differ in government organizations are the elected officials in the central, top administration and elected and nonelected officials who are heads of highly specialized departments and agencies with authority over their own domain and budget.

Subordinate positions such as the chief technology officer (CTO) and the chief network officer (CNO) work alongside the CIO to handle other strategic areas. Ideally, the CIO has subordinates who provide expertise and supplement the CIO's leadership by contributing to enhancing the information systems strategy of the organization.

The CIO requires being not only technically knowledgeable but also a general understanding of how the departments and agencies oper-ate within the government organization and the ability to focus on the role of supporting the business strategies through the organizational and information systems strategies. CIOs need top-level support and need to communicate effectively with the department heads and their business managers, IT directors, and senior IT managers by collaborating and cre-ating a shared vision so that there are no conflicting agendas (Pearlson & Saunders, 2006). There can be conflicting agendas between the CIO and the departments and agencies. In some situations, the CIO can be too controlling by wanting others within the organization to do things as he or she wants it to be done without regard to the suggestions, ideas, and feedback from others.

In many organizations, the CIO is viewed as the IT spokesperson but may not be viewed as the strategic planner by the functional departments and agencies within the organization. Grover, Jeong, Kettinger, and Lee (1993) investigated Mintzberg's ten managerial roles. The results from 111 participants in the study indicate that the CIOs and the IS managers ranked the importance of their roles as *entrepreneur, monitor,* and *liaison* roles as the same. The CIOs rated their *spokesperson* role more important than the information systems (IS) managers. The IS managers rated their role of *leader* and *resource allocator* as more important than the CIOs. Surprisingly, the senior executives in the functional area of the finance departments had similar rankings of their managerial roles as the IS managers.

In contrast to the private sector organizations in this study consisting of manufacturing and sales departments, public sector organizations have specialized functional areas within the departments and agencies as the organization's *primary* activities. Another important fact is that depart-ments and agency heads determine their project priorities based on their individual budgets. *Information systems maturity* and *information systems centralization* can have an impact on the roles of the CIOs. As organizations depend more on information systems, and when some of the technology functions become more centralized, there can be different expectations of the managerial roles of the CIOs.

So what does this all mean to government organizations? The importance of the managerial roles, specialization of the functional departments and agencies, and distribution of authority in government organizations can create role conflicts. In fact, the impact of leadership styles and term limits of elected officials can have a direct impact (Benton et al., 2007) on the roles of the CIO. Organizational IT standards and policies developed and updated as a collaborative approach to IT decision making within the organization can assist in reducing some of the conflict.

Elected Officials and Constituents

Many elected officials in the organization's central administration and department heads who are elected into office by the voters feel that they have some responsibility to their constituents. This can make the role of the both the CEO and CIO even more difficult because of the political environment. Even though the CIO does not have authority over elected officials, this individual can work toward trying to create a shared vision in relation to the organizational strategy and the organization-wide computer networks and systems that support both the business strategies of the many departments and agencies.

One of the most important roles of the CIO is building positive relationships with the top-level executives, peers, department heads and their business managers, and IT directors in the organization by demonstrating *authentic collaboration* and integrity, not just giving the appearance of collaboration by establishing central technology committee with no shared vision.

Information technology directors and senior IT managers in the departments and agencies in government cannot have two top-level groups directing them: (1) the elected officials, and the CEO and CIO in central administration, (2) and the (elected and nonelected) department heads. Some IT managers may find themselves in situations in which they have to make a choice of who they will serve when there are conflicting agendas. In most cases, their choice will be the department head and that is why shared visions and authentic collaboration are critical to the success of the organization as a whole.

Often a CIO can be caught in conflicting agendas when there are changes at the top-level executive leadership in the organization. The very nature of a political environment can mean that the top-level executives often prefer to make the selection of someone to fill the position of CIO who will support their agenda.

Employees and Performance

CIOs operate within the existing limited budget and often inherit the technology staff from the central IT department within the organization for organization-wide projects. Some of the technical staff may be valuable to the CIO and others may be mediocre or unproductive. The CIO must find ways to achieve the goals and objectives of the organization with the existing personnel or find ways to augment staff with consultants and contractors with specialized technical expertise.

In many private sector organizations, unproductive employees can be promptly terminated from their positions due to poor performance. Employee unions in government organizations require managers to go through the lengthy process of documenting employee performance, attend meetings with the employee and the union representative, develop employee performance improvement plans, and document the work performance prior to starting any termination procedures. Working with problem employees can be a time-consuming and laborious process with no guarantees of the end result. In fact, "State laws that recognize the right of county employees to organize unions and bargain collectively" (Benton et al., 2007, p. 975) can complicate a manager's role with regard to work performance issues, terminations, or layoff of government employees.

You would want to know why I put all this importance on employee performance. It is because I had my own experiences as a manager with problem employees. In each case, I met with each individual employee regularly attempting to improve the employee's performance. I was required to put the employee on a performance improvement plan outlining the areas that the employee needed to work on for improving his job performance. I completed an employee evaluation every three months discussing with the employee his progress or lack of progress and things he needed to do to improve his performance.

In total, I spent over one year documenting and working with each employee with no visible signs of improvement. Problems like this took many hours away from my other important job responsibilities. The regular meetings with the employee included the employee's union representative. The end results of such an effort on my part went absolutely nowhere. I do believe that some people with job performance problems are just moved around from one division to another with the hope that someone else will deal with the problem.

Laying off problem employees in government organizations can be difficult because of employee unions. However, during the many years I spent working in government, there were only two employees who had serious job performance problems. In my opinion, in both the cases, these two individuals selected the wrong field to work in and could never acquire the necessary skills needed for performing their jobs because their potential and talents were not in the field they chose for their career. Everyone has talents, but some people discover their talents early in life and others later. Some people may go through their entire life without ever discovering their real talents and remain in a job out of necessity. These are the individuals who need to find a career that better suits their personality and skills. These two individuals were assigned to several divisions and eventually left government employment as a result of their inability to perform the job tasks.

CIO and Vision

Ideally, the CIO will assist the CEO and the top-level managers in supporting their visions using technology and is instrumental in establishing information technology standards and policies for the organization. The CIO needs to be able to provide IT leadership and have experience in software engineering for designing, developing, and implementing information systems.

Some organizations have positions such as a chief technology officer (CTO) or chief network officer (CNO) and a chief information security officer (CISO), who are subordinate to the CIO and manage other strategic areas because one person does not have all the qualifications to fill the role of CIO (Pearlson & Saunders, 2006).

Another area important to organizational success is supporting the information technology infrastructure and networks that are important to ensure that things run smoothly; however, sometimes, these kinds of projects are not always visible to the department heads and their staff. Information technology governance is important in government in order to have a clear definition within the organization as to who has responsibility for information technology in terms of the information technology infrastructure, use, and project management (Sambamurthy & Zmud, 1999; Weill & Ross, 2005).

The question that needs to be asked is: What is the responsibility of central IT, the departments and agencies (decentralized), and shared responsibilities (federal) between central IT and the departments? The IT governance model adopted by the organization identifies who has decision rights over the three distinction spheres of IT activities.

The CIO needs to provide leadership to support the business strategy of the departments and agencies, which is supported by the organizational strategy and the information systems strategy for providing governmental programs, products, and services. The CIO with a transformational leadership style, the ability to communicate, is trustworthy, has vision, and has people skills can be more successful in the position than those who do not demonstrate these qualities.

I have observed several individuals who were hired as CIOs in the 23 years of working in county government and most served for a short term in the position ranging from 1 to 5 years. In addition, during the 23 years I spent in the county government organization, only one CIO hired was a female and all the others were males. She served in the position of the CIO for two years. I often thought of applying for the job, but realized that my tenure in the position would probably be short-lived, based on the observations of the duration that most of the CIOs stayed in the organization. Several IT directors and managers in other government organizations report similar observations of the short-term tenure in their organization for many CIOs and they have seen several CIOs come and go over the years.

Although some people will not admit it, there is still some discomfort with women being in top-level leadership positions, especially in professions that are predominately male. There is a gender gap in some organizations with few women in top-level management positions and some not getting equal pay for working in the same job as males. In other organizations, in both the public and private sectors the "good old boys club" and the "glass ceiling" does exist, which limits advancement of women, people of color (e.g., Hispanic or Latino, multiracial, African American, and Asian) and even some white males to top-level management positions. Individuals who make decisions on who is promoted can bring their own biases into different situations and circumstances.

I have even observed some males who strive to be in top-level positions, but they were not in what is referred to as the "good old boys club" and did not advance to higher-level management positions. You can find much literature on these two topics and I will provide you with more information on this subject in Chapter 7.

Some individuals may view the short time they serve in a top CIO level position as a stepping-stone to CIO positions in other organizations with the hope that they will be able to get another long-term position. Many may or may not be interested in staying with one organization for a long. For some it is matter of career-path choices.

For many years, people decided to stay and work in public-sector organizations long term for employee benefits such as medical benefits, sick leave, vacation time, and a retirement plan; and others opted for higher-paying salaries in private sector organizations. However, because of the economy in the United States in the past few years, fewer jobs offer the higher-paying salaries and better employee benefits.

Now let's discuss the government organizations and look at a more complex situation. You may feel at times the CIO and his subordinates, the CTO or CNO and the technical managers, in the organization's central IT department are not providing you the support you need and at times create barriers to getting your project done—especially when you are a manager in a department or agency within the organization. By observing the organization and looking at the problems from another perspective, there can be three visible areas of conflicting agendas:

1. The central IT organizational strategy that fully supports the business strategy of the departments and agencies within the government organization is lacking.
2. Development of some of the organization-wide IT standards and policies do not enable the departments and agencies to perform their work and can adversely impact their operations.
3. The CIO's ability to secure funding to upgrade or enhance the organization's central IT network infrastructure (e.g., WAN, LAN, VPN, intranet, and Internet) is lacking.

In some organizations, the information technology standards and policies established by the organization actually create barriers to the departments and agencies. Another problem is that the CIO can often experience difficulty with obtaining resources and support for organization-wide projects such as funding for upgrading the networks and acquisition of new hardware and software, and other resources.

Upgrading or enhancing the network infrastructure is important to organization performance, but in some cases, it can be overlooked by top-level executives and managers because of other priorities within the organization. In some situations, the CIO does not receive top-level management support for funding the central, organization-wide network projects.

Ideally, the CIO needs to be able to lead the organization in creating IT standards and policies that allow the departments and agencies within government to work effectively. Some of these policies should be reviewed on a regular schedule and changed to support the business strategy of the departments and agencies within the organization in addition to being aligned with the organizational strategy. You should encourage your department head or top-level manager to request review meetings as a collaborative effort with the CIO.

But wait! At times, there can be an environment of conflicting agendas between the CIO, the central IT department, and the departments and agencies. In this situation, leadership at the top of the organization when working with the departments heads will assist in defining a collaborative

IT governance model essential to success. IT governance agreements and standards need to be reviewed periodically and updated by the organization as a whole.

Organizations that create collaborative and shared visions between the top-level managers in the central organization and the top managers within the departments and agencies assist in reducing conflicting agendas. Without this *authentic collaboration*, the roles and responsibilities of the CIO remain blurred. If the role remains blurred, it can cause conflicting agendas between the CIO and the department heads and their business managers and IT managers.

It may be that the role and responsibilities of the CIO in many organizations have been predefined by the top-level executives in central administration and the department heads; and they feel there is no need for radical changes. After the IT standards and policies have been defined for government-wide planning, security, privacy, system acquisition, and the adoption of an information technology governance model on decision rights have been agreed upon, the role of the CIO may be viewed as more of a monitoring and central spokesperson role instead of a strategic one.

Importance of the CIO Position

The CIO is important to the organization for establishing a balance between the business, organizational, and information systems strategies of central administration and the many departments and agencies. The business strategy is driven by the business objectives. The general responsibilities of the CIO may change over time based on the views of the central organization's top-level managers, especially when newly elected officials are at the helm. The role of the CIO depends on the organizational culture. If the CIO is hired and it does not work within the organizational culture, it can result in the CIO not being retained on the job for long.

CIOs in some government organizations do not stay in the job long enough to establish strategic plans and see the results of those plans. Even for CIOs in the private sector organizations, there is a "higher-than-average corporate dismissal rates compared with other top executives" (Grover et al., 1993, p. 109). If CIOs are in the position from one to five years, most do not see the long-term impact of their decisions. As a result, they do not know if the decisions they have made actually improved organizational performance or have resulted in additional challenges for the organization.

The role of the CIO in government may not be viewed by some as being in the strategic area but being more narrowly focused on the responsibilities of the organization-wide infrastructure networks and the central IT department and its computer support services. Since most CIOs report to the CEO and not to department and agency-level department heads, the department heads and their IT directors are most often viewed as the strategic decision makers by the departments or agencies for their business strategy.

Middle space is where there is no shared vision and there are conflicting agendas. In middle space, you can be pulled between those above and below or even experience those above (tops) with conflicting agendas. Let's take the concept of middle space and look at it in relationship to projects from the perspective of the department and agency IT directors and IT managers who handle all forms of technology projects. There are the

- tops (above), who are the elected officials overseeing central, administration, and budgetary controls, the CEO, the CIO, and
- the tops (above), which are the departments and agency heads who are nonelected and elected officials and their assistants;
- the middles, who are the business managers, project managers, IT directors, and senior IT managers and their technical staff;
- the belows, who are the end users of technology, and the workers in the organizations, who are the professional, business, technical, and office support specialists; and
- the clients and general public the organization serves.

In this situation, there were two top groups from the perspective of the department and agency technology directors and senior technology managers. One of the problems that can arise is if there are conflicting agendas coming from the CIO in the central organization, it puts the department IT directors and senior IT managers in a position where they must choose who they will serve: the CIO or their department head. In most situations, it will be their department heads. More on middle space and no shared vision are discussed in Chapter 6.

A few years ago, there was a project in which three department heads, who are elected officials, considered having the integrated mainframe computer information system hosted by an outside company to lower the costs of doing business. The mainframe information system was located in the data center in the organization's central IT department. The central IT department was a hosting site for the computer system operations. The IS support, maintenance, and projects are handled by the technical staff within each of the three departments. Two other large departments recently moved their computer information systems off the mainframe to other computer information systems not located within the central IT data center. Both of these departments notified the the CIO and the CTO in the central, organization's IT department of the move two years prior to actually moving off the mainframe computer.

As a result of the move, the central IT department's plan was to shift the costs of the two departments to the remaining three departments. There was no reduction in costs. This shift would require an increase in each of the three department's annual budget and would require the respective department heads to terminate some of their employees to stay within their total operating budget. There was no shared vision. In fact, the three department heads tried to seek information on why the organization's central IT department planned on shifting the costs to their departments but received no clear explanation.

This approach by the organization's central IT department was not supported by the three department heads; therefore, they instructed the IT director (middle) in one of their own departments to develop a request for proposal (RFP) to bid for services to host the mainframe computer information system elsewhere with another company that provided similar hosting services without significantly increasing the costs to the three departments in addition to what they were already paying for services from the central IT department.

After the draft RFP was developed, the organization's central IT department was given the opportunity to review the draft document. From the start, there were conflicting agendas between the three departments and the central, organizational IT department. The CTO and the organization's central IT department's staff were not supportive of the RFP and the three department heads. They identified what they considered major flaws in the draft RFP document even though none existed; and there was hypercriticism of the IT director (middle) who completed the RFP document.

It was only after involvement of the newly hired CIO, the central organizational IT department's staff worked on a plan for not increasing the cost of hosting the mainframe information system. As a result, the system costs were not shifted to the remaining three departments. In this particular case, the CIO (top) was instrumental in providing leadership for solving the problem and creating a shared vision instead of the three departments heads (tops) and the CTO overseeing the central, organizational IT department working in an environment of conflicting agendas.

Another important strategy that influenced this particular project is that these three department heads as elected officials worked together and actually formed a peer relationship to address the problem. The IT director (middle) in the department who developed the RFP was working under the directives from the three tops who, in this case, were the elected officials rather than the tops in the central organization.

Group empowerment as elected-officials and as department heads was beneficial in this case. The department IT director was aware of the fact that the tops who are the three department heads have authority over their own information systems decisions and was able to stay out of conflicting agendas. Often managers have more influence on changes as a group instead of one department head acting alone or even one manager acting alone.

Summary

Stakeholder management is important to project success, and stakeholders can be internal and external to the organization. External stakeholders can be political interest groups. Internal stakeholders can have concerns over centralized versus decentralized projects. Centralization or decentralization of computer systems often appears as a topic of concern from newly elected officials or newly appointed CIOs and is not a simple decision, and needs to be driven by the business strategy and organizational strategy. The information systems strategy is a support strategy. Organizational history is important for those trying to shape the future. Elected officials at the top, central, administrative level of the organization and those within the departments and agencies who have authority over their own domain are important to organization-wide decisions. Understanding who is really in charge of information technology means an organization needs a well-defined IT governance model, which identifies IT decision rights.

Organization culture is established at the top level of the organization and it can influence the behavior of others throughout the organization. Organization culture can be seen and observed by all those at different levels of the organization. The CEO and CIO play an important role in establishing IT governance, communication, and leadership. However, the CIO can be limited by employee performance within the central, organizational IT department and by organization culture. The CIO's position is important in leading change using a collaborative approach to IT management. It is important for managers to recognize that some of the technology managers at different levels in the organization are often viewed by the department heads as the strategist for information technology projects.

Review Concepts

- Identifying and managing project stakeholders
- Internal and external project stakeholders
- Centralized versus decentralized systems

- Economies of scope and breadth of diversification
- Who is really in charge of information technology?
- Organizational culture
- Information technology governance model
- The chief information officer (CIO)
- Elected officials in central administration and as department heads

Discussion Questions

5.1. Discuss the importance of identifying and managing project stakeholders.

5.2. Describe one of your experiences with stakeholders external to the organization.

5.3. Discuss some of the reasons why mainframe information systems were centralized within government organizations.

5.4. Describe economies of scope and breadth of diversification.

5.5. Explain the difference between an information system's boundaries and system interfaces.

5.6. Describe the concept of information technology governance and discuss why it is important to an organization.

5.7. Do you think every organization needs a CIO position? If so, explain why or why not?

5.8. What role can the CIO take in establishing organizational information technology standards and policies?

5.9. Why do you think the subordinate positions such as the CTO, CNO, and CISO are important?

5.10. Describe how elected officials often view their responsibility for managing a department or agency.

CHAPTER SIX
MIDDLE SPACE

No doubt, you as a project manager have encountered many different kinds of challenges at one time or another in your work environment. Project managers work within organizational systems, and within these organizations, there are projects that can be successful and those that fail or do not increase organizational performance. When things do go terribly wrong within organizations, it is not unusual for top-level executives to start pointing fingers in an attempt to identify the individual who is the problem (Jick & Peiperl, 2003). Many managers have their own theories as to why specific projects fail or have major problems and others can only guess as to what are the real problems.

This chapter focuses on middle space where there is no shared vision and there are conflicting agendas. In the organizational environment of systems where there are tops (executives and department heads), middles (managers and supervisors), the belows (specialized workers), and the clients and citizens they serve, it is important for project managers to understand how to master the space they are working within rather than focusing on trying to fix people.

Barry Oshry provides a different way of looking at the organization. He wrote several articles about being in *middle space*. For those in middle space, there is a gradual disempowerment. When you are in middle space, "you are caught between the conflicting agendas, perspectives, priorities, needs, and demands of two or more individuals or groups" and it pulls you between others (Jick & Peiperl, 2003, p. 403). Some people can be more in the middle than others are. Often supervisors and other kinds of workers can be caught in middle space; and the space can have multiple contending forces from the top and bottom, and both vertically and laterally. Whenever you are caught between conflicting agendas, needs, and demands of two or more people or groups, you can be working in middle space. Perhaps, you have been in the same situation.

For project managers, middle space is when you are between the top group (above) and the below (workers) group, see Figure 6.1. The tops have

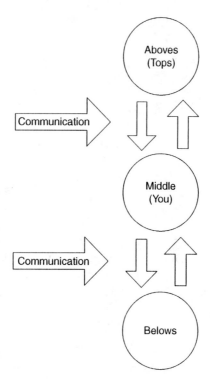

Figure 6.1   Working in middle space.

Source: Adapted from Barry Oshry as cited by Jick and Peiperl, 2003.

their agendas and priorities that are different from the belows. Because of the circumstances that have developed in recent years within some private sector organizations, I add the words *ethics* and *values* to the definition of middle space.

Ethics is defined as "the principles and standards that guide our behavior toward other people" and as the "law either clearly requires or prohibits an action" (Haag, Cummings, & Phillips, 2007, p. 13); and the definition of the word value means what is right in relationship to principles and standards. My revised definition is that you are in middle space when "you are caught between the conflicting agendas, perspectives, priorities, needs, demands and/or ethics and values of two or more individuals or groups" and it pulls you between others.

I expanded the definition of middle space by including *ethics* and *values* because of the studies about individuals called *whistleblowers*, who challenged the unethical practices in organizations such as Enron Corporation,

Arthur Anderson, and World Com. You can read more about this in the study by Stevens (2004). Stevens reported that in 2000, the Gallup Poll rates nurses as the most ethical and car salesmen as the least. Business executives were rated much lower than the nurses, but not as low as the car salesmen. A more recent study might reflect different results. These whistleblowers were really caught in middle space and they could see how decisions by the top group could potentially have negative consequences on the bottom group, on themselves, and the organization as a whole.

Some were probably unaware of the magnitude and how big the problems really were but chose not to be part of the top group because their own ethics and values determined what choices they would make for themselves. Perhaps, you have experienced being caught in middle space at one time or another in your work career.

I do believe that there are times that some individuals are not even aware of the fact that they are working in middle space. Sometimes you miss the obvious because the environment you are working in keeps you busy focusing on the incidentals. Those individuals who are caught in middle space and are in it longer than they should be begin to feel its effects on their well-being and a gradual disempowerment. Nothing is more disappointing and frustrating to managers (middles) and even to the specialized work groups (the belows) than the feeling of disempowerment.

How do you know you are in middle space longer than you should be? You know it when you become anxious, tense, pressured, have feelings of uncertainty, and you see too many unresolved issues between the top group and the bottom group. Your physical body is actually protesting and you can choose to recognize what is going on or try to ignore it. Eventually, middle space will lead you to gradual disempowerment because you are caught in "conflicting agendas, perspectives, and priorities of others" (Jick & Peiperl, 2003, p. 403). Longer work hours and increased work demands can add more pressure and stress to the middle space experience. It can impede your ability to develop meaningful work relationships.

The Human Resources IT Project

An interesting example relevant to this discussion about a project with no shared vision and conflicting agendas is a human resources (HR) information technology project. The project was initiated and sponsored by the organization's human resources director, and the CIO who were instrumental in putting together a central organizational committee.

The committee included the HR project manager, an HR consultant, the chief information officer (CIO), the chief technology officer (CTO) responsible for the organization's central IT department, and the IT directors and senior IT managers in the departments and agencies. The project mission was to change how technical employees would get promoted and paid for their technical skills and experience. Instead of using the traditional step increases based on job performance and length of time and experience in a position, pay increases would be based on competency pay. Therefore, employees would be paid on the basis of predefined competency skills earned and demonstrated in the job. Their performance would be evaluated and reviewed annually.

There were several problems with the competency pay concept after it was implemented and in operation that the organization encountered for approximately three years. It would take a long time to discuss the details, but as a result of the problems, the pay for competencies earned was changed back to the traditional pay schedule consisting of step increases based on an employee's tenure in a particular job position and the employee's performance.

From the start of the project, there was no shared vision between the top group consisting of the human resources director, the CIO, CTO, the HR project manager, and the HR consultant; and the middle group consisting of the department heads, and the IT directors and senior IT managers in the departments and agencies; and the below group consisting of the highly specialized technical employees. In this particular case, much time and resources were spent on working on the details for the competency pay concepts, which in the end did not benefit the organization as a whole and diverted many IT directors and senior IT managers away for their work performing the organization's core primary business.

Another problem surfaced during the HR IT project because the top group decided that IT directors and the senior IT managers who were responsible for managing an entire department or agency within the organization would be given the generic job titles of information technology officer (ITO) I, II, or III, at different pay levels. Even information system managers who reported to and worked as subordinates to the IT directors and IT managers would be classified as ITOs. In some cases, departments and agencies would have multiple ITOs.

The IT directors and IT managers responsible for a department or agency means being responsible for all of the technical staff; maintaining the computer hardware and software and the networks; developing annual IT budget proposals; handling computer hardware and software purchases for their department; and developing computer request for proposals (RFPs), agreements, and contracts. Pay levels for ITOs would be based on the size of their department, total amount of their IT budget, number of subordinate IS managers, total number of desktop computers, and total number of LAN servers.

What started out being communicated as a competency pay project focusing on technical employees actually was expanded to include the positions of the IT directors and senior IT managers with changes to their job description, titles, and pay rate. Because of the changes, these individuals felt they no longer had *autonomy*. Their job titles would no longer identify them as being responsible for an entire department or agency but as an information technology officer. In some departments and agencies there would be multiple ITOs at different levels.

In addition to these concerns, many of these IT directors and IT managers felt that the scope of their management responsibilities, college degrees, professional and technical certifications, and work experience were not taken into consideration in the new ITO job title classification. As a result of the IT project's implementation, several individuals in the central, organizational IT department were given job titles of ITOs and bureau chiefs.

The technical directors and managers within the departments and agencies felt that the CIO and CTO had powerful influence on the HR director and project manager leading the IT project. The ITO job title change was not considered a shared vision and there was no prior agreement on the project mission with the department and agency heads. As a result, these IT directors and managers in the departments and agencies were actually caught in middle space because of the conflicting agendas.

Another concern of these managers was that the new ITO job classification substituted experience for an associate's degree, bachelor's degree, and even a master's degree, and made other changes to the position qualifications they felt would have a negative impact on the government organization in the long term. Many felt that the changes made the path to management positions *ambiguous*, meaning that the criteria for getting promoted into management is open to several different contradictory interpretations. Therefore, they referred to it as the generic ITO job title.

The HR IT project and the proposed changes did not develop a clear path to leadership positions in information technology management. Many directors and managers felt that it did not assist in retaining and recruiting qualified IT directors and promoting others from within the organization to IT management positions or even the CIO position in the future. They felt that when the criteria for selecting leaders decline or are lowered, so does the quality of leadership.

Integrate Middle Space

How did the technical directors and managers within the many departments in this organization manage being in middle space when it came to the ITO job titles? They did it through peer-group association and decided that they would continue to refer to themselves as the IT directors or IT managers of their specific departments or agencies. They did not let the formal payroll job title limit them. Some even added their degree to their personal business cards. As middles, they learned to integrate with one another and developed their own support network and strengthen each other, see Figure 6.2.

I do not know if the compensation pay and qualifications for managing an entire department or agency was ever resolved, but not long after the ITO job title and compensation changes were implemented some IT directors left the organization:

- One department IT director opted for an early retirement from the organization to work as a consultant;
- Another department IT director communicated that his job title and pay were determined by the state court system and it was not subject to being changed;
- An agency IT director left the government organization for a position elsewhere;
- Another agency IT director decided to work on a plan to eventually leave the organization to work in the private sector;
- Another senior IT manager in a medium-size department left his job for a position in another department with a higher pay rate.

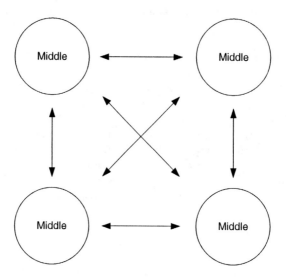

Figure 6.2 Coming together, integrating, and sharing information.
Source: Barry Oshry as cited by Jick and Peiperl, 2003.

The new ITO job title did not help to retain a few of these highly qualified and experienced individuals. In the end, some of the technical directors and senior IT managers responsible for a department or agency felt the effects of disempowerment and the path to IT management positions was blurred. Unfortunately, top-level executives in the organization's central, administration were blind to its future impact on the organization as a whole.

The most important question that needs to be asked is: What impact did the results of this IT project have on the overall organizational performance? In this case, the results from the project implementation introduced many problems that the organization and its resources had to work on resolving and it diverted people away from the organization's primary business activities and had a problematic impact on the overall organizational performance.

By looking at this project in another way is that CIO and HR director (top) could have collaborated with the department heads (tops) and their IT directors and managers (middles) within the departments and agencies to create a shared vision and agreed upon project mission that could have avoided some of these major problems. In fact, organizations need to develop career paths that encourage leadership development and education with a high commitment to employees gaining new skills and competencies to lead. Education should be one of the many criteria for promotion within the organization (Jick & Peiperl, 2003). Another topic to consider is that relatively low public sector salaries in some organizations can cause problems in recruiting and retaining highly qualified and experienced IT managers, project managers, and technical workers.

What about the IT directors in the departments and agencies who left the organization behind? Those IT directors who left the organization had options and took advantage of those options. It is important for you to have the skills, qualifications, and education so that you can consider options. Why? Because leaving a position is always a choice you can make when you feel that staying is not in your best interest. Maybe you feel that you have reached a block wall and the organization does not value you or your contributions to organizational performance.

If you do plan on leaving, a good approach is to plan your departure carefully because there is the saying that the grass always looks greener on the other side of the fence. It may not be greener after all when you are there on the other side if you have not made a good career choice. Do not despair if you think you have no other options. An organization does not have to necessarily limit you or your abilities if you think beyond the boundaries of your current position and that of the organization. Do not let your work environment fit you into a mold. You can learn, observe, and work on organizing your life around *who you are* as an individual, as a manager, as a supervisor, and as a leader. In some situations, it is good to think about other options or move on to other opportunities.

You can consider accepting another position or work on completing additional training, professional certification, or an advanced degree. You can find it advantageous to focus on the positive things you can do and reinvent yourself looking at new goals and opportunities. Out of challenges and adversity can be your own progress. Do not dwell on the negatives. Winston Churchill once said, "We make a living by what we get, we make a life by what we give" (Moncur, 2013, para. 2236).

In contrast to not having a shared vision, there are many top-level managers, CIOs, IT directors, and business managers who do work collaboratively in an organization. They do work on shared visions with other managers at all levels in the departments. Unfortunately, the few who do not work collaboratively on a shared vision create an environment in which some individuals are caught in middle space where there is a gradual disempowerment.

Facilitate Middle Space

As a project manager, you want to be a leader and also be a facilitator and bring people together to empower the tops (above) and the belows (specialized workers) to productively interact with one another (Jick & Peiperl, 2003), see Figure 6.3. Using this approach, you are working on managing middle space. In some situations, you can take problems or challenges and find ways to turn them into opportunities. There are probably several approaches you can take by reading literature about project management, but the most simplistic one is to facilitate middle space by looking at the organizational system and identifying the top, middle, and the below groups, and the clients they serve.

A good example relevant to this discussion is an information systems project that was recently completed for an organization. The scope of this project was for the entire organization versus a project that is a subsystem (i.e., department or agency) of the organization. Several department heads involved with the project are the tops (above); the project manager and team members are the middles; and the belows are the user committee chairperson as a spokesman (a manager) from one of the participating departments and many end users of the information system and the staff they manage. The clients are identified as those who use the products and services produced by the organization.

The next step is to look at how communication takes place for the project. In this case, the project manager meets with and updates the steering

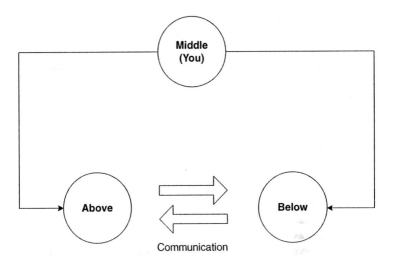

Figure 6.3 Facilitate middle space.
Source: Adapted from Barry Oshry as cited by Jick and Peiperl, 2003.

committee on a regular schedule. The steering committee consists of several key department heads and the chairperson from the user committee. In addition to attending the steering committee meeting, the project manager attends the user committee meetings chaired by its chairperson. During the meetings, questions are directed to the project manager by the chairperson only if there is a need to clarify the discussion items or system design requirements.

If you are a project manager, be prepared to respond to the questions asked by the committee members. If you do not have all of the answers, make sure one or two of your team members attend with you who can provide the information. It is important to have a strong chairperson who will lead the user committee meetings and an alternate chairperson as a backup. Looking at this project differently will assist you in facilitating communication between the aboves, the middles, and the belows. You have to learn to see systems, not just people. When "we don't see system spaces; we see only the effects these spaces have on us" (Jick & Peiperl, 2003, p. 403).

Endorsing Communication

Communication is important and can be a valuable asset for those in the organization. John is a CIO who has an open door policy and strongly endorses two-way communication and is interested in feedback from his staff. He will at times walk around and talk to employees. He told me that he does the things that he believes is right and that both formal and informal communication is a way of understanding what is going on in the organization. He is instrumental in tapping the ideas and creativity of those within the organization. He elaborated that he is interested in the skills and expertise of those who work in the organization, and that good managers use the talents of their staff where it is most beneficial for the organization. Successful leaders value the high-quality IT staff within the central organization and within departments and agencies. When things go well with information technology support in the departments and agencies, information technology goes well for the entire organization.

This CIO believes it is important that managers know the people who are working in the organization and find out their talents, their expertise, and use those talents where it benefits the organization as a whole. He believes that is how really good managers lead and this is how you can be successful in business and how you can improve organizational performance.

The Influence of Politics

In comparison to private sector companies, various governments including US state, county, and city government organizations are faced with different kinds of challenges because of the nature of the political environment. The private sector's priorities are focused on gaining strategic competitive advantage and can organize projects to accomplish the business goals; whereas the public sector's priorities are more significantly influenced by politics and comprise internal and external interest groups (Caudle, Gorr, & Newcomer, 1991; Dufner, Holley, & Reed, 2002).

No matter how much you try to avoid it, politics can often drive poor information system decisions. There is nothing mysterious about some decisions made by top-level managers. Pinto and Kharbanda (1996), in their research on information system projects, report that decisions may be narrowly scoped because they are built on a political agenda. In some situations, the project becomes a hostage to a personal game of keeping power at the expense of the overall effectiveness of the organization; and political environments of this nature make it difficult to implement successful projects. When an information system project is narrowly scoped, little time is spent in understanding the business initiative (if any exists) that is driving the change nor is there collaboration among top-level managers affected by the decision.

If you are a novice manager, be aware of politically driven projects that are not aligned with the business strategy nor are they aligned with the organizational strategy. In some situations, these projects focus on the information systems strategy driving the change instead of the business strategy based on business objectives driving the change and are not led by the business managers and their decisions. These types of projects can be costly, time consuming, and provide no added value to the organization in terms of efficiency or organizational performance or any other kind of value.

Peppard and others (2007) report that all system projects have outcomes and not all outcomes are benefits. The project must be actively managed so that the benefits can be obtained. No matter how good your intentions are for the organization and despite your best efforts, some projects do not always go the way you expect them to go.

How do you avoid narrowly scoped and politically motivated projects? First, if you are not a top-level manager, you may not have a choice. As a project manager, you can provide information on what you see as potential problems with the project and the information that supports your views. If top-level management decides to move forward with it anyway, you will have to support management regardless of your own feelings about the project. If you are representing the end users (the belows) of the system, you can present their concerns about the project. In this case, you are a bottom when you have to be a bottom.

If the concerns of the end users of the computer information system or other stakeholders in a particular project are not being considered by the tops in their strategic decisions, it is important that you provide the appropriate information to the belows and move on to the next step in the process. This can be a very difficult situation to accept but you have to move on. Create an on-the-job behavior that focuses on the project work that has to be done, and find ways to fulfill some of the requests of the end users after the project has been implemented. If you are the project manager, then you need to learn how to manage being in middle space. If you cannot move on, now is the time for you to consider other options and exit gracefully.

Second, if you are not the project manager and you have expressed your concerns about the project and got no support from top-level executives or managers, it is best not to negatively impact others in the organization including the project team. If you think about it, this is the same kind of behavior that you expect from your own staff. Top-level organizational culture impacts the direction that organizations will take in making decisions about their projects. This means that change must take place at the top level of the organization and it may be difficult to make changes as a middle-level manager. If you are not successful in communicating your concerns with top-level managers, you can communicate with your peers and collectively express your concerns to top-level managers through the appropriate channel of communication through your department or agency. In this way, you are communicating as the middle group to the tops.

For example, I mentioned earlier that in many US county governments, the top central organization's executive is the chief executive officer (CEO) or the chief administrative officer (CAO), who in some counties can be appointed to the position by the board of supervisors who are elected officials. In the departments and agencies, there are top-level department heads; some elected into office and some not elected. If you are fortunate enough to be a manager who is not directly involved with the politically motivated project, you can communicate your concerns and then devote yourself to more productive projects and activities.

The plan for change by developing a custom-built system or purchasing a new commercial, packaged software system should result in a system that benefits the organization in achieving efficiency and effectiveness. Research by Jick and Peiperl (2003) on change management describes the importance of identifying the need for change. First, as a business manager, you want to identify the need for change; second, you want to develop a detailed vision of the organization after the change has been implemented; and third, have a vision statement. There should be a shared vision by collaborating with the departments affected by the change.

Navigating in Fog

Sometimes you may use your own true, authentic feelings and perspectives about what is going on and make incorrect choices. I remember reading a story about Doug Batchelor (2012), who was flying a plane in Northern California in the wilderness area where there are a lot of trees and mountains and it was sparsely populated. He was flying to a small town and had two friends with him, who were husband and wife, when he came upon clouds and fog. The airport instrument tower was not operating that day so he had no way of communicating with the airport where he was planning on landing.

He did not want to alarm his friends and tried to remain calm, but he became really concerned because he had no visibility. He said when pilots are flying in clouds or fog and have no visibility of land they lose their bearings on where they are because they cannot see any visible landmarks such as the mountains, the terrain, rivers, and cities or towns. In some situations, they will fly out the cloud to discover they are really flying the plane upside down. Pilots are instructed in this type of situation to trust their instruments in the plane and not their feelings. In this particular situation, he decided to trust his airplane's instruments and not his feelings because your feelings can get you into serious trouble. By trusting his instruments, he finally flew out of the fog and was able to see the blue sky and land safely. He realized after seeing the blue sky that he was previously flying toward the mountains, which would have been disastrous if he continued to follow his own feelings instead of the plane's instruments. Sometimes, our feelings can make us lose our bearings as to what is really going on in a particular situation or with a particular project.

If you are feeling frustrated or overwhelmed, it may be a clue that you need to look at the organization in a different way. It is important to look at the system of tops, middles, belows (workers), and the clients and citizens you serve. Identify the groups of tops, middles, and belows. If the direction from the tops is ambiguous, you as a project manager can be caught between different individuals and their contradictory ideas about the project, which can result in several possible meanings or interpretations. Try to find out the real problems. Determine if there is a shared vision or there are conflicting agendas and their reasons. Work on communicating with other middles to get a different perspective of the situation. Another question to consider is whether or not you will get a realistic appraisal from each member in the top management group. If you cannot convince the tops of your views and why things should be done differently, as a project manager you have to be supportive of the top group with the assumption it does not compromise your own ethics and value system.

Ideally, a sufficient amount of time needs to be spent on identifying the business initiative for changing the organization and investing in a new information system or making major system upgrades and it should not be driven solely by a single top-level executive because it needs to be a business strategy decision. When political decisions are narrowly focused and the decisions are made, some novice project managers will move forward with the project anyway. As a result of the project implementation, the organization may have to struggle with making the system work to support its business operations long after the top-level executive who initiated the project leaves the organization.

The system may be costly to maintain with no significant improvement to organizational performance. These types of projects do exist and sometimes even if you are a project manager or even an IT director for a department, you are caught in middle space because a top-level executive has much greater influence on the project decision. Sometimes the best decisions you make will not be supported by the top management.

Bill Cosby once said, "I don't know the key to success, but the key to failure is trying to please everybody" (Byrne, 1996, para. 322). The simple fact is that top-level executives and the CIO who do not work collaboratively with the department heads and their business managers, and the IT directors or IT managers within the organizational system create an environment of conflicting agendas where managers are at times caught in middle space.

In the organizational system of tops, middles, below groups, and clients and the general public that the organization serves, no one really knows the relationship and interaction tops have among each other and with the CEO and CIO. Middles and belows are often excluded from meetings where important decisions are being made all the time that can affect the middles and the belows.

In some situations, tops in the central, administration level of the organization have their priorities on organizational strategies for administration and budgetary control; and then there are the tops who are department heads who are highly specialized with their priorities on the business strategy for their departments or agencies; and there are the middles (managers and supervisors) who work for the tops, and then there are the belows (workers) with specialized skills.

More importantly, do not forget about the general public who are the citizens and clients who feel the government organizations should be fulfilling their expectations, needs, and wants. In fact, they depend on the government departments and agencies to provide those services. When computer information systems do have problems, it is usually the middles and the belows (specialized workers) who have to communicate with the public and handle their dissatisfaction with how those services are delivered.

Do you ever wonder why some very good CIOs encounter problems? Perhaps the very nature of the CIO position with the expectations and direction of the tops in the central organization and the expectations of department and agency heads make it difficult for some CIOs to be successful. There can be those individuals at the top of the organization involved in IT/IS decision making who are not aware of some of the most important essentials that promote project success. Frequency and the type of communication between the CEO and CIO can assist in creating a shared vision on how to use IT to support the organization's strategy (Johnson & Lederer, 2007).

Establishing central information technology committees without real empowerment can give the appearance of collaboration without actually giving the members authority to make the decisions on the information systems strategy that supports both the business and organizational strategies. It is only the atmosphere created by *authentic collaboration* that makes organizations successful. When there is true collaboration, the organization as a whole and its various departments and agencies do better.

What are the information system project expectations from the tops, middle management, and the end users of the system (belows)? What is the organization supposed to be able to do differently after the information system project has been implemented?

At this point you may be asking why all this fuss about communication and collaboration. To help avoid the negative consequences from information systems project implementations, business managers must be involved in information systems decisions and need to identify the business initiative that drives the change and, in doing so, develop the vision of what the organization will be like after the project has been completed and develop the the project mission. CIOs who work in collaboration with the organization's central, top administration and with the top-level executives, who are the department and agency heads, assist in supporting the business strategy.

Opportunities

Let's take a few minutes to talk about you as a project manager or IT manager and opportunities within the organization. Sometimes, opportunities for your career development can be around you if you look at the organization differently.

There was an IS project manager in county government who was involved in an organizational-wide information systems project that was a politically driven. Under the project managers' leadership, the older information system was totally removed and the new system was installed using the same commercial software system, which was considered one of the best of breeds for government. The project was not considered an upgrade to the existing information system but was a complete replacement of the older system with all the new system programs and functionality. As part of the project, minor enhancements were made to accommodate for the business practices within the departments and to ensure the system could be upgraded when new versions of the software were released.

The information system was year 2000 compliant, meaning that it was able to handle the century change going from a two-digit year (99) to a four-digit year (2000). The information system had an in-house developed warrant reconciliation system and a data warehouse that provided the end users the ability to generate their own customized reports. Maintaining the systems and in-house support was cost-effective. The benefits exceeded the cost of implementing the project.

Within a short time, a new CIO was hired into government and the priority was established to replace the computer information system even though it has been totally replaced just three years earlier. The objective was to replace the systems with an enterprise resource planning (ERP) system. In this case, the project manager felt that there was no business initiative that justified getting another new information system because the existing system had recently been implemented and had all the functionality for the departments.

Rather than being caught up in middle space and with all the politics and spending a large amount of money on something that the project manager felt would not provide a lot of added value to the organization, this individual decided that it was time to pursue other options. This person applied for and accepted another position as an IT director within the same government organization but in another agency.

As an IT director, this individual did not have to be involved with the problems that surfaced as result of the politically motivated implementation of the information systems project. As a result of the new ERP project, the organization had to divert many resources and management away from its core business procedures and activities to work on resolving many problems that later developed.

The decision to leave the department gave the IT director broader experiences with directing technical staff who managed the local area (LAN) networks, web servers, and many different kinds of computer systems. The technology division included network administrators, computer support technicians, and database administrators, which added to the director's prior experience of directing IT managers, technical supervisors, systems analysts, and computer programmers. All of these experiences were valuable and provided the director different opportunities.

Sometimes the decision to leave a position is not always monetary but provides other kinds of career opportunities. In the new position, the IT director was able work for an elected official who was head of an agency and was able to direct a new project by automating one of the departments in the agency from a paper-driven process to a computerized information system. In hindsight, this individual said it was one of the best decisions he had ever made because of being able to focus on more productive projects and at the same time pursued a graduate degree in the evenings.

In some situations, it may be necessary to leave the job or even the organization behind because you can spend too much time working in middle space or trying to reach the top in an organization where there are no opportunities for being promoted to top-level positions. This is something that may be difficult for you to recognize at times. However, the advantages of working for large organizations in both the public and private sectors are that you have more opportunities and flexibility to apply to different jobs and move horizontally or vertically to other departments or agencies. Large organizations offer some major advantages and opportunities because of the size of the organization there can be many opportunities to work in other departments and agencies.

But wait! Suppose you recognize that you are working in middle space with no shared vision and conflicting agendas and things are not getting any better. You have applied all the essentials of project management that you learned in your textbooks and training courses. What do you do next?

First, recognize that in most situations it is not about you but it is about the organizational system of the aboves, the middles, the belows (workers), and the clients and the general public the organization serves. In fact, the tops "need to direct their attention to fixing what's systemically wrong with a space in which competent middles are pulled into becoming stressed, disempowered, and ineffective" (Oshry, 2003, p. 4). Second, when working as an IS project manager, there can be some individuals at the top of the organization who do not have a full understanding of the essentials that contribute to successful information systems projects. It is not unusual for there to be interpersonal conflict in some situations (Barki & Hartwick, 2001).

If you are working in middle space, it is time for you to step back and reflect on your situation, and decide where you are and where you want to be in the near future; and then determine what you need to do now to build yourself toward that future. Politically initiated projects can often result in conflicting agendas and no shared vision of the business strategy.

If you are at the point of considering leaving, you do not have to stay in a job position if you feel you are not getting the proper level of support from top-level management. The most important question is: Can you identify the advantages and disadvantages of staying in the position? Do the disadvantages outweigh the advantages of staying? Work on making a list and review it.

I always feel that work is suppose to be something a person likes doing because it can be motivating to go to work each day by focusing on doing tasks that you find are productive and rewarding. There is a program on television about the US coast guards in Alaska and how they are constantly building their skills daily through training and working together as a team. There is a shared vision of their mission, and each person knows exactly what his or her responsibility is as a member of the team. Several coast guards said their mission is to "save the lifes of those that need them." One coast guard said that he loves his job so much that if he had to do it without being paid he would do it. How many people can actually say that about their job? These are individuals who will go into the worst conditions to save a person's life.

Working in information technology, of course, is not like being a US coast guard but each day you go to your job the work should be something you look forward to doing. When I was working as a computer programmer, the information technology manager was redesigning the office space to make room for more technical staff. Some individuals were complaining because they felt their office cubical would be too small. I did not care if the office space was too small. In fact, I told one of my coworkers that I did not care if they put my office in a closet as long as I had ample lighting and was able to work comfortably, perform my job tasks, and work on developing software programs. I was really content with what I was doing and the size of my office space did not really matter to me.

Information systems project management has its challenges, every job does, and that is why information system project managers have both education and experience in computer programming and software engineering because if it were easy anybody could do it. I found it to be an exciting and challenging field to be working in and there were no dull or boring days. There is always something challenging to accomplish and many people need the information system services and the technical support. As a systems analyst and IT manager, I spent a lot of time working with business managers and the end users of the various information systems. Sometimes people visualize you as being somewhat isolated working in a corner by yourself. In my job, there was a lot of communication and dialog with the end users of the system and involvement in writing program design specifications.

Computer software engineering for designing and developing information system is something you have to be educated and trained in doing. Even minor changes to a software program can cause major problems in the computer system. One missing decimal point or one missing period in the software code can cause major errors in the program logic and in the program computations. The program design and logic is either right or wrong and there is no in between.

Relationship with Your Employer

Once you are able to see organizational systems and the connection of middle space, and the tops, the middles, the belows, and both the clients and general citizens, and the slow disempowerment of working within it, you learn to integrate with your peers and you can think about and view the organization differently (Jick & Peiperl, 2003). Remember the important point here is to think about the organizational system and try to identify the problem areas of the project. Think about how this project compares with past projects that ran smoothly. The focus here is not on complaining. If you find that a project is both politically motivated and narrowly scoped and you have no influence on the direction that the top-level management is taking, the decision to leave is a personal decision and each person must weigh the advantages and the disadvantages of leaving. If you feel that changing your position is something you need to do then it is a decision only you can make as you evaluate your own beliefs and values. The decision is not an easy one and there are no easy answers. If leaving is not an option, then work within the goals of the organization and be supportive but start working on developing yourself outside of the box so that you can take advantage of other opportunities when they do come your way.

Another word of advice is that before you accept a position find out who you report to and who has control of the project team members. Several years ago, I accepted a position as a project director for an organization-wide information systems project as I wanted to broaden my work experience. I interviewed and accepted a position in another government department.

I should have known from the start that I was stepping into middle space because even though the project team members were under my direction in one physical office location, the project director's position was actually in the auditor-controller's budget; and the project team member positions were actually funded by the central, organization's information technology department and its budget.

In theory, the project team members were to serve in the role of contractors with the project being under the direction and control of the project director. As a project director, I was responsible for reporting to the auditor-controller, who is a department-level executive, and to a top-level central, administrative steering committee. The steering committee members comprised a senior manager from the central organization's executive office and several department heads and their representatives from several key departments and agencies and the CIO representing the organization's central IT department. There were conflicting agendas from the start from several sources:

1. My perspective as a director supporting the business strategy for the project and the perspective of the end users of the system,
2. The steering committee members from several key departments, and the
3. CIO and the central IT department.

In the real world of project management, there was no shared vision and there were conflicting agendas between the tops. No doubt, the top-level executives in the central organization who came up with the idea for the structure of the project director and team member positions thought it was going to be in the best interest of the project and the organization as a whole.

Prior to me accepting the position of Project Director, there were two project directors who filled the position for only one year each, which was really a good indicator that I was stepping into middle space. There were obviously good reasons why these two people left the position. I have a philosophy that I cannot be responsible for something I do not have control over. In this particular position, it was a slow progression of disempowerment as a project director.

It did not take long for me to realize that I was working in middle space. As a result of the conflicting agendas, I built strong peer relationships that provided me resources and support. I remained in the position for two years, which was long enough to complete the project with many different kinds of challenges, but in the end, the project was implemented successfully. In this situation, I could see there was nothing wrong with the competent IT directors (middles) who served in this position before me but it was the tops and their conflicting agendas, no shared vision, and a project that was not driven by the business strategy and not supported by the organizational strategy and the information systems strategy.

More about Middle Space

When I was working in middle space, I actually developed a plan that I felt would work for me at the time. In addition, I developed strong peer relationships at work. You can do the same thing. I actually started working on my master's degree during that time and completed it shortly after I left middle space. Even more surprising to me was I developed peer relationships with my university class members. We arranged study groups and luncheon meetings together on weekends, because we all had a common goal and that was to learn what we needed to know and to finish our courses. Two of my class members who were CIOs provided me a wealth of information about politics and the organization.

In the work environment, I did not plan on working in middle space any longer than I had to so I accepted a position of IT director in another department within the same organization and was in charge of the technical division. All of the positions were under my direction and were funded within the one department.

In the circumstances of working in middle space, I was soon able to recognize the environment I was working in, the conflicting agendas, different priorities, and lack of a shared vision. I eventually developed the people skills required to master the environment and was able to build strong peer relationships and other resources for support within the organization. I was actually able to grow and develop myself through my experiences and came up with my own plan. You may not be aware of it, but learning new things can be a secondary outcome and provide benefits from working in this position (middle space).

Since the information system was a commercial, packaged software system, I learned how to revise the contractual agreement for the software system and how to develop the appropriate forms for submitting the contractual agreement to the board of supervisors for approval. I learned how to write other types of computer system RFPs and contracts. I was able to work with the legal counsel (attorneys) in government who reviewed my contracts to make sure they were in proper form. I learned to work with the state, other counties, company vendors, and contractors. Even though I was in middle space, I was able to develop myself and broaden my experiences and was able to learn how things were handled within the government organization. I eventually became an expert at developing RFPs and information system contracts.

I was able to facilitate different meetings at the state level, meet different people, and be a facilitator at conferences held by the professional government association meetings that I attended with my department head. I learned to manage the environment in which I was working. You can do the same and grow from your experiences if you are aware of middle space. As a project manager, it is important for you to recognize the environment you are working in and not live in the dark ages of organization behavior (Jick & Peiperl, 2003). You can learn a lot and develop yourself on the job if you start to look at your environment differently. The environment can give you warning signs, and it is important to recognize that you do not have to be limited by the environment. You can break out of the mold.

Some people say that you can't see the forest for the trees. I do believe that when working in the field of information systems project management many individuals do not recognize the real problems in the environment and therefore some projects fail and do not succeed or do not provide the benefits in terms of system functionality. Often people have been caught in middle space at some time or another in their work career.

Do tops in organizations ever get caught in middle space? Yes, tops can be caught in middle space. I have observed department heads caught in middle space when decisions made at the top central, administrative level of the organization have a negative impact on how they direct and manage their departments' business operations. In some situations, conflicting agendas laterally may be perceived as territorial, power struggles, see Figure 6.4.

Let me take a few minutes to tell you about the experiences of Michael who is a department head and an elected official. He received several requests from another elected official at the top, central administration level of the organization. Michael said that he could not show any favoritism by complying with the other elected official's requests because he

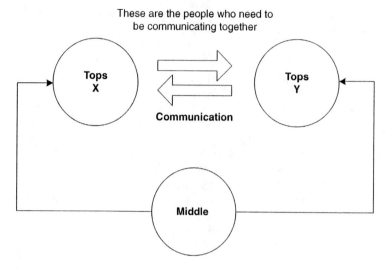

Figure 6.4 Tops with conflicting agendas.

Source Adapted from Barry Oshry as cited by Jick and Peiperl, 2003.

would be subject to violation of the law on how specific business activities are performed.

Michael's initial thoughts were that this elected official did not have a good understanding of how the business procedures are performed by his staff. Michael said that he explained to the other elected official why he could not comply with his requests. However, from that point on, there was an environment that made it difficult at times for Michael to get things approved at the top central, administration level of the organization because of this elected official. He told me that he would like to be able to work with the other elected officials and even other department heads and managers in the organization, but if he is asked to do something that violates his own ethics and value system, does not comply with legislation, does not take into consideration the well-being of all the constituents that voted him into office, and adversely impacts the manner in which he manages the business operations, he will make his own decisions in the best interest of his department. As an elected official, he has authority over his own domain or agency.

This department head was actually working in middle space, laterally, for several months but did not compromise his ethics and values. If you will recall at the beginning of this chapter that middle space can have multiple contending forces from the tops and below and both vertically and laterally. The managers (middles) in Michael's department actually had to deal with some of the problems that surfaced from the conflicting agendas between the two tops; however, Michael protected himself, his staff, and the organization by acting ethically. I cannot help but wonder if some of the tops in group X being the central organization's elected officials met as a group with the tops in group Y who are the elected officials in the departments and discussed the conflicting agendas whether there would have been some resolution to the problem. In this particular case, everything worked out in the end. Michael eventually retired from government and the elected official who made the unethical requests lost the next election and no longer works in the government organization.

Unfortunately, you do occasionally hear about some elected officials in federal, state, county, and city government in the news reports violating ethical practices and having to deal with the consequences of those actions. Unfortunately, there are some tops who have their personal, self-serving agenda. Stevens (2004) reports that, "Ethics and compliance programs fail when they are not true expressions of the company culture" (p. 168). Another study by Miller and Thomas (2005) found that relative position and relational closeness had an impact on reporting unethical acts. These types of ethical problems can be disruptive to the organization as a whole and can impact the morale of those working within the organization.

Anyone can get caught in middle space; however, middle-level managers are caught more in the middle and more often than others and can be in a position where they are constantly dealing with conflicting agendas and no shared vision. Both the organization culture and politics can be instrumental in information technology project decisions. Top-level executives in the central administration can be influenced by the CIO in their decision making within the organization, and the CIO can be influenced by top-level executives.

CEOs do not like conflict and rely on the CIO to assist them in making good decisions on the information systems strategy that affect the organization's technology projects and the network infrastructure. CIOs who have a shared vision and collaborate with top-level executives, department heads, and managers in the departments and agencies within the organization assist in eliminating conflicting agendas and create a shared vision. Organizational culture and politics can work together to make very good decisions or it can be instrumental in making some very poor decisions.

Office Space

There is a movie titled *Office Space* (Judge, 1999), which I saw when it first came out in the theaters about downsizing a company. In the movie,

Peter worked in an office cubical and, obviously, did not like the work he was doing. In the end, Peter said that he was not motivated because he had eight different bosses and a top-level executive who owned the company that micro-managed him and the other employees. Peter said the only thing that motivated him was to avoid not being hassled. Peter was in middle space and he was being pulled in eight different directions in a job he did not like doing.

Then there was Milton who had been moved several times until he ended up having a work in a cubical at the back of the office. I am sure this did not help his self-esteem. I often wondered if Milton was really ever good at his job or whether he was in the wrong kind of job and needed a career change early in his life. Perhaps it was a case of gradual disempowerment in which he became anxious, tense, and nervous and finally became a self-doubting and ineffective, mumbling wreck. Eventually, Milton's office was moved to the basement storage room. The only thing he had to hold on to during every office move was his bright, red stapler. Maybe holding on to the stapler was the only thing he felt control over and it gave him a sense of stability.

In the movie, Milton had actually been fired five years previously, but for some reason there was a glitch in the payroll system and he was still working at the company every day and getting a paycheck. In the end, his paycheck was stopped. The boss took away the red stapler, which was the only thing Milton had that he really cherished. Milton continued to work because no one officially terminated him. The boss, the consultants, and others were thinking that Milton would eventually just quit and not come in to work each day.

Although the people described are just characters in a movie and the improper words should be eliminated, you can see the conflicting agendas and the gradual disempowerment of Peter and Milton. Peter's solution created more problems for him because he had a plan but it was not a very good one and the consequences were not well thought out. Peter and his friends' approach was unethical and against the law. He and his peers introduced programming code into the computer systems that calculated a fraction of a cent from each transaction and put the remainder into another account they had access to for withdrawing the funds. One of Peter's peers, the programmer, later discovered he put the decimal in the wrong position in the program code and they ended up a balance in the account over $305,000 in just a few days. Things went from bad to worse when they tried to figure out how to give the money back to the company.

First, Peter had too many tops with conflicting agendas directing him; and second, even Peter had a peer group that he could talk to about his problems and just vent and to discuss solutions. Although Peter did go for professional help, which in the movie complicated his problem, it would have been better for him to find someone as a role model or a mentor who is successful in working with others to provide him some guidance. Unfortunately, Peter influenced his peers into doing something they should not have done. He would have been better off evaluating his situation to determine what he really wanted to do in life and leave the company behind. In the end, Peter actually ended up working on a construction cleanup crew. He discovered that he really enjoyed doing physical work and being outside and not in some stuffy, office cubicle doing a job that he did not like doing. It is difficult to be really good at something you do not like doing.

If you are in middle space, strive to associate with your peer groups and integrate with others because this helps you survive in such an environment and helps you develop a powerful and supportive network (Jick & Peiperl, 2003). By associating with peers, you will be able to have more good experiences and you will be able to reflect back on good conversations; and it can help you to focus on the positive things. You can learn a lot from your peer groups. They can be an important support network for you. It is important to find a balance between your work and your own personal life. The presence of friends in your life can be resources that will provide emotional support.

Agendas

If you are working in middle space, be informed on what is going to be discussed in meetings. Before going to a meeting with the above (tops) group and the below (bottoms) group, ask for an agenda to be published and distributed to everyone prior to the meeting so that you can be prepared for the topics to be discussed and avoid surprises. Ask for an estimate of how long the meeting will be and request that it be put on the agenda.

During the meeting, avoid being pulled into other people's conflicting agendas; and whatever happens keep your professional composure. Think about the system of the tops, middles, belows, and the clients. Do not take it personal. If you have to, excuse yourself, step outside of the meeting room and slowly count to fifty, get a drink of water, and then go back into the meeting. Try to focus on having diplomatic, open, and nonconfrontation dialog with others.

Mood Regulation

How do you prepare yourself to deal with conflicting situations? It is a good idea of be aware of mood regulation and control your behavior during stressful meetings. I attended a meeting in which a top-level executive who is a department head was so upset over what was being communicated in the meeting, he actually excused himself from the meeting and did not return. His assistant quickly announced that something came up and he had to leave the meeting. After the meeting, his assistant told me in confidence that the executive left the meeting because it was his way of staying in control. He was actually high enough in the organization to be able to do it. This was his way of emotionally handling the situation without displaying negative behaviors and regulating his mood responses. I would not recommend using this approach as a project manager.

Mood regulation is an important skill that leaders must work on managing, especially, in stressful situations (Baruto & Burbach, 2006). Later this department-level executive told me that he did not agree with what was being communicated at the meeting. He said that if things do go wrong with the information system that is being redesigned and changed, he would ultimately be responsible for the computer system problems as a public official and take all of the criticism and heat. The truth is that he was absolutely right. The tops usually start their finger pointing as to who caused the problem and it is not normally blamed on a computer program but on the person or persons responsible for making such poor decisions.

It should be no surprise to you that people react in different ways to stressful situations. I live in California where there are many earthquakes. I was chairing a meeting in a building downtown on the eleventh floor when all of a sudden there was an earthquake. The building began to slightly sway because it is built with expansion joints just for earthquakes making it potentially earthquake safe. This is really a good thing. I have experienced several earthquakes while working in this same building and learned not to panic after working there for several years. Young children in school are instructed to stop, drop, and cover.

Some people just quickly got up and the left the meeting during the earthquake and others including myself stayed in the room and got under the conference table. In our previous earthquake drills, we were told to find protection under a table or a safe place, which made a lot of sense because the building we were in has many large glass windows. After the earthquake was over, I told those who did remain in the conference room to leave the room because I knew that nobody would be able to concentrate on the meeting. There were two people who I know are very afraid of earthquakes and would not be able to concentrate on their work during the remainder of the day. These two individuals notified their superiors that they wanted to leave for the day and actually went home.

I found it interesting to see that we practiced many earthquake and fire drills as employees on a regular schedule, but when it came to the actual earthquake, some individuals did not follow the procedures and just reacted to the situation. This is the same approach that some individuals use when they react to specific conflicting or stressful situations instead of thinking about what they were trained to do next. All the training during the drills just went out of the door with the wash water and becomes an afterthought. Do not react to conflicting situations. Try to think it through, then respond, and act appropriately. If your behavior follows these principles, you know that you are acting ethically and responsibly.

Distancing Strategies

As a project manager, you want to avoid meetings that pull you away from the project because it could potentially increase project risks and impact the project completion date. Normally you want to "seek out information— rather than run from it" (Jick & Peiperl, 2003, p. 408) and use it in formulating your own perspective of the conflicting agendas. However, when you cannot identify the reasons for the no shared vision, distancing strategies have been found to be successful in dealing with some conflicting situations. In looking back on my own experiences, I regret the fact that there were times when I was working in middle space as a project director that I was not able to recognize what was going on in my work environment.

There were meetings with two department heads and two assistants that I attended with no published agenda. This was a clear warning sign. There were those in attendance with several conflicting priorities even though the project plan was already in place and being worked on. At the time, I lacked the experience to regulate my own mood responses because I did not understand the concept of middle space and the organizational system with tops, middles, belows, and clients; and conflicting agendas among the tops with no shared vision.

I eventually recognized that the meetings were not intended to offer solutions but they actually created barriers to the project. It is important that you recognize the environment you are working within. I expressed my concerns to the top-level executives. As a result of my communication, future meetings with these individuals were cancelled and became nonexistent, because they actually took time away from focusing on the project and the work that had to be accomplished.

Exactly what was the motivation of the individuals who arranged the meetings? I do not know and it was not worth my time trying to figure it out because my focus needed to be on the project and getting the work accomplished. Do not waste your valuable time trying to figure out why people do the things they do. Some managers may have their own personal agendas not focused on improving organizational performance. I received support by communicating with my department head and those at the top, central administrative level of the organization. You may run into similar situations, and it is essential that you look at the organization system of tops, middles, belows, and clients or citizens they serve and work on getting the tops to support you when you need it. Your focus needs to be on goals and objectives of the project and getting the work that needs to be completed.

As a rule, I do not recommend distancing strategies because you cannot change things unless you actually confront them and have meaningful discussions with others. However, if you see what is happening is preventing you from focusing on the work that has to be done, you need to work on making decisions that are in the best interest of completing the project and meeting the project target dates by distancing yourself from obstacles or barriers. If there are other types of central, organizational IT meetings that are pulling you away from the project, send your subordinate manager so that you are in the channel of communication with the things that are going on within the organization as a whole.

Leadership Styles

Let's take a few minutes to talk about another very important topic, that is, leadership style. Transformational leaders are actively engaged within the organization. Some of these leaders find out what is going on in the organization just by walking around and talking to others. When it came to my technology staff, I found that it was good to integrate with others by just walking around and communicating with the people I managed and with other individuals in the department. There were occasions when I was able to learn much more about how well things were going not only in the department but also in the organization by walking around and talking to people than I did in formal meetings or through e-mails and text messages.

There are some managers who do not leave their offices because they do not want to communicate any more than they have to because they feel like they have too much work to do. They work within their own space and never venture outside the boundaries of what they consider is their safe zone. Really good project managers are competent, trustworthy, and dynamic. As a result, they have a lot of credibility. They communicate well, have good management skills, and are competent in their field. These managers follow through on their promises, show no biases, never try to demean or embarrass others, and are flexible. They normally have high energy and try to relate positively to others (Avolio & Bass, 2004; Bass, 1990, 1999; Bass & Avolio, 1993; Bass & Avolio, 1994).

Interpersonal relationships and face-to-face communication with your team members is a good thing. I worked with a project manager on a very large project. He sent e-mails to the people in the cubical next to his office rather than getting up and walking ten feet to have face-to-face, meaningful conversations. How can you manage people if you have no face-to-face interpersonal communication when they are within walking distance?

Technology using computers, laptops, webcams, e-mail, cell phones, electronic notebooks, and other technological devices for communication provide many benefits, but there needs to be a balance so that technology does not overshadow more important priorities, tasks, and opportunities to have meaningful conversations with others and form meaningful relationships. Establishing your priorities is really important.

There is nothing wrong with limiting your time during the day to the tasks of reviewing and answering text messages and e-mails. I check my messages periodically during the day in the morning and in the afternoon. If others have emergencies, I inform them to call me on my cell phone and not to send me an e-mail or text message.

In today's technology environment, we can be faced with information overload. Sometimes we can be too busy for face-to-face conversations with other people. We may have a great amount of activity in our life but accomplish little; receive and send many e-mails and text messages each day but have very few real conversations; and we can use a lot of technology but experience very few results. Take time to ask yourself: What kind of results are you getting from your use of technology each day? What have you actually accomplished?

There was a meeting I attended in which the top-level executive said that he wanted everyone in attendance to silence their cell phones, put them away, and pay attention to what is being discussed in this meeting. Imagine if you are in the physician's office because you are not feeling well, and in the middle of an examination the doctor reaches in his pocket, pulls out his cell phone, and starts calling or text messaging someone. Your first thoughts would be that he has the wrong priorities at a time when he should be giving his full attention to you as his patient.

Peer Relationships

This following section examines the topic of peer relationships. Why are peer relationships so important? It is important because it is a way of getting the kind of support you need within the organization as a manager or even as a supervisor. In fact, peer relationships can actually improve your leadership performance. Peer relationships are important to develop and maintain. A study by Parris, Vickers, and Wilkes (2008) is about middle managers in the workplace and their friendships. Twenty middle managers participated in the study over several months. The results found that the work life of middle managers has changed over the past 20 years. Longer work hours and the development of new technologies increased their work demands long after they physically left the office. The managers experienced a wider scope of responsibilities because of downsizing of employees within many organizations.

Because of the demands in the workplace, there can be an increase in the workload for both managers and their subordinates. The manager's personal relationships, friendships, and physical exercise became a lower priority or even be nonexistent. Some managers even experienced a sense of loneliness in their middle management positions. Others said they experienced what they considered a hostile work environment due to the political environment in their organization. Some respondents felt both anger and sadness that the impact of their workload had on the quantity and quality of their time with friends. Many individuals recognized the value of friendships and the workplace experiences with others have on their well-being, but felt they had little time to develop relationships (Parris et al., 2008).

Friendships can have relevance both at work and in your personal life. Friendships actually provide stability, support, a channel for venting your emotions, and helps to alleviate some of the work-related stress and demands. It is important for you to recognize the value of friendships in the organization. Managers need to take time to make it their priority to work on relationships with peers, especially, if you are working in middle space.

Peer relationships with others as a manager or even as a supervisor within your peer groups are important to your well-being and health and will help you to work in middle space. You will have the opportunity to discuss issues and find out how your peers would approach various problems through informational support and with the goal of problem solving and at the same time have social support.

This particular study reported the experiences of several middle managers and said that, "The ability to vent their emotions or let off steam was expressed by many respondents. In particular, they spoke of the stressful aspects of their work and personal lives, and that their friendship provided an opportunity to discuss these and restore a since of equilibrium" (Parris et al., 2008, p.410).

I was part of a peer group in which one member had several personality flaws. Even though he had several flaws, this person was never vindictive and never tried to demean or embarrass others. It was interesting to see how the group dismissed his flaws because of the many good qualities of this individual. Perhaps, you have had similar experiences and you have found the good qualities of a person with many flaws. In fact, we all have some flaws. Recognize that you may not be fortunate enough to work in a secular environment where you are going to like everyone you work with within the organization. Groups can overlook the negatives about a peer and accept the individual regardless of the person's shortcomings. They become more tolerant. Peers can provide a lot of support to you for communicating and sharing experiences. It gives you an opportunity to discuss and see their views on certain topics, situations, solutions, and circumstances. Do not go through your life with no peer relationships. You have more power and positive experiences as a group than as an individual working alone.

Types of Peers

It is advantageous to have different types of peers. I was fortunate enough to work for a large government organization with 37 different departments and agencies. There were many people I could select as my peers. You should find peers in the following categories that can be part of your support network:

- Mentor
- Coach
- Best friend
- Younger person
- Older person
- Celebrator
- Optimist
- Spiritual person

These kinds of peers can be supportive in many different areas of your life. The following describes the various types of peers.

Mentor

A mentor is a trusted teacher or counselor within the organization. This person can serve as your advisor because the mentor has many experiences in different kinds of obstacles or challenges you may face in the work environment. Most mentors have a lot of experience and can give you good advice in handling specific projects or situations.

I met my mentor in my early years of working in information technology in the private sector. This mentor had a lot of experience and offered sound advice. If you are a woman and have a male mentor, it is important to consider whether you are working in a predominantly male profession and carefully evaluate the advice from your mentor, mainly because men sometimes do not face some of the same challenges as women in management. It is important to consider the organizational culture and whether a few women and minorities are in top-level management positions in the organization where you work. Even so, a mentor can give you a lot of valuable advice and information because they know the politics and working within the organization and can be a sponsor and recommend you to others for future promotions.

Coach

Another important peer is the coach, who can help you stay focused on your goals and personal career path. This person does not do anything to inadvertently sabotage your plans. The coach is a person who is supportive of your goals and plans and can be a valuable asset to you when working on your classes, your degree, your certification, or other career training plans. Everyone needs to have a coach to keep them motivated and focused.

Best Friend

Everyone needs a best friend. The best friend is an individual who is supportive, someone you can trust, and who can offer you advice. A best friend will not share information that you both discuss. This person will listen to you when you need someone to listen. The person in the work environment is a one you can share work-related experiences. It is good to have a best friend just to vent and let off steam. In some situations, you may not really want any advice. You just need someone to talk to about the situation or the specific problems. Do not share your personal non-work-related experiences with your best friend at work and work peers. The best friend at work should be related to things you can discuss professionally about work. It is important to keep your personal life separate from the work environment.

A personal best friend outside of work is a person who you can trust and share your personal experiences. I have a peer best friend who I met when I was working in city government when we were both working in administration. We both eventually left the city and went on to work elsewhere in two different organizations. I stayed in government employment and my best friend went into establishing a corporate business. We have been best friends for many years now. I can share confidential information with my best friend and know that this person will not share it with anyone else.

Younger Person

Do not forget the peer who is younger and brings new and different ways of thinking. There was a younger person who was new to the organization. He asked me to go to coffee break with him because he did not want it to appear as if he did not have any friends. He was totally honest and thought about not having friends, which he really valued. He could see the importance of peers at a young age in his career. This young man eventually became a successful CIO for a private sector organization. Feelings of isolation can come from not having peer relationships and not being part of a group.

Older Person

Another type of peer to consider is an older person, who brings their life experiences and can offer good and sound advice. This type of a person can put a different perspective on certain situations and circumstances. They know who they are and they have already defined themselves and are not afraid of what others think about them. They will communicate their thoughts, express their feelings about different topics, and provide a different perspective. This person brings a wealth of knowledge and information to your peer group.

Celebrator

Another peer who should be in your support network is the celebrator who will help you plan and celebrate your accomplishments in different ways. It is important that you work on celebrating both small and large accomplishments because many small ones lead to larger ones. The celebrator creates a fun environment. Celebrating can be just going out to lunch together or going to Starbuck's for coffee. I know a person who would order flowers for her friend and have them delivered to her office as a way of celebrating. I know another person who orders flowers for herself when she had a major accomplishment.

Optimist

The optimist is one who says a glass is half-full and not half empty. The optimist helps you stay positive and look at the favorable outcomes and good things that can occur when faced with the challenges and negative events happening in your life. This individual will help you to take bright, yellow lemons that are juicy but really tart and make sweet lemonade out of them. The optimist keeps you focused on the positive things and not on the negative things in life.

Spiritual Person

Finally, there is a spiritual person who supports your religious views and value system. This peer may be someone within or outside of the organization. Some believe that because of their religion, they can keep everything together and work through any obstacles. The spiritual person shares your spiritual views and convictions. The spiritual person can provide you support when you need spiritual support.

When you think about selecting your peers, focus on finding supportive peers. You may find a mentor who is a celebrator or a best friend who is an optimist. Just remember to broaden your peer group at work to include these positive qualities in individuals. The reason I recommend that you broaden your peer group is because some individuals may leave the organization for employment elsewhere or even retire and move away to another state or another demographic area. Some of my peers moved on to other opportunities and left the organization behind. You do not want to limit yourself to just two or three peers. If you broaden your peer relationships, you will not feel the impact of those who eventually leave for other job opportunities. New individuals may be hired within the organization but it takes time to develop the peer relationships. You will find in the end that *group empowerment* supports individual empowerment (Jick & Peiperl, 2003).

Suppose you work for a small organization and there are very few peers to choose from within the various departments and agencies. In this case, you do not have a choice in selecting your peers. Remember that integrating with other middles at work builds cooperative, collaborative, and supportive relationships. Look for the qualities in the peers to see if any of them fall into any of the categories I described previously. In addition to peers at work, you can consider looking at professional organizations to network with others who can support you in areas that are not supported by your peer group, such as a coach, an optimist, a spiritual person, and a best friend. However, your organizational network is most important.

I know of an individual who works for a small company and said that it is difficult to integrate with other managers because most of the other managers are located in various company locations throughout the United States. She joined the Project Management Institute (PMI) professional organization and said that she is able to network with other individuals who work in the same kind of business and she is able to get the kind of support she needs.

Take control over the things that you can control and work on making changes from the middle down (the belows) and the middle upward (the tops). You can control focusing on the positive things and not the negatives. Try to stay positive despite the challenges at work. You can control having a positive outlook. You can control identifying with the positive people in your life. You can control surrounding yourself with supportive individuals and peers. You can control making some time for yourself. You can control working on your own career plans and professional development.

Retirement Parties

Some people have more of a difficult time handling middle space than others and that is another reason why peer support is really important. If you think you do not need peers and that you can go at it alone, I would like to tell you about two of many retirement parties I have attended.

I attended a retirement luncheon for a middle-level IT manager who worked in government for 24 years. Many people were in attendance at the luncheon. It was ironic that the top-level manager did not make time to find out the work history of the middle manager and no attempt was made to speak about her 24-year journey in the organization, her accomplishments, and her likes and dislikes while she worked in county government. No doubt, the top-level manager was thinking that her peers would have a lot of things to say about her.

During the luncheon, there were no personal stories about her to tell others. She had one friend with whom she, occasionally, went to coffee break and lunch together. This one person got up and tried to save the day by saying something nice about the manager during the luncheon, but nothing of real substance. It was a very sad experience when it should have been a joyous occasion. I thought about the entire situation and felt really sad for this person. I actually had nothing to say about her either so I could not contribute anything to the luncheon. I would often see her passing in the hallways and say hello, but she never reached out to others or had any meaningful conversations.

This middle manager did not build any peer relationships over the years that she worked in government. There was no one to speak about her journey in a meaningful way and the closeness with others was missing. Other individuals were not able to speak about their own personal experiences with her. The entire situation gave me the feeling of such a sense of loss when a person can work for an organization that long a time and leave under these kinds of circumstances. Unfortunately, I have attended other retirement parties and luncheons that repeated the same situation. Middle space can be a very lonely place. I do not believe people were created to be loners and to be disconnected from others and that is why peer support is so important.

In contrast to having no peer relationships, I attended another retirement dinner party where the manager actually took control of his own party. In fact, he made plans with his peers and coworkers on what he wanted to do for his party and had input to the agenda. He even made the arrangements for the location where the dinner party was to be held and paid for the facility himself.

He found out that some of the coworkers play musical instruments and sing in a band on weekends. He arranged for them to provide the singing and the music for dancing. He decided to make it a country western, costume party. He did not leave everything in the hands of others. He had his own speech written, arranged for music, dancing, and even told humorous stories about some of the peers and coworkers during the dinner.

He bought throw-away cameras and had them placed on the tables and people were asked to take group pictures and leave the cameras behind so he can put the photos in his own photo album. Now, you can use cell phones and iPads for taking and sending digital photos. He has a network of peer relationships and has the respect of many employees. It was actually a very joyful occasion. If you are working in middle space, take control of the things you have control over. This manager took control even as he was leaving the organization behind. He was involved in the planning of his own retirement party.

In my own situation, I still have long-lasting friendships from the government organizations. I meet with a group of friends from the peer relationships I formed while working in city and in county government. Some of these same individuals left the government organization to work elsewhere, others are still working within the government organization, and a few of them actually retired.

I took a different career path, but I kept my friendships with several of the people I worked with when I was working for the government organization. I attend luncheon meetings with the group of about 10 people on a regular basis and we meet at different restaurants in the city where I use to work even though I now live 50 miles away. One member of the group occasionally travels by plane from Arizona to California to have lunch with everyone. This person moved to a nearby state that would normally be about a four-hour drive one-way, but is 50 minutes by plane. We have been meeting for lunch for several years now. In fact, I have built new peer relationships where I now work and maintain my government peer relationships even after leaving the government organization behind. This is a way to actually expand your scope of friendships.

I do have some words of caution about peer relationships. If you are looking to develop peer relationships at work, remember to stay within your peer group, meaning managers need to develop friendships and integrate with other managers. Supervisors need to develop peer relationships and integrate with other supervisors. Avoid showing favoritism to specific individuals and developing close friendships with subordinate staff. Try to treat everyone in a balanced way.

There was a situation in which a top-level manager developed peer relationships with a supervisor and a nonsupervisory employee. The other employees felt that the manager was showing favoritism to these two individuals. He would, occasionally, go to coffee breaks and lunch with these two employees. When it was time to complete employee performance evaluations and writing reference letters, this manager put himself in a situation where he could not objectively evaluate the performance of these two employees because of his work relationship. In fact, another employee filed a grievance with the personnel department stating the manager was giving preferential treatment to these two individuals.

Collaboration

Knowledgeable CIOs, IT directors, and business managers who work collaboratively with the departments in the organization to establish information technology policies and standards work to support not only the goals of the organization but also the business strategy of the individual government departments (Grover, Jeong, Kettinger, & Lee, 1993). Organizational-wide information technology standards and policies assist in reducing conflicting agendas and reduce the feeling of managers being caught in middle space.

Many organizations, including government, devise information technology policies and standards on computer use, security, hardware and software purchases and many other IT policies in an effort to support the organizational and business strategies through collaboration with other managers within the organization. Without this collaboration, many managers at different levels within the departments will feel as if they are caught in middle space and are not part of the shared vision. The CIO or the IT director in the central information technology department who overlooks the needs of the departments may very likely run the risk of creating an environment of *conflicting agendas* that is counterproductive.

Because of the political environment in government and in public sector organizations, there may be a time when some project managers may be required to lead major projects he or she feels is not in the best interest of the organization. In some situations, project managers may be able to find ways to work through these problems, as previously discussed in this chapter, or evaluate the advantages or disadvantages of making major career decisions.

Organization Structure That Supports Departments

Many government organizations rely on the CIO and the central IT department to monitor and support the organization as a whole and to work with others to establish standards and policies and direct organizational-wide technology. Because of the close relationship with the CEOs, the CIOs are extremely powerful and can influence either strong or weak support of the operations of IT at the organizational-wide level and IT at the department and agency level of the organization.

The organizational IT standards and policies that are created need to allow the departments to work effectively, which in turn will improve overall organizational performance in providing the programs, products, and services to the public. Some novice CIOs and organizational central IT departments have created major barriers to departments and agencies for implementing information systems and making technology changes. There needs to be an organizational-wide assessment of the organizational and the business goals of the departments within the organization, and periodic changes need to be made to the IT policies and standards. As middles working with your peers, you as a group can communicate this to the tops. There needs to be a balance between the business, organizational, and information systems strategies, and this will assist in promoting collaboration.

Summary

Middle space is where there is no shared vision and there are conflicting agendas. If you are working in middle space, you experience gradual disempowerment. Middle space is not where you want to be for long. Managers need to learn to integrate middle space, and in some situations facilitate communication between the top and the bottom groups. Several real-world experiences are given of those working in middle space, including mood regulation and distancing strategies. Peer relationships are important to managers and provide support. Politics can influence good decisions or poor decisions for information system projects; however, there are different choices and decisions you can make when working in middle space.

Review Concepts

- Middles space and disempowerment
- Integrate middle space
- Facilitate middle space
- Endorsing communication
- Influence of politics

- The movie *Office Space*
- Making choices
- Agenda distribution
- Mood regulations
- Leadership styles
- Types of peers:
  Mentor
  Coach
  Best friend
  Younger person
  Older person
  Celebrator
  Optimist
  Spiritual person
- Collaboration

Discussion Questions

6.1. Discuss the concept of middle space.

6.2. Discuss the meaning of slow disempowerment.

6.3. What are the advantageous of integrating middle space?

6.4. Describe the importance of facilitating middle space.

6.5. Why is the movie *Office Space* used as an example of working in middle space?

6.6. Can you describe your experiences with middle space?

6.7. Discuss the need for peer relationships. What type of peer support do you have in your work place?

6.8. Why is it important to have an agenda prior to a meeting?

6.9. What does mood regulation mean to you?

6.10. Why is education and professional development important?

6.11. Have you thought about your career options or choices in your current job? If so, describe some of them.

CHAPTER SEVEN
THE CAREER PATH AND WORKING WITHIN THE ORGANIZATION

Nothing can be more disappointing to a project manager than feeling disempowered or thinking that you have no choices in your career. Why do so many people have difficulty with this subject? It is because it is about you, your own personal goals and ambitions, and your own personal decisions. There are both horizontal and vertical careers paths, but the path for promotion within an organization is not always visible. Observation of who is promoted in an organization is important because there may be advantages to the horizontal career path.

The goal of this chapter is not to advise you, but its intent is to present different experiences of others to assist you in sorting out your thinking and examining the choices you can make by considering your own educational and professional development, looking at the organization where you work, considering the wait-and-see approach, and examining the horizontal and vertical career paths. Another part of the problem is that some managers have not prepared themselves to be in a position to make choices. If you are reading this book, then you are taking steps to looking at your environment differently and to educating yourself, which will help you pave the way for developing your own goals, priorities, and career plans.

Choices You Can Make

There have been people caught in middle space from the work environment or from their schedules. Maybe you are one of them. Before you decide that you have no other choices, let me tell you about Jason. One of my students, Jason, in a health information systems course I was teaching, told me that he was giving serious thought to making some major career decisions. Based on what he told me about himself, it was a clear indication that he was caught in middle space.

This young man was working as a paramedic and supervisor, but felt that he wanted opportunities to enhance his career with other experiences and gain additional benefits for retirement in the future. I think most people start to seriously think about long-range plans somewhere in their thirties. Jason said that he really liked his job, but it kept him so busy that he had little time outside of his work because of his 24-hour work shifts and rotating schedules. In fact, Jason told me he loves his job as a paramedic and that people really need him.

Jason was 36 years old at the time, and he felt like it was time to start thinking about the long-range future. Even though he really loves what he was doing on the job, he felt he was caught in middle space because of the conflicting situation with his work schedule. He had developed strong peer relationships with the other paramedic supervisors. Some of the relationships were within his local office and others were with peers in other divisions.

One day, a discussion came up among the supervisors on how much a couple of the paramedics liked being in the US Military Reserves and the benefits and satisfaction that resulted from their involvement in different assignments. So after researching his options, Jason gave it some serious thought and applied for the military reserves. It is amazing what information you can get from peer relationships. Associating with peers at work gave him insight into doing something that would provide him more options.

Jason went on to basic training for nine weeks and then went into military training for an additional four months in another state. He said the training was not easy, because most of the people in training were younger than he was and were in their early twenties. There was a lot of physical, mental, and survival training. After successfully completing his basic training, followed by specialized training, he was recognized as one among the top in his group. He went back to his full-time job as a paramedic and supervisor, but he was assigned to another division that gave him more opportunities and professional growth and he was assigned to weekend duty at a nearby air reserve base.

Jason told me that when he went into the US Reserves, his position or a comparable one with his employer was available to him when he returned from his training. He was able to receive comparable pay while he was in reserve training, and on completion of his training, he received other benefits including a sign-on bonus. Long-term benefits for him means additional funds for education and health insurance coverage in addition to doing things on base to broaden his experiences. The military reserve duties occasionally require him to travel to different places that he would have never been able to travel on his own time. He is planning on a trip to Europe soon.

I saw Jason a couple of years later and he told me that it was one of the best decisions he had ever made. It was because he started thinking out of the box. So what am I really saying? If you feel that you are in middle space, then it is time to reflect on where you are; and where you want to be in the near future; and make a plan to take steps to get to where you want to be. Imagine what would have happened if Jason had no peers.

When I was a student in college, one of my professors said that if a job is not working out for you, then you always have the choice of leaving the position. In theory, this may be true, but in the real world, choices are based on your own situation and circumstances. Your education, work experience, job skills, qualifications, geographical region where you live, and even your health all have a bearing on the future choices you will be able to make in life. The main consideration is that you invest time in yourself, and by investing in yourself, you are opening the door for other choices and opportunities.

Previously, I said that your health can have an impact on your choices. There is an IT director in my peer group who was diagnosed with a serious illness. He went through treatment and he is in remission and returned to his job. He said that his opportunities were limited if he wants to go to another organization because of his health history. He feels that he would not be able to pass the physical exam because of preexisting conditions and would not be totally covered under a new organization's medical insurance plan if he were hired. This is one of the reasons why I said people have choices, but in most situations it is based on their own circumstances and qualifications.

You may very likely be in middle space as a director, as a manager, as a supervisor, or even as a college student. Moving forward with making a decision may not result in immediate monetary rewards, but in the long run it can turn into other opportunities that can be rewarding and in some cases monetary. Making the decision and actually starting to do something is a major step. Regardless of your current situation, it is always best for you to focus on making sure whatever you do is professional and ethical. Do not be discouraged when things do not happen when you expect them to happen. Some things may take some time before you begin to see changes.

Peter Drucker, a well-known management speaker and educator, wrote several books on servant leadership. He reports that servant leadership means leaving your ego at the door and making sure that priorities of other people are being served. Humble leaders do not flaunt their egos, but they suppress them for the good of the organization and focus on the goals of the organization and take into consideration the well-being of the people who work for them. If more top-level executives and managers followed

Peter Drucker's philosophy, many of the problems we have seen during the past few years with private sector companies and public sector organizations could have been avoided. This is a good philosophy and approach but invest time in developing yourself, which will benefit you in your long-range plans.

Although this book focuses on project management, you do not have to be a manager or supervisor to experience the impact of working in middle space. Middle space can have multiple contenting forces from above (top), below (bottom), vertically, and laterally; and there is a gradual disempowerment.

Julie is a young lady I know who once worked for me when I was a project manager and she accepted a position in another company. She put all her time and effort into her new job. She would communicate with me about her work experiences. I must have been her outlet for communicating her concerns because of our past working relationship.

Julie was working in middle space because of the environment in which she worked and was caught between conflicting agendas of her manager and her personal responsibilities as a parent. At that time, she was the secretary to a project manager and was a single parent with one child. She said that she was so busy that she did not have the time to work on her college degree. She previously went to professional development courses through her employer, but the courses did not result in any type of certification but did help her to become proficient in using workgroup office system software.

Later the work environment changed when the manager whom Julie reported to decided to leave his position and go to another company and a new person was hired. Things did not go so well for her because the new manager she worked for had different views on what she should be working on for the team project and was not supportive when she put in request for her vacation time off or additional time off because of her obligations as a parent. Julie was caught in middle space with conflicting agendas and she decided it was time to think outside the box.

This young lady found that there was a Microsoft Office Specialist certification she could obtain by going through online training courses for Microsoft Word, Excel for spreadsheets, and PowerPoint. These were office support systems software that she uses daily on the job. So she went through the online training courses and took the exams and received her certification. Julie joined the International Association of Administrative Professionals (IAAP) and attends the chapter meetings near her home in order to network with other professionals. She worked at home on the training courses and earned her certified professional secretaries' (CPS) certification by passing the exam. She has a network of peer relationships within the association and at work that provided her support, encouragement, and guidance.

Julie eventually applied for another position in a different department in the same large organization. Her work experience, Microsoft certification, and her CPS certification and membership were things she was able to put on her job resume when she completed the application. She was interviewed for the job and was selected for a higher paying position. She is still valuable to the organization as a whole, but in another department.

The main point is that Julie put together a plan and invested time in herself by getting her certifications that provided her other opportunities when the time was right for her to make the change. She did not want to stay in middle space any longer. She felt that without the certifications and positive association with others at the local chapter meetings she would not have been selected from the many applicants who applied for the position. She is involved with a peer group at work, has peer associations outside of work, and she took the time to invest in herself and it was to her benefit.

Learn to recognize the fact that there may be no other career options or opportunities within the department or within the organization where you work. There was another young lady, Lisa, who was working in a similar situation as an administrative assistant. She previously worked for a family-owned company. The company is a small private sector company with just 300 employees.

Lisa stayed with the company too long with the hope that things would change for her because there were no opportunities to transfer or be promoted to other departments. Some of her friends told her to move on and leave the company behind, but she decided to stay to see if things would change. Things never did change and the only other option she had was to eventually leave if she wanted to move up in her career. She did say that she waited too long to make the decision to leave, especially, with the job market being as it is today with very few jobs. Lisa told me that she wished that she had listened to other people and had made the decision to leave sooner rather than later. She finally did make a decision to leave the company and found another job in a different organization.

In contrast to making career decisions and politically initiated projects, there are projects that do follow the organization procedures for prioritization, and get support from top-level management, and result in a positive impact on information system projects and the organization. Project priorities using predefined procedures collaboratively established by the organization and the departments have the potential of not being politically motivated by one person's own agenda. Managers who have an understanding of the types of computer information systems that support organizational performance, the business strategy, strategic and support systems, issues with centralization and decentralization, the influence of politics on projects, and understand who has authority over the information technology decisions for the organization and within the departments have a better understanding of the human factors necessary to make projects succeed.

Education and Professional Development

College degrees, technical and professional certifications, and professional development courses and training are really important for those in the information technology field. Some organizations include employee training costs within their budget and are willing to pay for training their employees who request it. You can ask about your department's criteria for going to training programs. Ask for information on their policy on sending you for training and taking college courses. People may be *good* at what they are doing but that they can even be *better* at their job when they stay current with their skills and the technology. It may be time for you to do an inventory of your skills and find out what skills are important in the market place for the position you are interested in working and work on a plan to upgrade your skills. Improving your skills gives you opportunities to make more choices in your career.

When my youngest daughter was in middle school, I encouraged her to take keyboarding because she always typed with both hands but with only two fingers. She told me she could get all of her typing done with just two fingers and had no interest in taking keyboarding. I told her "yes," and that is good, but think about how much *better* she could be by typing using the proper form. She would not have to search the keyboard to find the letters and will be able to focus on the tasks she is trying to complete.

My response was that with practice that she will be able to type even faster without a lot of effort. By taking the course she will learn the correct form of typing by placing both her hands and fingers on the home row and on the proper keys. I told her the initial emphasis is on proper form, and by practicing her typing skills, she will be able to develop her speed. After some lengthy discussions, I convinced her to take the course anyway.

"You don't know what you don't know until you actually know it" (Jick & Peiperl, 2003, p. 414). After completing the course, she said that it was really a good decision taking keyboarding and that she said she now knows the difference between typing with two fingers versus using the proper form to keyboarding, which is a lot better and faster.

Horizontal and Vertical Career Paths

The topic of horizontal or a vertical career path is worth discussing in detail because of the discussions I had with some of my students a few years ago. Several students told me about their experiences trying to get promoted while working in government organizations. The question my students asked was: How do you know whether there is a career path for getting promoted? My response to the students was that it all depends on the organization where you work and each department or agency within the organization. You may have your own experiences and concerns about your own career or just want to have a better understanding of the environment. The following sections talk about other case studies and my observations of what individuals can do to help maximize their chances of success.

Career expectations from long-term employees at one time was based on learning as much as you can within the organization by accepting different positions, and eventually you will be promoted to a higher-level management position. Today, there is no concrete rule on how to rise to the top of the organization (Jick & Peiperl, 2003). Over the years, many organizations shifted from the vertical career paths to the top to the horizontal career path where individuals can broaden their experiences and advance by moving sideways and then move up vertically when the opportunity arises. By moving horizontally, you can become more knowledgeable about the organization as a whole. Experienced top-level managers often consider promoting those who have climbed through the ranks and having an understanding of the organizational business environment. In some cases, individuals leave the organization behind by working for private sector companies that provide services to many organizations, including the organization they left behind, and some start their own business. Big organization careers are "no longer the principal route to success" (Jick & Peiperl, 2003, p. 325).

The Organization Where You Work

How do you know what is the career path in your organization or department? You will know it through observation of who gets promoted, their work experience, and their educational background. Just observe, observe, and continue to observe! Some organizations provide a clear career path to the top while in others it is not so clear. The path can even be blurred at times and at times there may be no career path for you at all.

When you observe, you are actually watching and listening to what someone else is doing and saying, and you experience the reality of what is going on. This is referred to in some studies as observing experiences. You may find that there is a clear career path to the top or you may find out there is no career path at all within the organization. Do not spend your time trying to move up in an organization where there is no career path. The sooner you find this out the sooner you can consider other options, opportunities, and investing in yourself.

Take some time to examine yourself and where you are; examine your strengths and weaknesses; observe what is going on around you; and decide where you want to be in the very near future. Then decide on what you have to do to get where you really want to be.

I have observed top managers in several different departments and organizations inform their staff that if you want to be promoted to a management position, you need to have at least a bachelor's degree in a specific major or a closely related field of study. I have often observed the importance of obtaining professional and technical certifications in some technical positions for project managers, computer support technicians, network administrators, and database analysts. Continuing your professional development and training is important.

In some situations, an individual may have a lot of technical expertise but may lack management skills. Therefore, professional development courses or obtaining a professional certification is beneficial. Even if someone has the title of a manager, it does not mean the person has the required project management skills. In fact, many different kinds of jobs require continuing education units for individuals to keep their certifications or licenses such as nurses, teachers, paramedics, technicians, computer specialists, and many other professions.

In some organizations, the path to a top-level position is very limited because there are fewer positions at the top, whereas in other organizations, the management structures are flatter, making it difficult to climb to the top. In fact, you may find out that there is no career path in the organization where you work. Often, there are top-level managers who feel that getting someone from outside of the organization brings in valuable expertise with a different perspective. Because of the limited organizational career opportunities for moving to top-level positions in some organizations, many individuals leave the organization on their own choice. Therefore, it is importance to observe what is going on in your organization.

Are there opportunities for women to be hired into top-level technology leadership positions? Fisher (2013) conducted research on women in top leadership positions and reports that they are underrepresented in the field of information technology. Many "women who enter and stay in the technology field, may find themselves struggling to reach executive ranks" (p. 2).This quantitative study explores several barriers to women being promoted to top-level leadership positions such as the *glass ceiling* and being promoted to *glass cliff* roles that are highly visible positions but are high risk. The study examines enablers to top-level positions using five factors of negotiation, mentorship, sponsorship, competitiveness, and networking. The 218 participants in the survey from corporate America are leaders and nonleaders and members of several professional organizations including but not limited to the Society of Information Management (SIMS), Association of Information Technology Professionals (AITP), National Association of Female Executives (NAFE), Professional Business Women in California (PBWC), Women in Technology International (WITI), and the American Association of University Women (AAUW).

The results of the study found *sponsorship* as being an important factor for women obtaining top-level leadership positions and the women who had a sponsor also had mentors. Sponsors are those who have a close working relationship with top leaders in the organization. Mentoring focuses on growth and development of a person, whereas sponsorship can navigate a person's career and nominate a person for promotions and to top leadership opportunities (Fisher, 2013). The study identifies the importance of top-level managers in organizations establishing formal mentoring and sponsorship programs that will assist in promoting women to top-level, technology leadership roles.

Wait and See Approach

So maybe you have observed and analyzed the situation and decided to use the wait and see approach to being promoted. What is the wait and see approach? It is when you wait to see if a position opens up for recruitment so that you can submit an application for the position. The question you need to ask yourself is: How long do you plan on waiting for a position to be available so that you can apply for it? I have seen some of my peers not selected for a position within the organization and determine that they will wait to see if another position opens for recruitment in the near future. In the meantime, some continue their education and professional development and others do not. This approach has worked for a few individuals and for others the wait can be a long, long time with no guarantee there will be the opportunity to apply for new job opportunities. It is really a matter of choice as to how long you plan on waiting. It may be six months, a year, or it may be two years or more.

If you wait too long for a position to be open and available for recruitment, you may experience what is called missed opportunities. These are opportunities that could have come your way if you left the organization behind but you are not at the right place at the right time to take advantage of the opportunities. Your choices are individual decisions only you can make for your career path. If the job does eventually open up for recruitment, there is no guarantee you will be hired for the position if someone else applying for the position has better qualifications or has a sponsor. You may be fortunate enough to be the one with the best qualifications and be promoted to the position.

More Choices

Now, let's assume you have considered your options and you feel that it is time to leave the organization behind. I have observed several situations in which individuals left the government organization by their own choice to work for Microsoft Corporation and provide services to the government organization they left behind. These individuals have really good careers now. One is working in New York and loves it. Another individual left the government organization because he was interviewed for the CIO position but was not selected for the position. He recognized the career limitations and felt it was not in his best interest to stay in that particular government organization. He actually obtained a better position elsewhere. The individual who was actually selected for the CIO position was from within the organization's central IT department. Other individuals stay long enough to earn their master's degree and then leave the organization behind. Some leave an organization to work as technical professionals, consultants, contractors, professors, researchers, and others form professional partnerships.

If you choose a different path and leave the organization behind, you are able to identify with your profession and network with others in your profession. There are a growing number of professional organizations that offer memberships based on your professional experience and qualifications. The Internet makes involvement and communication with these professional organizations very easy compared with the days before the Internet. There is no longer the need to identify with the single company or organization. The Internet, globalization, and telecommuting provide different opportunities to work for different organizations, countries, and to work away from the office by telecommuting.

Some individuals are not aware of the benefits of a horizontal career path. By moving horizontally within an organization you can gain broader work experience moving sideways and then taking a vertical career path by moving upward *outside* the organization (Jick & Peiperl, 2003). You can actually develop your knowledge in different areas of the organization and you can have a better understanding of specific tasks and of the entire organization. To be successful in your career does not mean you have to stay within the same department or even within the same organization.

I do have some words of advice if you do decide to leave an organization. Suppose that you feel there is no longer the possibility of promotion or there are no longer the opportunities for different kinds of work experiences or growth. It is important to stay in the job long enough to see the results of the decisions you have made as a manager or supervisor. If you do not, you having no way of knowing if you are successful or not in your leadership role.

Serious consideration should be given to leaving an organization. Many employees are more reluctant to leave the organization behind due to the economy and the risk associated with a new position and their job security. The economic situation and the high jobless and unemployment rate in some states in the United States can have a major impact on many individuals when making the kind of career decision of quitting their job and leaving the organization behind.

Some people are underemployed, which means they are working one or two part-time jobs at a lower pay rate with either limited or even no benefits such as medical insurance and a retirement plan. In some cases, individuals have gone into totally different professions after they leave the organization behind either after being laid off from their job or leaving on their own choice.

I have seen a couple of individuals leave the organization, and they were, eventually, laid-off work in the new organization because of downsizing or budget cuts. This can be a devastating experience for anyone, especially when a person had a previous job and is laid off from the new job in a different organization. Being laid-off from a job is a difficult situation to deal with and both of these individuals said they felt really sad and lost after losing their jobs. I can only imagine what this feels like because I never went through this type of experience. One person told me he had a pity party and then decided it was time to do something about his situation. Both of these individuals have jobs today, but said they would have done things differently in hindsight.

Changing jobs has its own risks because you do not have the seniority in years of service when you are a new employee in another organization. This happened to a friend of mine. He was working for a community college and he decided to change jobs because of the opportunities and the pay increase. At the time, he thought it was really a good decision. It was only after working there for a few months, he received notification that several positions would be cut from the budget, including his position. This situation was something that neither he nor his employer was not able to foresee. He worked in a part-time position for a few months. However, because of his experience, skills, and college degrees, he was soon able to get a full-time job rather quickly elsewhere.

In another situation, two individuals actually left the United States and went to other countries for employment and have been very successful in their jobs. In some countries, English is the primary or the second language. Both of these individuals were fluent in another language, which is an asset when going to another country. Being bilingual or knowing multiple languages can be an advantage when looking for jobs in other countries. If you do not know another language, you can start by learning one. There are many language books and different kinds of learning programs on DVD and websites that you can purchase if you do not want to enroll in a language class.

Investing in yourself is important. Have a pity party and move on to the next step by working on a plan. Some people have even gone into working for themselves in their home office or in a completely different type of business. The days of working hard and long-term employment in one organization is not always a guarantee that you will be promoted to a higher position (Jick & Peiperl, 2003). You need to work toward being in a position to broaden your career options regardless of whether there is a potential promotion within the organization. Whatever career path you choose, put together a plan so you can work toward getting the skills, the educational qualifications, and the experience you need. When other opportunities do come your way then you will have the flexibility of taking advantage of those opportunities and making choices. Some good old boys clubs do exist that can limit both women and even some men from being hired for leadership positions. Sometimes it is easier for you to make changes instead of waiting for those in the organization to change.

What about those individuals who work in the same position for years? I observed many individuals in government organizations who have not been promoted and work in the same position they were hired into several years ago. It is important for you to recognize that these individuals are valuable to the organization because many of them continue their education through professional development courses and training. Many of these individuals are professionals, others are technically skilled, some are highly specialized in many different job areas, and others are knowledgeable office support workers. The organization needs all of these people to support the overall organizational performance. Many people are happy and content with what they are doing and have no desire to change jobs and do not want to be promoted to supervisory or management positions. These workers are valuable to the organization because they have years of expertise and work experience and have found total job satisfaction doing what they like doing.

Working in a job that you like doing is great. You can be thankful that not everyone is a manager or wants to be a manager or a supervisor, because then we would not have project team members and no highly specialized and skilled workers in organizations. I attended a special event a couple of years ago and had the opportunity to have a conversation with a very talented and popular singer. I told him how much I enjoyed his singing and that I had no talent for singing. His response was: "Thank goodness you can't sing because if everyone could sing there would be no audiences." He said he is glad that people have different talents and that is why he has an audience for his performances. Well, you can be thankful that management and supervisory positions are not a career goal for everyone. There is a need for highly trained and specialized workers at all levels within an organization who can contribute to successful organizational performance.

Let me tell you about Tanya who is a computer programmer analyst and has a master's degree in software engineering. She really enjoys working as a software engineer and is an expert in her field. She worked in my technical division in government for about four years and was eventually interviewed and promoted to a supervisory position as a senior programmer analyst. Her long-term goal was to get into supervision and then eventually get promoted into IT management. After working in the supervisory position for a few months, she realized her real passion was working in the trenches of the technical area of computer systems design and programming.

Tanya said that supervising was something that she pursued for a long time, but after working as a supervisor she found out that she did not like supervising others and dealing with the various situations that surfaced while performing the job. She realized after working as a supervisor she had to deal with supervisory paper work and personnel problems like someone calling in about being sick near a holiday weekend and other kinds of administrative tasks.

Tanya eventually left the government organization and went to work as a software engineer contractor in the private sector. The good thing about Tanya is that she was able to recognize what she wanted to do and where she wanted to be in her career. She keeps her skills up-to-date by taking technical classes at the local college or professional online training courses whenever she feels there was a need to apply it to her projects and other work-related activities.

Summary

Others' experiences can assist you in thinking about your choices. Educational and professional development is important. There are both horizontal and vertical careers paths, but the path for promotion within an organization is not always visible. Observation of who gets promoted in an organization is important. There can be advantages to the horizontal career path. However, it is important to recognize when there are no career opportunities within the organization and consider other opportunities and options for your continued growth and development.

Review Concepts

- Choices of others
- Educational and professional development
- The horizontal and vertical career path
- The organizational where you work
- Wait and see approach
- Career choices

Discussion Questions

7.1. What impact did peers have on Jason's decision?

7.2. Explain the importance of education and professional development.

7.3. What does it mean to consider the horizontal and vertical career paths?

7.4. Describe the wait and see approach.

7.5. Discuss the advantages or the disadvantages of the horizontal and vertical career paths.

7.6. Discuss whether you have considered your choices.

CHAPTER EIGHT
THE PROJECT MANAGER

Project management involves many different kinds of skills, such as technical skills, the business knowledge, people skills, management and leadership skills, and the knowledge of the human aspect of management. Many people have their own opinions on the qualifications of an information systems (IS) project manager. I believe there are four essential skill areas important for being a project manager:

1. Knowledge of the business
2. Technical skills
3. Completion of project management courses or training
4. Leadership style

Novice project managers sometimes may not have the experience or appropriate training to manage large projects. Those who have the understanding of how to manage a project assist in and minimize risks. They understand the business strategy for the project and the business requirements, and are better able to manage the work effort required for the project team to implement the information system. This chapter explores some of the skills of the project manager, including their leadership style of being a transformational leader, transactional leaders, or laissez-faire leader.

Leading the Project

At times, it may be a challenge for government organizations to find someone with the experience and required skills to manage a project. Even if they did find this person, the organization may not be able to pay the higher salary because of the competition with the private sector organizations. Many private sector firms require the applicant to have project management experience and a minimum of an associate degree and some additional project management courses or certification or even a bachelor's degree in computer information systems, computer technology, and computer science or a closely related major subject. Some individuals have master's degrees and doctorates. Completion of project management courses or a project management certification is important to project success.

In Chapter 6 there is a description of a human resources IT project in government that resulted in the job descriptions for IT management positions being changed and substituted experience for having college degrees for management positions. This is unusual because many of the departments and agencies within this same organization required a minimum of a bachelor's degree in a particular field of study as a prerequisite to the various management positions. Eliminating the requirement for college degrees and professional certifications sends mixed messages to employees about the importance of a formal education. More importantly, there is no clear path to IT leadership and management positions within the organization.

In the future, this same organization may find it difficult to draw from its pool of employees to promote from within the organization because of lack of employees with specialized management qualifications. Some technical staff may not have developed themselves beyond the technical skills. The project manager and IT manager need to understand the business strategy of the organization or department they are responsible for managing in addition to the technical skills. Hence, many organizations in the private sector promote from within the organization.

Managers who have worked for different divisions or departments within government often broaden their knowledge and experience of the business strategy and organizational strategy. In other situations, IT managers who work in the business division within an organization learn the business operations and strategy because they work closely with the business units.

Some students in college may major in computer science, information technology, or computer information systems as an undergraduate student and obtain a master's degree in business administration or management. Other students may major in management as an undergraduate and obtain a master's degree in MIS or closely related field as a graduate student or take courses to obtain technical or professional certifications. This approach to education gives those interested in managing information systems a broader knowledge of both the business and technology in order to have a more holistic understanding of the business goals and objectives of an organization and help in solving business problems. A fairly recent approach to education are degrees in informatics that combine a particular field of study such as business, biology, economics, healthcare, sociology, statistics, telecommunications, information security, and many other majors with various computer courses (Groth & Mackie-Mason, 2010). The focus is on an interdisciplinary approach to technology design. Informatics certification programs are available to those who currently have a degree in a particular field of study.

A project manager does not have to be an expert in all the technical areas but needs to have a general understanding of the technology (software, hardware, and network) and the business specialization. The project team members should have the functional and technical expertise that complements the project manager's skills. Many project managers have access to several experts within the organization specializing in the technical details and, in some cases, hire consultants and contractors to augment their project team or staff.

So what about the novice project manager who does not have the knowledge of the business operations within a department or for the organization? The manager who has taken the project management courses or training and has the technical skills but does not have the background knowledge of the business should take time to understand the business by interviewing those who are involved with the day-to-day business activities and become familiar with the documents generated by the department or agency (reports, documentation, diagrams, processes, flowcharts, etc.) that support the business functions.

A general understanding of the technology and the business operations of the department or agency in which the information system is to be implemented will give you as a project manager the ability to make informed decisions on how the business strategy for a given project can be best supported by the information systems strategy. If you are working on an organizational-wide project, a general understanding of the organization and the impact on the departments and agencies is beneficial. If you do not have this background, develop strong peer group relationships and networking to broaden your knowledge about the business operations.

There are other areas that can impact your success as a project manager. Pinto (1986), in his study on project management, identifies four areas that can impact project success:

1. Power relationships and political activity;
2. Characteristics of the project leader;
3. Environment effects; and
4. Sense of urgency or importance of the project (p. 45).

The result of the study found the "characteristics of the project manager" and "the sense of urgency or importance of the project" important to successful projects. The survey participants were project managers from several organizations in both the private and the public sectors, so this may be the reason why the other two areas of power relationships and political activity; and environment effects were not significant in this particular study. However, more recent studies show that the political environment and the availability of project resources have a major impact on project priorities and decisions in government organizations.

I include *resources* and *history*. Without resources such as funding for the project and the appropriate personnel, the project will experience major risks. Knowing the history within the organization in relation to the project is very important because those who do not know the history run the risks of repeating the same mistakes of the past, see Figure 8.1.

A consultant who was hired by the top-level managers in the central county organization contacted me regarding a project that I had implemented several years earlier. He asked me some pointed questions about any issues I experienced when working with two key department heads. He wanted to have a better understanding of some of the history of the project within the organization. I answered his questions and provided him some background information.

The information system he was inquiring about was actually implemented in the early 1990s prior to me becoming the project manager. The initial implementation had some major problems because it was later discovered by a different project manager who took over the system that some of the information system's program modules were never installed and

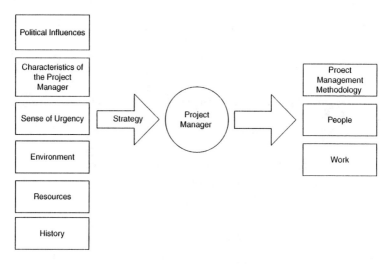

Figure 8.1 The organizational effects and project management.

implemented. When information systems have numerous problems, many times it is the result of the project not being planned properly. Another problem was the person originally managing the project had no experience in IS development and implementation. After the new project manager and his project team implemented these missing program modules, the problems were resolved.

When I took over directing and managing this same information system, the goal was to find a year 2000 solution. The final solution was to implement the newest version of the same commercial, packaged software that was year 2000 compliant with newer user functionality. The old system was totally removed and the new system installed without any major problems. The postaudit review of the system was completed, but for some reason it could not be found in the system document. For this reason, there needs to be some procedure of retaining the history of major projects, which was discussed earlier in Chapter 5.

The Project Manager's Skills

Another study by Turner and Müller (2005) reported that, "Rarely does literature on project success factors specifically or overtly mention the project manager and his or her leadership style and competence" (p. 57). The study suggested that an IS project manager's leadership can affect project success and that project managers may not attribute their own success to the project. Because there is the potential that the project manager's abilities and skills can impact project success, project management, and success factors should include the project manager's leadership style in determining project success.

The study by Pinto (1986) identifies the importance of the project leader's characteristics as essential to project success and empirically tests the relationship of the two variables.

The theory on leadership uses the Multifactor Leadership Questionnaire (MLQ) to determine transactional, transformational, and passive-avoidant (laissez-faire) leadership styles and reports that transformational leadership has the greatest positive influence on success. Transformational leaders motivate others to perform above expectations in order to achieve the goals and visions (Bass, 1990). These types of leaders are engaged and connected with the individuals they lead. They demonstrate qualities that result in respect and pride from their subordinates and they become role models. They are instrumental in getting groups to focus on the mission and encourage their followers.

Transactional leaders focus on the day-to-day transactions in achieving the goals by working through others. It is an exchange relationship based on rewards for a job well done. If subordinates make errors or fail, then there is negative reinforcement such as criticism or even punishment. If the transactional leader runs out of rewards, there is a problem with the ability to continue the exchange relationship. Studies have shown that transactional leaders have a greater need to dominate others and have a high ideal of themselves.

Project management is an approach to achieving the goals of the organization and reducing project risks. The impact of leadership style has been researched in literature, but few studies include leadership style and its relationship to information technology project and project success. The project manager works through others to achieve the goals of project and the leadership style may have an impact on project success.

Characteristics of the project manager are described in the study by Pinto (1986) as possessing adequate administrative skill, has interpersonal (human) skills, adequate technical skills, has presence (the project leader is perceived by the team members as being visible and involved), has the ability to motivate subordinates, has the ability to maintain a cohesive team, and has sufficient authority from top level department officials for the project.

The results of the study found the relationship between project leader characteristics and sense of urgency to be important to project success, but two other moderating variables were not supported. Although Pinto (1986) found leadership to be significant to project success, other studies in literature focus more on the project manager's leadership style as being more transformational, transactional, or laissez-faire (nonleader). Several theories have evolved over the past few years in relation to information technology and leadership styles.

Pinto (1986) reports that the project manager's leadership skills and competency are important to project success and tests its effect as a moderating variable in the project management study of essential success factors important to project success. Seven items measure project leader characteristics: technical skills, interpersonal skills, administrative skills, visibility, ability to maintain a cohesive project team, the ability to motivate the team, and authority bestowed by top management. The study tests the characteristics of the project leader and its significance on the independent variables and project success and found significance in the relationship between project leader and project success.

Project Manager's Leadership Style

If you consider leadership closely, you need to recognize that your leadership style is the total of everything that you do as a leader. You may have the tendency to overlook that your leadership style is your tone of voice, how you communicate, how you interact with others, how you respond to others, how you use your hand gestures, and philosophy about yourself as a leader. Your project management style is a mirror reflection of your leadership style and how you do things. Really good project managers are constantly improving their leadership style in search for better ways to relate to others. Good project managers realize that some leadership styles are more ethically appropriate than others by not degrading others or making them appear as if they do not know what they are talking about when trying to express their ideas or concerns about a particular subject or project.

Several studies in literature report that a person's project leadership style has an impact on successful information systems projects. Bass (1990) conducted research on different leadership styles. He identified transformational and transactional leadership style and laissez-faire as a nonleader and developed the Multifactor Leadership Questionnaire (MLQ). The questionnaire tests the tendency of the leadership style to being more transformational, transactional, or laissez-faire (nonleader). The three leadership styles are discussed in the following sections.

Transformational

Transformational leadership style is distinguished by the leader's ability to motivate employees to perform above expectations and to achieve a shared vision (Bass, 1999). Transformational leaders accomplish goals through directing the work of others, have the confidence and respect of others, attempt to simulate creative approaches to solving problems, and become a source of inspiration to other employees. This study reported that transformational leaders can motivate others to do more than what each thinks is possible. Transformational leaders can discern, comprehend, and articulate the opportunities and threat to the organization and can create methods for achieving the organizational goals.

The transformational leader views each employee as an individual by sharing and understanding concerns of others and attempts to stimulate individual growth and instill in other employees inspiration and motivation, and finds ways to promote positive expectations about what needs to be accomplished. The transformational leader can be transactional when appropriate for achieving the defined goals depending on the situation (Avolio & Bass, 2004; Bass, 1999). It is important that you strive to be a transformational leader when managing your projects because these types of leaders are more successful. Avolio and Bass (2004) described the main components of the transformational leader as idealized influence, idealized behavior, inspirational motivation, intellectual stimulation, and individualized stimulation.

A diagram of the evolution from a novice to a mature transformational leadership style is shown in figure 1 of the case study of a Hong Kong IT project by Ng and Walker (2008) that explores leadership styles in relationship to a Confucian culture. The research found that this public sector organization lacked a top-level project sponsor, a clear vision, and a mission statement. The project experienced several leadership problems, including lack of positional authority and required management skills to lead the project. In addition to their findings, this project seemed to lack the SDLC approach of performing the preliminary analysis, the feasibility study, and information analysis phases as outlined in the ten-phased SDLC outlined in Table 3.1 of Chapter 3 for developing the system's functional requirements before awarding the contract to the vendor company. The vendor took the role of the chief planner for the project instead of the project manager from the public sector organization.

Transactional

Transactional leaders focus on changes through the day-to-day transactions by working with and through others (Bass, 1990). This leadership is characterized by management by exception (active) and the presentation of rewards to subordinates for their accomplishments. It is an exchange-based relationship and the presentation of rewards to followers for their accomplishments. Transactional leaders and their followers or subordinates are in a transactional relationship and have an understanding of the value and the economics. When the transaction is completed, both parties can agree on a new transaction.

Transactional leaders may offer other types of rewards such as bonuses, pay increases, promotions, and vacation time as awards to those who fulfill mutually agreed-to objectives. The leader can lose the ability to influence followers if there is no ability to provide rewards. Leaders who perform management by exception tend to focus on their subordinates' mistakes and delay decision making or intervening until something has gone wrong and are more likely to be found in lower-level rather than upper-level management teams (Avolio & Bass, 2004; Bass, 1990).

My own experiences with government organizations is that top-level managers cannot arbitrarily give rewards or bonuses, mainly because of public scrutiny on the use of taxpayers' money and organizational policies and regulations. Pay increases and compensation are a formal process of promotions and step increases and are normally tied to the annual budget. Increases in pay and promotions are based on length of time in the job, passing the probationary period, experience, skills, and job performance evaluations.

In any organization in both the private and public sectors, some individuals may be promoted more quickly to top-level positions because they have more support from the CEO or other top-level managers as their sponsors. Government employees can be compensated for overtime hours worked and by being promoted to higher-level positions. Although pay is an important factor, managers can give nonmonetary rewards to employees in the form of employee recognition and awards, provide different kinds of tasks assignments, and be assigned to new projects that may provide more job satisfaction and enrichment. A study by Melkers and Willoughby (2005) surveyed 277 participants from county and city government on measuring performance and reported that recognition is the most frequently given reward but "some pointed to pay-based rewards, including pay for performance even additional pay or gain sharing" at the department level (p. 184).

Non-leaders (Laissez-Faire)

In contrast to both transactional and transformational leaders, there are passive-avoidant (laissez-faire) leaders who actually have the tendency to be more of a nonleader. Tasks are usually delegated to subordinates with little oversight. The passive-avoidant leadership style usually avoids direct and frequent contact with subordinates and tends to treat workers as individuals rather than workers being team members. The laissez-faire leader keeps communication through a strong open door policy, productivity records, conferences, and reports.

The prerequisites for the laissez-faire leaders are usually highly skilled and independent workers who show initiative and endurance in their work. This leader establishes controls other than frequency of contact to monitor the performance of the subordinates. Studies suggest that employees who work under this leadership style may become insecure if they are not getting continuous reassurance and have frequent contact with their supervisor (Avolio & Bass, 2004).

Depending on the size and the scope of a project, an individual usually has the tendency of demonstrating one of the three leadership styles. An individual may be at times more of a transformational leader and at other times be a transactional leader depending on the tasks and project activities and duration of the project. The leadership studies do not attempt to categorize individuals into one category of leadership style, but suggests that most leaders have a tendency to be more transformational than transactional or more transactional than transformational, or more laissez-faire than one of the other leadership styles.

When looking at organizational systems, there are primarily three levels of influences: the tops, middles, and the belows, who are the professional, specialized, and technical workers within the organization. Tops have major influences on shaping the organization but the middles as leaders are in a position to integrate with each other and carry out the work that has to be done within the agencies, departments, and units "often spending their time in other people's territories" (para. 9); and need to learn how to use their own unique power potential to strengthen each other (Oshry, 2003).

In addition to the various leadership styles, a project management methodology or approach will help to ensure success of information system project implementation. A project management approach provides a framework for managing and tracking information systems projects. Project tracking is necessary to determine whether a project is on time, is within the project's estimated costs, and has the appropriate project team resources. It provides a channel for identifying problem areas so the project manager can respond with the appropriate decisions to reduce overall project risks. A good project management methodology is important but there are many other factors that influence the project outcomes, which are discussed in Chapter 9.

For many years beginning in the 1980s through the 1990s, information systems managers had no other option than to develop their computer information systems internally. Now, there are several different options available to organizations. Packaged, commercial software offers some organizations the option of purchasing software rather than the organization dedicating time and resources to designing and developing their own computer application software.

Many organizations in both the private and public sectors buy commercial, packaged software systems when the business functions are not unique such as those functions found in payroll, financial accounting packages, and other commonly used generic software systems (Dennis & Wixom, 2003). The ability to purchase packaged software has provided organizations more options. As organizations become more dependent on packaged software, there is a need to carefully evaluate the software products before buying it. Lawlis and others (2001) reported that a formal process for evaluating packaged software purchases is essential to ensure the product will support the business functionality within the organization.

Summary

Project managers should have many different types of leadership skills in addition to the technical skills. They are impacted by the environment within the organization. Education and professional development are important along with having an understanding of the organization. There are several areas that can impact project success, including the political environment, the sense of urgency, history within the organization, and the availability of project resources. The project manager's skills are important, including the leadership style. There are three different types of leadership styles: transformational, transactional, and laissez-faire. Managers should strive to be a transformational leader. These types of leaders motivate others to perform above their expectations.

Review Concepts

- Interdisciplinary skills of the project manager
- Characteristics of the project manager
- Power relationships and political activity
- Environmental effects
- Sense of urgency
- Leaderships styles: transformational leader, transactional leader, and laissez-faire leader

Discussion Questions

8.1. What is the meaning of organizational effects on project management?

8.2. Discuss the advantages and the disadvantages of commercial, packaged information systems and in-house developed information systems.

8.3. What project manager skills do you feel are most important to successful projects?

8.4. Discuss the three different types of leadership styles.

8.5. Describe the main components of a transformational leader.

CHAPTER NINE

CRITICAL SUCCESS FACTORS AND PROJECT SUCCESS

Managing a project requires some form of information systems approach to project planning and implementation. The project manager is critical to the success of the project and he or she must focus on those areas that are important to project success. This chapter describes in detail the factors essential to project implementation success.

If you are an information systems (IS) project manager, it is important for you to focus on the key factors that contribute to project success. The Project Implementation Profile (PIP) identifies the ten critical success factors (CSFs) for project implementation success. Pinto (1986) reports that priorities of CSFs may change during the four phases of project development implementation life cycle: conceptualization phase (start), planning phase, execution phase, and termination, but overall project success is based on the ten key factors.

The PIP model can be applied to various stages of a project and as a postimplementation review to "allow lessons learned from past projects to assist future projects" (Finch, 2003, p. 33). Finch (2003) recommends when using PIP as a postimplementation project review, the project manager should complete the profile but that the ratings should be reviewed and agreed upon by those who were on the original project team. There can be lessons learned by conducting reviews of post-project implementations and post-project failure reviews (Pinto & Kharbanda, 1996; Pinto & Slevin, 1992).

The ten-factor model of project implementation success by Pinto and Slevin (1987) as shown in Figure 9.1 suggests that communication, monitoring and feedback, and troubleshooting occur throughout the project (Pinto & Slevin, 1988; Schultz, Slevin, & Pinto, 1987).

The postimplementation review of successful projects and failed projects allows project managers to detect and avoid problems in future projects and identify factors that contribute to success (Pinto & Kharbanda, 1996). The project manager is involved with managing all aspects of the project and communicating with team members, clients, and other managers and

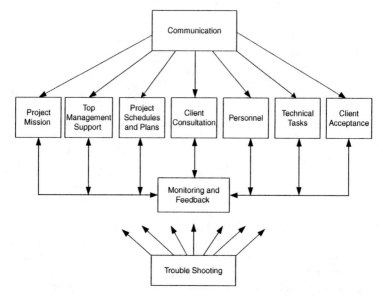

Figure 9.1 Ten key factors of the project implementation profile.
Source: Pinto and Slevin, 1987.

is in a position of having a holistic view of the project when completing the survey questionnaire, and should obtain input from the clients on the measures of project success.

Ten Critical Success Factors

My study includes ten CSFs: project mission, top management support, project plans and schedules, client consultations, personnel, technical tasks, monitoring and feedback, client acceptance, communication, and troubleshooting. The measures for the ten CSFs are from the original study by Pinto (1986), consisting of a 7-point Likert scale, and are the same measures that were converted to a 5-point Likert scale (Rosacker, 2005), see Figure 9.2. The ten CSF variables are described in more detail in the following sections.

Project Mission

First, there is a vision and, then, there is the project mission. The project mission is the general goals and objectives that are understood by all those

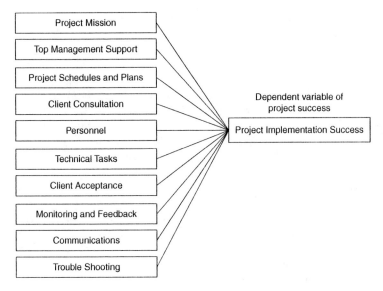

Figure 9.2 Ten critical success factors of the project implementation profile.
Source: Pinto, 1986.

involved with the project, including project team members and key stake-holders from the organization who are interested in the project outcomes (Pinto, 1986; Pinto & Slevin, 1987; Rosacker, 2005; Rosacker & Olson, 2008). Project mission is the need to share a common focus of the organization's objectives to fully integrate the information systems (Reich & Benbasat, 2000).

I need to emphasize the importance of the project mission. The project goals and objectives should be agreed upon by all interested parties. The project mission must be a shared vision by all those involved in the project. According to Jick and Peiperl (2003, p. 403), "When there is no shared vision middle space is caught between the conflicting agendas."

If one or two top-level executives or managers make a decision that impacts and leads change by not considering others in the organization, it can cause conflict. I found that this type of thinking creates conflicting negative relationships with the department heads and their IT directors, and senior-level IT managers who are caught in middle space. The project mission is important to all projects. A clearly defined mission and vision statement is a roadmap and is essential to the success of the organization. Dennis Hightower once said, "If you don't know where you're going, any road will take you there" (Jick & Peiperl, 2003, p. 91).

The project mission and vision of what the business will look like after the project has been implemented will create a better understanding of the organization's purpose as it relates to the diverse business objectives of the departments in providing customer products and services. A bottom-up visioning approach from department heads and their middle-level managers to top-level management will contribute to the success of the vision. This is really important when there is an organization-wide project that impacts all the departments in a government organization. If some of the department heads and managers feel like they are in middle space, the business strategy is not aligned with the organizational and information systems strategy.

Top Management Support

Top management support is described as getting support and approval from top-level management for all the project resources necessary to achieve success, including financial and human resources (Pinto, 1986; Pinto & Slevin, 1987; Rosacker, 2005). In a study by Kearns (2007), a survey questionnaire was sent to participants and responses were received from 269 chief information officers of US corporations in various medium to large size companies. Results from the study indicate that top management support and participation influence IS planning, reduce problems in implementation, and improve project success.

If your organization has a CIO or a central information technology director, top management support means having the support of the CIO and the central information technology department in addition to the project stakeholders. Studies report that CIOs with an understanding of the different types of information systems within an organization realize the importance of the unique information systems in the various departments and agencies within the government organization that support the business strategy.

In some government organizations with a decentralized or federal (mixed) environment, the central information technology department supports and maintains the technical network infrastructure, the intranet, and Internet. Back-office systems, workgroups systems, decisions support systems, and transaction processing systems (TPS) or specialized information systems are linked through the network for access by end users from various locations within the organization.

Project Plans and Schedules

The project planning and scheduling factor is described as developing the detailed project plan and schedules, the work breakdown and tasks assignments with milestones for completing the project tasks within the estimated time frames, and defining the equipment requirements (Pinto, 1986; Pinto & Slevin, 1987; Rosacker, 2005). It is important to identify the stakeholders at the beginning of the project and have collaborative and participatory involvement of all stakeholders at the beginning of the project (Lim, Tan, & Pan, 2007). Stakeholders are those individuals or organizations that have a shared interest in the project; and consideration should be given to the impact on the stakeholders' business operations. Another study by Scholl (2004) reports the importance of a team approach and identifying stakeholders' interest in the project so that their needs are met in the planning phase.

Technical Tasks

The technical tasks factor is described as having skilled and knowledgeable personnel and the appropriate technology resources required to implement the IS project including hardware and software (Belout & Gauvreau, 2004; Pinto & Slevin, 1987; Rosacker, 2005). Problems can exist with computer systems because of the lack of architectural interoperability and incompatible standards.

Internet portals may provide greater access to e-government information by providing one point of access to services, integration of services, and may assist in increasing e-government efficiencies (Haung, 2007). Commercial, packaged information systems software and vendor information systems software can provide technical solutions and support the information systems strategy. Information systems and e-government integration can result in the seamless flow and sharing of transactions and documents with the appropriate integration of Internet application system software with internal information system using telecommunications infrastructure of networks (Internet, intranet, and virtual private networks) to connect these systems.

The network is defined as being able to connect to information systems using networks. Information systems and telecommunications have created networks to support business systems by connecting Internet and internal information systems to users, other businesses and agencies, and to customers (Housel & Skopec, 2001). The application service provider (ASP) model can be beneficial for organizations for accessing the hosted information systems for economies of scale by managing the operations and providing the necessary skilled technical personnel (Walsh, 2003).

There can be barriers to e-government application integration by the lack of architectural interoperability, incompatible standards, and lack of security models (Lam, 2005) and can impact other types of projects.

Another study examines the important issue of the integration of Internet application systems with existing internal application systems. Bhatt and Troutt (2005) examine the relationship between business process improvement initiatives (BPIIs), information systems integration, and customer focus. They tests the effect of IS integration and BPII on customer focus. The study found significant impact of data integration and the communication network integration on process improvement initiatives and customer focus of Fortune 500 companies in the United States.

Communication

The factor of communication is described as having the appropriate channels of communications with all key stakeholders in the project implementation. Within the context of the information system projects, it refers to listening and communicating with all key project team members and clients and end users, and communicating with the business managers and top-level managers and officials in the organization. All these channels of communication by the project manager are important to project success (Pinto, 1986; Pinto & Slevin, 1987; Rosacker, 2005). It is important for the project managers to have good listening and communication skill competencies and for managing the project team members (Henderson, 2008).

Client Consultation

Communication by consulting with those who are the clients and end users (stakeholders) of the resulting project outside the organization and within the organization is important for getting their feedback (Belout & Gauvreau, 2004; Pinto & Slevin, 1987; Rosacker, 2005).

Personnel

The personnel factor means having sufficient skilled human resources for the project, the ability to recruit for the project team, and the ability to provide training for project team members (Belout & Gauvreau, 2004; Pinto, 1986; Pinto & Slevin, 1987; Rosacker, 2005). Appropriate personnel means having a broad base of individuals to work on and support the project, the vision, the mission, and the work effort.

Monitoring and Feedback

Monitoring and feedback refer to communication between key personnel such as project team members and the project manager by continually reviewing project status, reporting project problems and deficiencies, and finding ways to correct them in a timely manner (Pinto, 1986; Pinto & Slevin, 1987).

Client Acceptance

Client acceptance is achieving users' acceptance of the project outcomes after the project has been completed (Pinto, 1986; Pinto & Slevin, 1987; Rosacker, 2005).

Troubleshooting

The factor of trouble shooting is taking corrective action for the problems that arise and taking action to avoid unforeseen problems (Pinto, 1986; Pinto & Slevin, 1987; Rosacker, 2005).

Summary

Ten CSFs important to project success are defined in this chapter. The ten factors are project mission, technical tasks, top management support, troubleshooting, client acceptance, personnel, project schedule and plans, monitoring and feedback, communication, and client consultation. It is important that there is a shared vision and project mission is one of the key factors. Top management support is important for getting the project resources, including personnel and funding of the project and for putting together the project plan. Technical tasks include the technical skills of the team members, the hardware, computer software, and the network infrastructure. Technical standards and interoperability is important to successful projects. Communication is essential for managing the project and communicating with all the stakeholders in the project, including managers and end users. Monitoring and feedback are important and so is troubleshooting any information system problems. Client acceptance means obtaining client approval and the acceptance for the completed information system project.

Review Concepts

- Project mission and the shared vision
- Top management support
- Project schedule and plans
- Client consultation
- Personnel

- Technical tasks
- Client acceptance
- Monitoring and feedback
- Communication
- Troubleshooting

Discussion Questions

9.1. Why is it important for the project mission to be understood by all those involved in the project?

9.2. Discuss the importance of top management support.

9.3. Describe the importance of the project plans and schedules.

9.4. Discuss the components of the technical tasks.

9.5. Why is it important to communicate with the project stakeholders?

9.6. Describe your experiences with any one of the ten critical success factors.

CHAPTER TEN
MEASURING PROJECT SUCCESS

There are many studies in the literature on measuring project success. Some studies include measures based on the original budget, cost, and original plans/schedules, but differ on measuring project success outcomes (Sumner, Bock, & Giamartino, 2006). Most managers feel that the overall benefits from the information system project should exceed its costs. This chapter describes an information systems study on measuring project success using the ten critical success factors (CSFs), the variable of project success, and its relationship to leadership styles in county government.

Several studies measure performance using sales, costs, profits, and buyer/seller relationships. These measures are not applicable to public sector organizations consisting of many departments with different types of business operations and services. The sheriff's department, department of public social services, county clerk, hospital, treasurer-tax collector, assessor, auditor, district attorney, and county recorder are some of the departments within county government with different business objectives. Performance measurements for the public sector are developed for each organization's unique strategy because each organization needs to determine what is relevant (Bryant, Jones, & K. Widener, 2004).

The Balanced Scorecard

The Balanced Scorecard (BSC) model by Kaplan and Norton (2005) identified four key perspectives of performance measures: financial, customer, internal business, and learning and growth. Chan (2004) examined the use of the BSC by municipal governments in the United States and Canada. There were 184 respondents with 132 from the United States and 52 from Canada. The study found that only 7.5 percent of the 184 respondents have implemented the BSC and that most governments adopted some other form of performance measures, but the greatest emphasis is on financial performance and the least is on technology innovation and change.

The time frame for accomplishing project goals in government is usually based on achieving results within two years or less, mainly due to elections and budget cycles (Dufner, Holley, & Reed, 2002; Melkers & Willoughby, 2005). In government, the annual budget is prepared by each department and is a tool for measuring financial performance based on direction from central executive administration. In the public sector organizations, "efficiency measures and outcome measures are less extensively developed than output measures for programs" (Julnes & Holzer, 2001, p. 699).

In summary, there are no universal standards for measuring public sector performance. Much of the research on public organization performance is qualitative. Many studies of organizational performance in literature focus on marketing, production management, innovations, research and development, and few are on county government. Departments within government work on putting together their annual budgets. The proposed budgets are submitted to the central top-level executives for review and approval by top-level officials. Priority is on timely submission of departmental budgets and staying within the budget for each fiscal year starting July 1.

How to Measure Project Success

Let's examine some of the original studies on project success. According to Pinto (1986), in an unpublished dissertation, the original project implementation profile (PIP) survey developed by Slevin and Pinto (1986) consisting of 100 questions was reduced to 62 questions in the 1986 study. Pinto (1986) reported that 418 project managers evaluated the importance of different factors relating to project success using a 7-point Likert scale ranging from 1 (strongly disagree) to 7 (strongly agree). The research identified the ten CSFs.

Respondents were asked to rate 13 items that described the value of the project in terms of project outcomes after project completion and in terms of project success. The goal in the original PIP study (Pinto, 1986) was to construct a general scale to incorporate a wide range of measures for project success. Another study by Pinto and Slevin (1988) on definitions and measurement techniques used the same 12 items of project success, but reworded the items to reflect the measures of project schedules and budgets to accurately reflect the measures, and identified two subcategories for the 12 items as (1) project and (2) client.

The purpose of the two subcategories is to understand the success measures that apply to the organization's project and the clients as end-users of the information system. The PIP has been used in other studies in literature with various moderating variables and its importance to project success (Pinto & Mantel, 1990; Pinto & Prescott, 1988, 1990).

Recent studies found that state, county, and city governments operate in a dynamic environment of politics and legislation that influences project priorities (Moon, 2002). In the government environment, project success or failure is visible to the public, whereas private sector organizations are more likely to keep project information within the organization boundaries for their own scrutiny.

Most studies about project success in the literature have mixed views on how to best measure project success in relation to net benefits and value to the organization. In contrast to most literature on e-government models, Coursey and Norris (2008) found that for e-government adoption, some presume that fully transactional systems are better and that more citizen interaction equals improved service and even questions the accuracy of the models. Project benefits should be identified at the start of the project. If clients, team members, and business managers perceive problems, then open communication is essential.

The Project Questionnaire

The questionnaire for this particular study on county government is based on the original questionnaire by Pinto (1986). This survey was chosen because the questionnaire measures project success in relation to ten CSFs in project management. The original questionnaire consists of 13 items to measure project success and 50 items to measure the 10 CSFs using a 7-point Likert scale. The 13 items were later reduced to 12 items (Pinto & Slevin, 1988).

The study by Rosacker (2005) on state government used an adapted version of the Pinto (1986) questionnaire in which the PIP questionnaire was converted to a five-point Likert scale and used a total of seven items to measure project success. Three measures on project success from the Rosacker (2005) study for plans/schedules and cost replaced two measures in the Pinto (1986) questionnaire.

The current study uses the three items from the adapted questionnaire by Rosacker (2005) and seven items from the PIP questionnaire (Pinto, 1986), therefore, resulting in ten items to measure success as one project success variable. The ten items are based on the following outcomes: plans and schedules are met, costs are within the original budget, and achievement of the functional goals.

All items were rated on 5-point Likert scale ranging from 1 (strongly disagree) to 5 (strongly agree). In the original study, Pinto (1986) used *not applicable* for each question related to the ten CSFs but not on the project success items. It was possible for the participants to choose "N/A" when the questions on the ten CSFs did not relate to the project.

Pinto (1986) reported that as a result of the pilot test the "unanimous piece of criticism that was received concerned the lack of 'Not Applicable' response for the items in the questionnaire" (p. 70). As result of the criticism, Pinto (1986) included "Not Applicable" to the items measuring the ten CSFs. The current study includes "N/A" for the ten CSFs.

The original Pinto (1986) questionnaire identifies four project life cycle phases of conception (start), planning, execution, and termination (completed) and includes projects in any of the life cycle phases and uses other moderating variables. The current study is based on the importance of the overall ten CSFs in relation to only those projects that have already been completed and considered successful. Therefore, the current study did not use the moderating variable of the project life cycle phases as described by Pinto (1986). The PIP questionnaire was used to evaluate general projects, successful projects, and those projects perceived to be unsuccessful (Pinto, 1986).

The PIP questionnaire for the current study is an adapted version of the original PIP questionnaire in an unpublished dissertation by Pinto (1986), see Appendix A. The PIP questionnaire was later published in a study by Pinto and Prescott (1990) on planning and tactical factors in relationship to project success.

Research on E-Government and Project Success

Many government organizations have taken advantage of the Internet technology and have web sites for both the public and business use to access information. State, county, and city governments are continually evolving their e-government technology plans and recognize that they can provide services to many groups that interact with government.

My interest in research was based on the use of the Internet and finding out how important the ten CSFs are in government projects; and if there was any relationship to the project managers' leadership style and success in the use of the Internet for eMortgages and eRecording applications that integrate with their internal information systems. I conducted a study on electronic government (e-government), project management, and the factors that contributed to its success. These are completed projects supporting the government business operations.

What is e-government? Electronic government is defined as the use of digital technologies to transform government operations for improving efficiency, effectiveness, and service delivery (Haag, Cummings, & Phillips, 2007). The study uses five stages of the e-government development model.

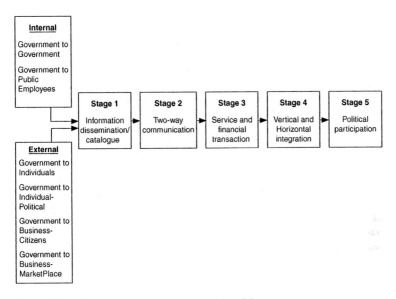

Figure 10.1 Stages of e-government growth model.

Source: Adapted from Moon, 2002.

Stage one is simple information dissemination or one-way communication of basic web services. Stage two is two-way request-and-response communication. Stage three consists of services and financial transactions. Stage four consists of horizontal and vertical integration of software applications, and, finally, stage five involves political participation (Moon, 2002), see Figure 10.1.

eMortgage

eMortgage is an electronic mortgage lending process that produces legally binding mortgages electronically and entirely without paper. Laws provide that electronic signatures can be used wherever existing law requires a *wet* signature. To accomplish fully electronic mortgages "SMART docs" (Secure, Manageable, Archivable, Retrievable, and Transferable documents) locks data and the document presentation into a single computerized file. End-to-end technology supports automating several steps that were previously done manually by electronically exchanging data. The process ensures that, "Information is transferred in a form that is readable both by computers and by humans, thereby enabling the requirements for filing with county recorders' offices" (Markus, Steinfield, & Wigand, 2005, p. 85).

eRecording

"Is the process of receipt, examination, fee calculation, and payment, endorsing of recording information and return of recorded electronic documents submitted for recording in a county's land-records office" using application software and telecommunications (networks) technology ("Number of electronic-recording counties tops 400," 2009, p. 78). Transactions of records that transfer interests in land must be filed in public records. The records are generally recorded and kept in each county in the United States and is available for public inspection or copying. If transfer of interest in land is not recorded in each county, "there is a risk to the beneficial holder that a subsequent bona fide purchaser may be accorded a superior interest in the property" (Brumfield, Newell, & Gordon, 2006, p. 6).

The focus of the study is on the advance stage four of the e-government integration with internal information systems. The study was guided by the following questions related to eRecording systems that integrate with internal information systems.

1. Which factors are most important in counties that have had successful e-government integration of eMortgages with electronic recording (eRecording)?
2. How do the characteristics of the project managers influence the factors that are important in integration of eMortgages with eRecording project success?
3. Which factors contribute to a high level of project implementation success (on schedule, on budget, functional success)?

Conceptual Framework

The study used the PIP survey questionnaire, originally developed by Pinto (1986), that identified ten factors important to information systems project implementation success. The study also incorporated another questionnaire called the Multifactor Leadership questionnaire (MLQ) originally designed by Bass (1990), which identified three leadership styles such as transformational, transactional, and passive avoidant (laissez-faire). These leadership style variables of interests are measured by the scores on the MLQ 5X by Bass (Avolio & Bass, 2004). The project manager variables are years worked in county government and years worked as a manager.

An adapted version of the PIP questionnaire was used, wherein project implementation success is measured on the basis of the following outcomes:

1. The project plans and schedules are met,
2. Costs are within the original budget, and
3. Solution implemented achieves functional goals of the system.

Population

The National Association of Counties (NACO, 2013) website reports a total of 3,068 member counties in the United States and 40 are city-county governments (cities that have consolidated government functions with their surrounding counties). The population for this study is project managers in county government within the United States. The list of US counties was extracted from the US Property Records Industry Association's (PRIA) excel spreadsheet of 496 counties in 34 states that have implemented e-government integration of eMortgages from mortgage companies, title companies, and other lending institutions with county government for electronic recording (eRecording) of real property/land documents. Information for distribution of the letters to participants was obtained by the researcher from Google searches of the association directories of state-wide county recorders, registers of deeds, and county clerks, and from the National Association of Counties website for distribution information and county population sizes.

The Hypotheses

In this quantitative study, the questions were put in a research form. Quantitative research means statistical methods are used for examining relationships and showing these patterns of behavior with numbers. The questions in the research are worded so that they can be studied and this is done by developing several questions and putting them in the study as hypotheses.

The first hypothesis was designed to test whether five of the CSFs (project mission, top management support, project schedules/plans, communication, and technical) are most important to project managers and the order of importance. The second hypothesis was designed to test whether the characteristics of the project manager (level of management, leadership style, length of work with the county, length of work as a manager) will affect the scores on the ten CSFs. The third hypothesis was designed to test which of the ten CSFs are most important when measured with the dependent variable of *Project Implementation Success*.

Results

There were 137 participants, and all were from different US counties in 33 states that participated in the study. Results are displayed in Table 10.1, with frequencies and percentages for region, county size, and manager level. The number of years worked in county government ranged from 1 to 41, with a mean under 18 years (M = 17.85, SD = 10.44). The number

Table 10.1 Frequencies and percentages for categorical demographic for US region, county size, and level of management variables

	N	%
US Region		
North Central	45	32.8
North East	12	8.8
West	44	32.1
South	33	24.1
County Size		
Over 250,000	44	32.1
25,000 to 250,000	52	38.0
Under 25,000	19	13.9
Level of management		
Top-level manager	71	51.8
Middle-level manager	25	18.2
First-level manager	9	6.6
Not a manager	13	9.5

Note. Frequencies not summing to 137 and percentages not summing to 100 reflect missing data.

of years worked as a manager ranged from 0 to 41, with a mean under 15 years (M = 14.66, SD = 10.77).

Hypothesis one found all ten CSFs significant and the order of importance as (1) project mission, (2) technical tasks, (3) top management support, (4) troubleshooting, (5) client acceptance, (6) personnel, (7) project schedules and plans, (8) monitoring and feedback, (9) communication, and (10) client consultation.

Hypothesis one was partially supported. All items in the survey of CSFs were rated on a 5-point scale ranging from 1 (strongly disagree) to 5 (strongly agree). It was possible for the participants to choose "not applicable" when the questions on the ten CSFs did not relate to the information systems project. The mean is simply the arithmetic *average* of the set of scores (sum of scores divided by the number of scores). The range of scores for each of the ten CSFs is 1 to 5. A mean of 1 or 2 indicates not important, a mean of 3 indicates neutral in importance, a mean of 4 indicates important, and a mean of 5 indicates the highest score in importance, see Table 10.2.

The results of hypothesis two show that having a higher score for transformational leadership was predictive of higher scores for all ten CSFs. Top-level managers (versus not being a manager) was predictive of higher scores for project mission, project schedules and plans, and technical tasks. Having a higher score for passive-avoidant (laissez-faire) leadership was

Table 10.2 Means and standard deviations of project mission, top management support, project schedules/plans, communication, technical tasks, client consultation, personnel, monitoring and feedback, client acceptance, and troubleshooting

	N	Mean		SD	F	P
CSFs					21.50	<.001
Project mission	93	4.49	a	.46		
Technical tasks	93	4.25	b	.57		
Top management support	93	4.13	bce	.70		
Trouble shooting	93	4.10	cdef	.60		
Client acceptance	93	4.07	def	.57		
Personnel	93	4.00	defg	.62		
Project schedules and plans	93	3.89	fgh	.65		
Monitoring and feedback	93	3.89	fgh	.68		
Communication	93	3.81	fgh	.66		
Client consultation	93	3.87	h	.67		

Note. Means with different superscripts are significantly different, $p < .05$.

predictive of lower scores for project schedules and plans, personnel, technical tasks, troubleshooting. Hypothesis two was partially supported.

US Region

The results of the US regions show that being from the west (versus North Central) was predictive of higher scores for top management support, project schedules and plans, personnel, technical tasks, and monitoring and feedback. It also shows that being from the south (versus north central) was predictive of higher scores for personnel, technical tasks, client acceptance, troubleshooting, and top management support, and communication.

Results of hypothesis three show that the overall model predicting project success from the ten CSFs was significant. The ten CSFs predicted 45% of the variance in project outcomes. Significant positive predictors (higher scores related to more project success) include project mission, client acceptance, and troubleshooting. Project mission was one of five CSFs included in the null hypothesis. Hypothesis three was not supported, but there were some interesting findings as a result of the study, which is described in the following section.

Conclusions

The following implications from the study are based on the survey results and from the rich source of postdata collection information from the participants:

For hypothesis one, the results show the importance of the ten CSFs and the order of importance. Postdata collection information from the participants show that project managers from counties in the study have integrated e-government systems that handle complex processing. The participants in the study are from different counties in 33 states.

It is evident from the study that the development of eMortgage standards and legislation are enablers to county eRecording system integration and the advance stages of e-government (eRecording) services is progressing at the department level of county government. The study strongly suggests that successful project managers of eRecording systems have support from the top management and top-level officials (county recorders, registers of deeds, and county clerks), have funding sources for the projects, and have support from top-level state officials. The study strongly suggests that clearly defined goals and objectives (Project Mission), third-party vendor eRecording software, and state-wide portals in some states are enablers to the advance stages of e-government services.

For hypothesis two, results show that the project manager's leadership style is important to successful projects. The study found it to be significant in relation to transformational leaders and higher scores on all ten CSFs. Transformational leadership has the greatest positive influence on success. Top-level managers versus nonmanagers had higher scores for project mission, project schedules and plans, and technical tasks, which seems reasonable since nonmanagers may not have the experience and knowledge of managers in general. Having a higher score for laissez-faire leaders may be attributed to the tasks being delegated to subordinates, as reported in previous studies on laissez-faire leadership.

As a result of the study and the postdata collection information, it seems reasonable to assume that project managers who align information systems strategy to support the business and the organizational strategies are important to eRecording system project success, and the higher scores for US Regions for some CSFs may be the result of shared communication and planning among regional US counties.

For hypothesis three, the results of the study found that all ten CSFs (when measured with the variable of *Project Implementation Success*) are important to project success but found project mission, client acceptance, and troubleshooting as most important to completed projects. If the goals and objectives are clearly defined at the start of the project, it seems reasonable to assume that the end results will directly influence client acceptance, which means obtaining users' acceptance of the project outcomes (results) after the project has been completed. It is reasonable to assume that troubleshooting is important because it means taking corrective action to problems that arise and taking action to avoid unforeseen problems when the eRecording system is supporting the daily operations.

Implications for Researchers and Managers

The research has some important implications for researchers and managers. A review of previous studies indicates that little information is reported on the progress of county e-government systems that are integrated with internal information systems, although there has been considerable progress in establishing websites for government services, publishing information, and providing online services.

The first implication from this study shows that project managers have integrated e-government systems that handle complex processing of receipts, examination, fee calculations, payments, endorsing of recording information, and return of recorded electronic documents submitted by the originators for recording in a county's real property recording department.

The goal of this research is to determine the priorities of county government in managing e-government projects for the advanced stages of e-government services and other factors that contribute to their success. Several previous e-government studies in literature focus on the Internet and online access to website information. However, e-government integration with internal information systems is not easily visible by examining websites. I believe that integration of information systems using Internet portals and virtual private networks is being utilized more than reported in literature and that integration is occurring between governments at the state, county, and city levels.

The second implication is that the participants are from 137 different counties in several states and provided a rich source of data from the questionnaire and postdata collection information. It is apparent that the development of standards for interfacing e-government with internal information systems is an enabler of the technical capability for eMortgages and county eRecording information systems. The extensible markup language (XML), mortgage industry vertical IS standards, and the Internet (Markus, Steinfield, Wigand, & Minton, 2006; Power, 2005; Wigand, Steinfield, & Markus, 2005) and legislation provide different approaches to providing services using IS innovation (Ewan & Ladd, 2008). Based on this study, it appears that e-government integration with internal systems is progressing at the department level of county government and is the result of eMortgage standards and legislation.

The third implication is that successful project managers of eRecording systems have support from top management and top-level officials (county recorders, registers of deeds, and county clerks). Earlier, I discussed the importance of peer association and building a network of relationships. The county recorders, registers of deeds, and county clerks and their project managers work through their formal state-wide associations and build strong peer relationships to assist them in achieving what they need to accomplish. They have associations in every state within the United States. It is obvious that they need top management support from their state government and from top management within each of the county government organizations.

Since most are elected officials, they are probably at times working in middle space between those at the state level and those in the top level of government in the county organizations where they work and the groups below who are the constituents that voted them into their elected positions and groups within the departments they direct and manage.

I really believe that their strong peer association with other recorders, registers of deeds, and county clerks in other counties within their states, and even in other regional states, assist them in obtaining top management support and skilled and experienced project managers, and this has a major influence on the success of their projects. They also received support and a close working relationship with their project managers and other resources such as the PRIA. Peer association is a very powerful tool for them and for project managers and also for you in your own job situation.

The survey study did not include questions on funding of the e-government projects but it was based on the feedback from participants that there appears to be funding sources for the projects and support from top-level state officials. Project goals and objectives (project mission), third-party vendor integration software, and state-wide portals in some states are enablers to the advance stages of e-government services.

The fourth implication is that the ten CSFs are important to making projects successful; and project managers must determine which ten CSFs are most important to e-government integration with internal information systems. The project manager's leadership style is important for successful projects. This study found it to be significant in relation to transformational leaders and higher scores on the ten CSFs.

Of particular importance is that there are 496 counties identified by PRIA as eRecording counties when this study was completed in 2010. At the time of the writing this book, there are 926 counties in 42 states listed on the PRIA (pria.us) website. It is evident that the 137 project managers who participated in this study are from those counties identified as being successful in implementing advanced e-government services and are using eRecording systems in which eMortgage transactions/real property record documents (from mortgage companies, title companies, attorneys, and other lending institutions) are electronically transmitted to county record-ers for electronic recording.

Perhaps, what distinguished the project managers in this study from those of other counties in the United States who have not implemented eRecording may be their management experience and knowledge on how to strategically align eRecording systems, as previously cited in Chapter 2, to support the business strategy. The information systems strategic triangle (ISST) framework is when project managers find a balance by strategic alignment of the IS project to support the organizational and business strategies as presented in the conceptual framework by Pearlson and Saunders (2006).

The study found the importance of the project goals and objectives being clearly defined in the task activities of the project mission as dis-cussed in Chapter 7 as most important to project success, and that pro-ject managers consider the technical tasks as a higher level of importance in relation to the other CSFs. In addition, the ability to secure funding sources for the e-government projects is an important factor that was not part of this study.

The CSF of project mission in which the goals and objectives of IS projects are clearly defined has more important role in information tech-nology projects than reported. It seems reasonable to assume that the goals and objectives in relation to the project outcomes and client accep-tance are most important to project managers and that troubleshooting is important to ensure that corrective action is taken when systems problems are encountered. A clearly defined project mission and strategic alignment of IS to support the business strategy is just as important to e-government project success. It is evident that many principles and factors including the ten CSFs identified in this study are enablers to the success of e-government system integration projects.

This research indicates that the managers' leadership style is important but not enough. Success depends on a broader scope including leadership style, strategic alignment of the project, the ten CSFs, top management support, peer support, skills of the project manager, and the appropriate technology and information system software.

Summary

There are several different theories and opinions on how to measure project success, but measuring success in public sector organizations differs from that in private sector organizations that measure performance based on sales, costs, and profits. The BSC is a method of measuring organiza-tion performance, but in most governments, the greatest emphasis is on financial performance and the least is on technology. There is no universal standard for measuring public sector performance.

Project success can be measured based on three items: (1) The project plans and schedules are met; (2) Costs are within the original budget; and (3) The solution implemented achieves functional goals of the system using the PIP questionnaire. Project leadership on transformational, transactional, and laissez-faire leadership style can be measured based on the MLQ questionnaire.

Research on county government provides several implications for project managers on project success. The results show the importance of peer relationships and top management support for successful projects.

Review Concepts

- The Balanced Scorecard
- The Project Implementation Profile (PIP) Questionnaire
- The Multifactor Leadership Questionnaire (MLQ)
- E-government and project success
- Research and hypotheses testing
- Implications for researchers and project managers

Discussion Questions

10.1. Discuss why the balance score card is not always a good measurement for government performance.

10.2. What are some of the items used in measuring of project success on the PIP questionnaire?

10.3. Discuss e-government systems in your organization.

10.4. Describe the hypotheses in the study.

10.5. Discuss some of the implications from the study on county government.

CHAPTER ELEVEN

THE ESSENTIALS OF GOOD MANAGEMENT PRACTICES

Essential core principles of information systems project management are important to managing projects. However, the essentials and supplemental concepts and ideas presented in this book will assist you in thinking of new ways to handle your quest for project implementation success. For many managers, this is a new way of thinking and means you have to make changes. Avoiding news ways of thinking and not developing yourself leads to stagnation, and in these circumstances you will not improve yourself and grow professionally as a project manager. It is important to value continuous improvement. This chapter is a review of many of the concepts you have learned in the previous chapters.

Everyone may at times experience various challenges when managing information systems projects. You will find that in some situations many individuals may have differences of opinions. The differences need to be discussed and worked out in order to create a shared vision. The differences help you to look at things differently. In battles, you take opposing views and in some cases you may win the battle but lose the entire war, which means that you should choose your battles carefully. Look at obstacles and challenges and learn how to view the organization differently as tops, middles, belows, and the public it serves. Be aware of the fact that you may do all the right things as a manager but realize that you cannot control everything around you in the organization. However, you can have a better understanding of the work environment with the hope that you will have more project successes and insight on managing certain situations and evaluating your choices.

If you have a small pebble in your shoe, it makes your whole body hurt. The pebble can be very small but can cause so much pain. It is so easy to just to remove the pebble from your shoe and you can walk with no problem at all. In some situations that you encounter, you need to remove the pebble in how you think and manage the situation. This is the reason why I include the information on the different kinds of barriers you may encounter, about working in middle space, and the options available to you so that you can achieve success and start to think about your environment differently.

After the information systems project is complete, it is important to assess the quality of the system by evaluating the technology being used and the computer information system. The postaudit evaluation and report needs to be included in the organizational history records. This needs to be a standard practice with all major IS projects. Many organizations make a large investment in information systems. Did anyone do a formal assessment of the project implementation that goes beyond the financial aspects of the project?

Did the organization get its money's worth? After all, some organizations have spent millions of dollars on information systems projects and it is worth assessing. Does the information system assist the organization in the various business functions and its business operations? Does the computer system or technology used assist the end users in accomplishing the tasks and activities based on the *shared vision* of what the organization will be able to do after the project is complete? Do the benefits of the system and organizational performance exceed the costs of the project?

It is good to take time to reflect on the project, and record your reflections in a project manager's journal as a way of assessing how you are doing. Write down the things that worked well and those that were problem areas. By writing things down, you can reflect on the information and attempt to find the meaning based on your own and others' experiences. Receive feedback from others as you lead others for improving your own leadership style. This information can be applicable to future projects. Personal experience makes managers more aware of good information systems design and implementation.

Some Essentials

During the many years I worked in government, I kept a journal and it helped me to reflect back on several key events in managing systems. I observed others in the organization and reviewed my IT management and organizational behavior books. Some situations I felt were difficult, but I found it to be a good practice to write in my journal as part of my quest for success and for improving myself. I wrote down the things that went poorly and what I could or should have done in the event I encountered the same problems again. You can do the same. It is good to keep a journal.

I found writing it to be good for me when dealing with challenging situations. It was always good to look back several weeks or months later to read my journal. It gave me more perspective of what I was dealing with at the time. I soon found that the sun always rises the next day and things do gradually get better and many situations are temporary.

Continued growth means learning from your mistakes and the mistakes of others, and recognizing the mistakes you and others make in handling specific situations or in making certain decisions. Many individuals make a major effort to learn from their experiences so that they do not repeat them. They find alternate ways or strategies for the solutions to problems. Ask yourself if you have learned something important. Learning has the potential of changing how you approach projects in the future. Think about the challenges you face with projects in a different way by looking at the organizational system of tops, middles, belows, and the general public and clients you serve.

Getting Started

If you never get started and make any major decisions, you will not make any mistakes at all. However, you will never accomplish anything significant in your life because you never get started. You may think about it for some time, but good intentions and thinking about it means you will never accomplish what you really want to accomplish.

When I was a student in college, my cousin kept talking about going to school and working on his bachelor's degree or on a technical certification. Every time I asked him how he was doing he said that he planned on taking a class *but* could not start because his time was being spent elsewhere on other unexpected priorities that surfaced. I really dislike the frequent use of the word "but" because everything someone says previous to this word seems irrelevant. Why? Because the words following *but* changes everything. He had been saying this for more than ten years.

I finally came to the conclusion that my cousin never started taking any classes because he really did not want to do it bad enough. It really was not a situation that he could not do it and go to college. It was the situation that he did not want to do it because it was not that important to him. He had no true desire or real passion to work on it. He never got started after all these years. Now he has little to offer when looking for other job opportunities.

You can get started by making a decision now and putting together your own plan and start working on it. Once you get started, you can begin to make progress until you reach your goal, whatever that goal may be for you.

Putting the Recommendations Together

This book makes several recommendations and some of these are for the organization while others are for project managers, IT managers, and those managers involved with information system decisions. The following is a list of some of the essentials discussed in the previous chapters:

- Project risks
- The internal and external forces of change
- The information systems strategic triangle framework
- Business initiatives
- The value chain of primary and support activities
- Portfolio management
- Project selection methods
- The project life cycle and software engineering
- Variations of the systems development life cycle (SDLC) phases
- Ten critical success factors and project implementation success
- Software project management methodology
- The Project Management Institute (PMI) Method
- Commercial, packaged information systems software
- Request for proposal (RFP)
- The contractual agreement
- Systems work requests
- Types of information systems
- The information systems strategic grid
- System boundaries versus system interfaces
- Information technology standards and policies
- Project planning
- Change control
- Expert opinion in business
- The three areas of measuring project success
- Stakeholders in government organizations
- IT centralization versus decentralization
- Economies of scope and breadth of diversification
- Organization history
- Elected and nonelected officials
- Organization culture
- The IT governance model
- Role of the CIO, IS/IT managers, and project managers
- Middle space
- The influence of politics
- Opportunities

- Agendas
- Mood regulation
- Distancing strategies
- Types of peers
- Collaboration
- Choices
- Education and professional development
- Horizontal and vertical career path
- Transformational, transactional, and laissez-faire leadership styles
- Research on e-government and project success

Working Together

Understand and use the concepts of what I have suggested in this book. Think about the organizational system of the above (tops) groups, the middles, the belows (workers), and the clients and the general public. See the connection between the multiple perspectives. Understand that a clearly defined IT governance model determines who has authority on specific decisions rights for information technology. Information technology governance is important to the success of the organization.

Your approach can be much better when the information technology decision rights have been defined in the organization and there is a shared vision. This can be accomplished by the CIO constituting a central committee of IT directors from the many departments and agencies within the organization to define IT organizational policies and standards and establish agreed upon IT governance decision rights. The standards and policies and IT governance decision rights need to be reviewed and updated periodically so that they do not create barriers to the central organization and the departments and agencies. Without clearly defined IT decision rights, there will be blurred visions, which can result in creating many kinds of problems. It can result in some managers at different levels in the organization being caught working in middle space.

The business strategy needs to be supported by the organizational and the information systems strategies. There is a balance in these three strategies in successful organizations. It is important for you to know the different types of information systems and how they support the organization. If there is a mission and a collaborative shared vision of information systems, those in the organization work in cooperation instead of working in an environment of confrontation or conflict.

When things do go well within the many departments and the agencies, they go well for the organization as a whole. When managers are pulled apart in middle space, it can become a no-win situation. In this type of an environment, a lot of time and energy are spent focusing on the differences and not on the work that needs to be accomplished nor on the general public and clients who rely on government services. Few benefit in this kind of work environment.

The most important thing you can do is to work on being positive despite the setbacks you may encounter and the challenges you face in your work environment. You cannot solve all the problems in the work environment. It can be very difficult at times, but understand the different categories of information systems and how each system supports the organization, its departments, and agencies.

Develop the skills you need to be a leader by engaging in lifelong learning. It is important that you value continuous improvement and continue to grow as an individual. Be aware of the different leadership styles. Some managers are transformational leaders, others are transactional, and some are not leaders at all (laissez-faire) even though they hold the position title of manager or supervisor. Having the position title of manager or supervisor does not make a person a good manager or supervisor. Work on being a transformational leader.

Oftentimes you may hear complaints about another manager and when someone on your staff asks you about the manager, avoid making any judgmental comments. In fact, you may not like the manager's leadership style either. You are entitled to your own opinion, but keep your opinions to yourself. Fortunately, you can distance yourself from this manager. Unfortunately, others who work for this type of manager do not have this option.

Employees can follow formal procedures through their department and through the human resources department in their organization for resolving complaints or grievances. It is a difficult situation for anyone to be in these types of circumstances, but it is up to the manager's superiors to handle the problems that may surface because of how the manager leads and interacts with others in his or her role as a manager. If you do not own the problem, avoid getting involved. However, it is not appropriate to keep quiet when unethical or illegal behavior is involved.

More about Peers

Recognize the need for peer support within the organization and value peer relationships. Build your own peer relationships and friendships. Understand the importance of relationships both at work and in your personal life. Do not forget to invest time in yourself and your own individual goals and career path.

Management Concepts and Principles

In summary, there are many good journals, articles, and books you can purchase and read as resources on how to manage information system projects. Focusing on the core principles of project management is important and it is just as important to consider the organizational environment. Project managers and business managers need to be aware of other essentials and the human aspects of project management by considering some the following management concepts and principles discussed previously in this book, see Figure 11.1.

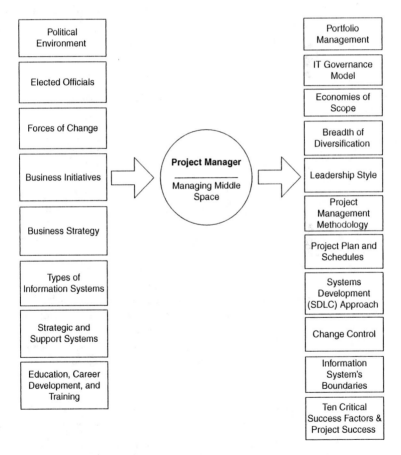

Figure 11.1 Information systems management concepts.

Project Essentials

- Align your projects by using the information systems strategic triangle framework in which the business strategy is supported by the information systems and the organizational strategies. These projects are more likely to be successful.
- Implement portfolio management procedures within an organization at the central, organizational top level and if you are a director or manager in a department or agency at the department or agency level.
- Work on obtaining the support from top-level management for your projects.
- Realize the importance of the portfolio management, project plans, change control procedures, the SDLC methodology, and a project management methodology.

Organization Essentials

- Recognize that top managers in the central organization focus on administration and budgetary controls and the organizational strategy.
- Know that the departments and agencies within government organizations operate largely independently because they are highly specialized with different goals and objectives with different business strategies.
- Recognize the different business initiatives that drive changes to information systems.
- Understand the IT governance model on who has authority over information technology decisions rights.
- Be aware of the economies of scope, breadth of diversification, and commonalities as drivers to IT centralization or decentralization.
- Recognize that some department heads are elected officials who have authority over their department or agency, budgets, the daily operations, and the information systems projects and priorities.
- Be aware of the importance of organization information technology standards and policies that are established at the top organization level through collaborative decision making are beneficial to the organization as a whole.
- Recognize that the top-level officials, the CEO, CIO, and department heads, who work together collaborate to support others in achieving the business strategies of the organization, avoid managers being caught in middle space with conflicting agendas.
- Be aware of the nature of the political environment and its influence on project decisions.

Project Manager Essentials

- Stay up-to-date with technology through education, professional and technical certifications, and professional training or development courses. Technology evolves constantly, and competent IT/IS managers and project managers know how to use the technology to support the business to provide different ways of doing business for improving an organization's performance.
- Promote awareness of the organization's strategic grid by educating business managers involved in IS decisions and others about the different categories of information systems that are strategic systems that focus on the primary business and those that are support systems.
- Be knowledgeable about the skills needed for information systems project management.
- Focus on a project management methodology (approach) and the ten critical success factors outlined in research studies.
- Acknowledge that project success is measured by three different measures as identified in the research study included in the previous chapters.
- Learn the different type of leadership styles of transformational, transactional, and laissez-faire leaders and work toward being a transformational leader.

Human Significance Essentials

- Be aware of the issues of centralization versus decentralization, the IT governance model, and who has authority over IT decisions rights.
- If you work in middle space, work on developing peer relationships for positive, long-lasting experiences. Learn to integrate with others for strong peer relationships and communication. Try to find a role model or mentor and a sponsor.
- If you are in middle space longer than you should be, work on your own individual goals and plan for moving out of middle space. Find peers who are coaches and cheerleaders that provide you the support you will need when working in the field of information systems.
- Make changes by working on those things you have control over and promote making changes from the middle up and from the middle down.
- Consider the choices you can make for moving vertically or horizontally in your career. Consider working outside of the organization.

Remember Lee, the IT manager described in Chapter 2? The following is my response to the problems he is encountering.

It is obvious that he is caught in middle space. Lee needs to develop strong peer relationships. Unless there are changes at the top level within the organization and within the department, he will be constantly faced with challenges. Lee's position as an IT manager needs to be placed at the top level of the department reporting to the department head instead of reporting to the assistant department head. This will give him more authority and he will be able to participate in the strategic decisions with other senior-level managers. Lee needs to be able to communicate with other managers on IT decisions within his department. A collaborated approach to IT standards and policies and a clearly defined IT governance model on who has authority over specific IT decisions will help reduce conflicting agendas and no shared vision within the organization.

It is important for Lee to work on implementing changes for the things he does have control over like portfolio management within the department and communicate the importance of the business strategy, being supported by the organizational strategy and information systems strategy. Lee and his technical staff need to have control over developing preliminary project plans for all major information system projects before starting work on project estimates or even starting work on a project plan. It is important that the department adopts a project planning methodology and SDLC methodology, focus on the ten critical success factors for project management, and evaluate project implementation success.

The primary business of government departments and agencies are its programs, products, and services. Central administration, budgetary controls, human resources, technology, supply services, finance, and accounting are support services. All of these functions contribute to improving organizational performance. The distribution of authority in the political environment of government organizations can create different kinds of challenges for IT managers and project managers.

The sense of urgency can be detrimental to project estimation and impact the project completion data and project costs. This can be a contributing factor to some projects going over budget. Lee as an IT manager and an expert in technology and information systems management should be communicating what needs to be accomplished in order to provide accurate estimates.

If you are caught in middle space and you are in the middle longer than you should be, start reflecting back on where you are, where you want to be in the future, and start making plans for taking steps forward to enhance your own skills, abilities, leadership style, and building your relationships with others.

It is my hope that you do not go at it alone. It is important to build strong peer relationships and integrate with your peers. Being in middle space can be a challenge, but nobody said that you have to be by yourself and be isolated from others in the process. You do not have to be alone.

A few years ago, one of the students in my university class was working and managing information systems projects, married and raising children, and going to school in the evenings. He said it was really difficult and he felt pulled between his job, family obligations, and the desire to improve himself for career advancement. He was in middle space without really knowing it—by being pulled between the tops in his job, the bottom with his family obligations, and sideways from his own desire to get his degree to increase his flexibility to move forward in his career. Many students are faced with this same situation.

I told him that if he takes one course each term, it will take him longer to complete all of the courses but he is one course closer to getting his degree or reaching his goal than if he did nothing at all. Many courses can now be taken online by participating in an online classroom instead of going to a physical campus. He said that he could manage one course using this approach and occasionally take two courses. He actually came up with his own plan and eventually completed all his courses and started work on his project management certification.

Many times you have to take small incremental steps to accomplish really big things. The most important point for you to remember is to develop your own plan. You may want to obtain a technical or professional certification, obtain a college degree, or complete professional development courses or technical training or even want to start your own business. Just remember that these are your goals and it is your own plan. You decide what you need to do and how you are going to do it. You can customize it and revise it to fit your own personal needs. Ask yourself the following questions:

- Where are you now?
  Evaluate the situation.
- Where do you want to be in the near future?
  Define your vision.
- How are you going to get there?
  Plan the path that you are going to take to achieve your goals.
- How would you know it if you got there?
  You experience less tension, less stress, develop more friendships, have real empowerment, and other feelings of well-being and accomplishments.
- How are you going to celebrate your achievements?
  Plan a luncheon or a dinner or other types of outings or events.
- Who and what can help you get there?
  Build strong networks and relationships with peers, peer groups, friends, and find other resources.

You Can Make a Difference

How do you view your success? You can make a difference by being in a position that will impact your environment in a positive way. You do not have to be a famous person or leader. Success is not always about making huge salaries. You can make a difference by implementing projects that help the organization fulfill its business strategy with successful information systems projects. You can make a difference by being a transformational leader and making others feel they are valued members of the team or work group. You can make a difference by positively affecting the organization and the people who work within it. You can make a difference by having positive peer relationships. You can make a difference by helping others achieve their goals. You can make a difference by balancing your work and your home life. You can make a difference by establishing your own career and educational plans and making the necessary adjustments along the way. All of these are opportunities that you can take advantage of in your life.

Reaching the top as not always tied to your job title in an organization with a higher paying salary. For many people, the amount of money they make indicates how much an organization values them as an employee, but a job is more than a paycheck. Obviously, no one likes the feeling of disempowerment; gender equally is important. Women should be paid the same salary as men for the same job. It is true that everybody wants to be able to make a good living; not worry whether they have enough money left over after they pay the bills; and would like to have some money for other things such as vacations, entertainment, savings, investments, and give to charity. There is a difference between basic human needs and wants. We need food, water, shelter, clothing, medical care when we are sick, and a feeling of belonging to survive. Many individuals I talk to say they enjoy what they are doing and if their salary increases because of it that is a good thing. They try to make time for themselves and their personal life.

There are some opportunities that come your way and you may turn it down and you may not ever get that opportunity again. It is important to think about where you want to be in life and what you want to accomplish, take advantage of opportunities, and work on getting there, but be considerate of others along the way. Success is about handling both your accomplishments and disappointments in a positive way and doing your best. You may have worked in many challenging positions and environments. Take time to view the organizational system of tops, middles, belows, and the clients and general citizens the organization serves. Do not focus on fixing people, but learn how to work on the things you can lead and change both at work and in your personal education and professional development. It is important to think about organizational system spaces. You may never be able to fix people but you can work on changing how you view things.

Summary

The chapter summarizes the essentials of good management practices and managing middle space based on the information from the previous chapters in the book. The forces of change, shared visions, portfolio management, the information systems strategic grid, the IT governance model, the project plan, detailed project plans, change control procedures, ten critical success factors, and making choices are some important concepts. Education, continued growth, and professional development are important for information systems professionals and project managers. A network of peer support is important to managers working in middle space. There is a need to find different types of peers: a mentor, coach, best friend, younger person, older person, celebrator, optimist, and spiritual person. It is important to develop your own career plans and learn to make your own choices. You may find it beneficial to get support from organizations like the Project Management Institute or other types of local or national professional management organizations.

Review Concepts

The chapter gives a summary of the following areas:

- Manager concepts and principles
- Project essentials
- Organizational essentials
- Project manager essentials
- Human significance essentials

Discussion Questions

11.1. Discuss whether you feel you are working in middle space and why.
11.2. Where are you now in your career position as a project manager or as a leader?
11.3. Where do you want to be in the future?
11.4. Discuss whether you think it is important to have peer relationships.
11.5. What type of peer relationships do you have now or want to have?
11.6. If you were to start on developing your own career plan, what would you include in it?

Appendix A

Request for Proposal (RFP)
Table of Contents

REQUEST FOR PROPOSAL

TABLE OF CONTENTS

5.2.1 English and Spanish Language Messages
5.2.2 Hardware
5.2.3 Software
5.2.4 Reports

Appendix B

Contractual Agreement
Table of Contents

ABC DEPARTMENT
CONTRACTUAL AGREEMENT

TABLE OF CONTENTS

BIBLIOGRAPHY

About us. (2013). *Project Management Institute—PMI.org.* Retrieved from http://www.pmi.org/About-Us.aspx

Ahadi, H. R. (2004). An examination of the role of organizational enablers in business process reengineering and the impact of information technology. *Information Resources Management Journal, 17*(4), 1.

Ahituv, N., Neumann, S., & Riley, N. H. (1994). *Principles of information systems management.* Dubuque, IA: Business and Educational Technologies.

Amescua, Antonio de, Garcia, J., Velasco, M., Martinez, P., Ruiz, B., Llorens, J., Garcia L., Calvo-Manzano, A., & San Feliu, T. (2004). A software project management framework. *Information Systems Management, 21*(2), 78.

Austin, C. J., & Boxerman, S. B. (1998). *Information systems for health services administration* (5th ed.). Chicago, IL: Health Administration Press.

Avolio, B. J., & Bass, B. M. (2004). *Multifactor leadership questionnaire: Third edition manual and sampler set.* Menlo Park, CA: Mind Garden.

Bajaj, C., & Bajaj, N. (2010). Business networks to design and market information technology products and solutions for organizations. *Global Management Review, 4*(3), 84–92.

Barki, H., & Hartwick, J. (2001). Interpersonal conflict and its management in information system development. *MIS Quarterly, 25*(2), 195–228.

Baruto, J. E., Jr., & Burbach, M. E. (2006). The emotional intelligence of transformational leaders: A field study of elected officials. *Journal of Social Psychology, 146*, 51–64.

Bass, B. M. (1990). From transactional to transformational leadership: Learning to share the vision. *Organizational Dynamics, 18*(3), 19–31.

Bass, B. M. (1999). Two decades of research and development in transformational leadership. *European Journal of Work & Organizational Psychology, 8*(1), 9–32.

Bass, B. M., & Avolio, B. J. (1993). Transformational leadership and organizational culture. *Public Administration Quarterly, 17*(1), 112.

Bass, B. M., & Avolio, B. J. (1994). *Multifactor leadership questionnaire (On-line) Abstract from Buros Institute of Mental Measurements.* Retrieved from http://www.mindgarden.com/products/mlq.htm

Batchelor, D. (2012). *Caveman theology.* Sacramento, CA: Mountain Ministry.

Belout, A., & Gauvreau, C. (2004). Factors influencing project success: The impact of human resource management. *International Journal of Project Management, 22*(1), 1.

Benton, J. E. (2002). County service delivery: Does government structure matter? *Public Administration Review, 62*(4), 471–479.

Benton, J. E. (2007). Conducting research on counties in the 21st century: A new agenda and database considerations. *Public Administration Review, 67*(6), 968.

Benton, J. E., Byers, J., Cigler, B. A., Klase, K. A., Menzel, D. C., Salant, T. J., Streib, G., Svara, J. H., & Waugh, Jr., W. L. (2007). Conducting research on counties in the 21st century: A new agenda and database considerations. *Public Administration Review, 67*(6), 968.

Bhatt, G. D., & Troutt, M. D. (2005). Examining the relationship between business process improvement initiatives, information systems integration and customer focus: An empirical study. *Business Process Management Journal, 11*(5), 532.

Booth, M., & Philip, G. (2005). Information systems management: Role of planning, alignment and leadership. *Behaviour & Information Technology, 24*(5), 391–404. doi: 10.1080/01449290512331335582

Brumfield, P. F., Newell, J. A., & Gordon, M. R. (2006). Coming to a screen near you—"eMortgages"—Starring good laws and prudent standards-rated "XML." *Business Lawyer, 62*(1), 295.

Bryant, L., Jones, D. A., & Widener, S. K. (2004). Managing value creation within the firm: An examination of multiple performance measures. *Journal of Management Accounting Research, 16*, 107–131.

Bryde, D. J. (2003). Project management concepts, methods and application. *International Journal of Operations & Production Management, 23*(7/8), 775.

Byars, L. L. (1991). *Strategic management: Formulation and implementation, concepts and cases.* New York, NY: HarperCollins.

Byrne, R. (1996). *The 2,548 best things anybody ever said.* New York, NY: Galahad Books.

Cats-Baril, W., & Thompson, R. (1995). Managing information technology projects in the public sector. *Public Administration Review, 55*(6), 559–566.

Caudle, S. L., Gorr, W. L., & Newcomer, K. E. (1991). Key information systems management issues for the public sector. *MIS Quarterly, 15*(2), 171.

Chan, Y. C. L. (2004). Performance measurement and adoption of balanced scorecard: A survey of municipal governments in the USA and Canada. *International Journal of Public Sector Management, 17*(2/3), 204.

Christensen, M. J., & Thayer, R. H. (2001). *The project manager's guide to software engineering's best practices.* Los Alamitos, CA: IEEE Computer Society.

Coursey, D., & Norris, D. F. (2008). Models of e-government: Are they correct? An empirical assessment. *Public Administration Review, 68*(3), 523.

Daniel, E., & Ward, J. (2006). Integrated service delivery: Exploratory case studies of enterprise portal adoption in UK local government. *Business Process Management Journal, 12*(1), 113.

Dennis, A., & Wixom, B. H. (2003). *Systems analysis design* (2nd ed.). New York, NY: John Wiley & Sons.

Doke, E. R., & Barrier, T. (1994). An assessment of information systems taxonomies: Time to be re-evaluate? *Journal of Information Technology, 9*, 149–157.

Dufner, D., Holley, L. M., & Reed, B. J. (2002). Can private sector strategic information systems planning techniques work for the public sector? *Communications of the Association of Information Systems, 8*(28), 413–431. Retrieved from http://aisel.aisnet.org/cais/vol8/iss1/28/

Eman, E. E., & Koru, A. G. (2008). A replicated survey of IT software project failures. *IEEE Software, 25*(5), 84.

Ewan, D. E., & Ladd, M. (2008). Race to the (virtual) courthouse: How standards drive electronic recording of real property documents. *Probate and Property*, *22*(1), 8.

Federal, State, and Local Governments (2012). *U.S. Census Bureau*. Retrieved from http://www.census.gov/govs/

Finch, P. (2003). Applying the Slevin-Pinto project implementation profile to an information systems project. *Project Management Journal*, *34*(3), 32.

Fisher, S. A. (2013). *Significant Factors in Securing Leadership Positions for Women in the Information Technology Organizations*. Unpublished D.B.A., Argosy University, Orange, CA.

Flak, L. S., & Rose, J. (2005). Stakeholder governance: Adapting stakeholder theory to e-government. *Communications of AIS*, *2005*(16), 642–664.

Gray, P., & Watson, H. J. (1998). *Decision support in the data warehouse*. Upper Saddle Back River, NJ: Prentice Hall PTR.

Groth, D. P., & Mackie-Mason, J. K. (2010). Education Why an informatics degree? *Communications of the ACM*, *53*(2), 26–28.

Grover, V., Jeong, S.R., Kettinger, W. J., & Lee, C. C. (1993). The chief information officer: A study of managerial roles. *Journal of Management Information Systems*, *10*(2), 107–130.

Haag, S., Cummings, M., & Phillips, A. (2007). *Management information systems for the information age* (6th ed.). New York, NY: McGraw-Hill/Irwin.

Haung, Z. (2007). A comprehensive analysis of U.S. counties' e-Government portals: Development status and functionalities. *European Journal of Information Systems*, *16*(2), 149.

Henderson, L. S. (2008). The impact of project managers' communication competencies: Validation and extension of a research model for virtuality, satisfaction, and productivity on project teams. *Project Management Journal*, *39*(2), 48.

Hillier, F. S., & Hillier, M. S. (2003). *Introduction to management science: A modeling and case studies approach with spreadsheets*. New York, NY: McGraw-Hill.

Hoffer, J. A., George, J. F., & Valacich, J. S. (2008). *Modern systems analysis and design* (5th ed.). New Jersey, NJ: Pearson Prentice Hall.

Housel, T. J., & Skopec, E. W. (2001). *Global telecommunications revolution: The business perspective* New York: McGraw-Hill/Irwin.

Huff, R. A., & Prybutok, V. R. (2008). Information systems project management decision making: The influence of experience and risk propensity. *Project Management Journal*, *39*(2), 34.

Janssen, M., & Kuk, G. (2007). E-government business models for public service networks. *International Journal of Electronic Government Research*, *3*(3), 54.

Jeffery, M., & Leliveld, I. (2004). Best practices in IT portfolio management. *MIT Sloan Management Review*, *45*(3), 41–49.

Jick, T. D., & Peiperl, M. A. (2003). *Managing change cases and concepts* (2nd ed.). New York, NY: McGraw-Hill.

Johnson, A. M., & Lederer, A. L. (2007). The impact of communication between CEOs and CIOs on their shared views of the current and future role of IT. *Information Systems Management*, *24*(1), 85(86).

Riedel, G., Rotenberg, M., Rappaport, D. (Producers), & Judge, M. (Writer/Director). (1999). Office Space [Motion picture]. United States: 20th Century Fox.

Julnes, P. d. L., & Holzer, M. (2001). Promoting the utilization of performance measures in public organizations: An empirical study of factors affecting adoption and implementation. *Public Administration Review, 61*(6), 693.

Kaplan, R. S., & Norton, D. R. (2005). The balanced scorecard: Measures that drive performance. (cover story). *Harvard Business Review, 83*(7/8), 172–180.

Ke, W., & Wei, K. K. (2006). Understanding e-government project management: A positivist case study of Singapore. *Journal of Global Information Technology Management, 9*(2), 45.

Kearns, G. S. (2007). How the internal environment impacts information systems project success: An investigation of exploitative and explorative firms. *Journal of Computer Information Systems, 48*(1), 63.

Keil, M., & Tiwana, A. (2005). Beyond cost: The drivers of COTS application value. *IEEE Software, 22*(3), 64–69.

Kemp, E. J., Jr., Funk, R. J., & Eadie, D. C. (1993). Change in chewable bites: Applying strategic management at EEOC. *Public Administration Review, 53*(2), 129–134.

Kerzner, H. (2003). *Project management: A systems approach to planning, scheduling, and controlling* (8th ed.). New Jersey, NJ: Wiley and Sons.

Lam, W. (2005). Barriers to e-government integration. *Journal of Enterprise Information Management, 18*(5/6), 511.

Lawlis, P. K., Mark, K. E., Thomas, D. A., & Courtheyn, T. (2001). A formal process for evaluating COTS software products. *Computer, 34*(5), 58.

Lim, E. T. K., Tan, C.-W., & Pan, S.-L. (2007). E-Government implementation: Balancing collaboration and control in stakeholder management. *International Journal of Electronic Government Research, 3*(2), 1.

Lundell, B., & Lings, B. (2004). Method in action and method in tool: A stakeholder perspective. *Journal of Information Technology, 19*, 215–223

Mantel, S. J., Jr., Meredith, J. R., Shafer, S. M., & Sutton, M. M. (2005). *Core concepts of project management* (2nd ed.). Hoboken, NJ: John Wiley & Sons, Inc.

Mantel, S. J., Jr., Meredith, J. R., Shafer, S. M., & Sutton, M. M. (2010). *Project management by practice.* Hoboken, NJ: John Wiley & Sons, Inc.

Markus, M. L., Steinfield, C. W., & Wigand, R. T. (2005). *The evolution of vertical IS standards: Electronic interchange standards in the U.S. home mortgage industry.* Paper presented at the MISQ Workshop. Retrieved from http://www.si.umich.edu/index.htm

Markus, M. L., Steinfield, C. W., Wigand, R. T., & Minton, G. (2006). Industrywide information systems standardization as collective action: The case of the U.S. residential mortgage industry. *MIS Quarterly, 30*, 439.

Melkers, J., & Willoughby, K. (2005). Models of performance-measurement use in local governments: Understanding budgeting, communication, and lasting effects. *Public Administration Review, 65*(2), 180–190.

Melville, N., Kraemer, K., & Gurbaxani, V. (2004). Review: Information technology and organizational performance: An integrative model of IT business value. *MIS Quarterly, 28*(2), 283–322.

Meredith, J. R., & Mantel, S. J., Jr. (1995). *Project management: A managerial approach* (3rd ed.). New York, NY: Wiley & Sons.

Miller, D. L., & Thomas, S. (2005). The impact of relative position and relational closeness on the reporting of unethical acts. *Journal of Business Ethics, 61*(4), 315.

Moncur, L. (2013). Laura Moncur's motivation quotations [Electronic Version]. Retrieved from http://www.quotationspace.com/quote/2235.html

Moon, M. J. (2002). The evolution of E-government among municipalities: Rhetoric or reality? *Public Administration Review, 62*(4), 424.

Morris, M. G., & Venkatesh, V. (2010). Job characteristics and job satisfaction: Understanding the role of enterprise resource planning system implementation. *MIS Quarterly, 34*(1), 143–161.

Moynihan, D. P. (2004). Building secure elections: e-Voting, security, and systems theory. *Public Administration Review, 64*(5), 515.

NACO. (2013). Overview of county government. Retrieved from National Association of Counties http://www.naco.rog./Counties/Pages/Overview.aspx

Nelson, Z., & Gentry, J. (2005). Face-off: Should your company replace its legacy systems? *Network World, 22*(16).

Ng, C. H., & Walker, D. H. T. (2008). A study of project management leadership styles across life cycle stages of an IT project in Hong Kong. *International Journal of Managing Projects in Business, 1*(3), 404.

Ngai, E. W. T., & Gunasekaran, A. (2004). Implementation of EDI in Hong Kong: An empirical analysis. *Industrial Management + Data Systems, 104*(1/2), 88.

Number of electronic-recording counties tops 400 [Electronic (2009). Version]. *Mortgage Banking, 69*, 78.

Orfali, R., Harkey, D., & Edwards, J. (1999). *Client/Server survival guide* (3rd ed.). New York, NY: John Wiley & Sons.

Oshry, B. (2003). Managing in the middle. *Management Executive Forum Series.* Retrieved from http://www.executiveforum.com/PDFs/oshry_synopsis.pdf

Parris, M. A., Vickers, M. H., & Wilkes, L. (2008). Friendships under strain: The work-personal life integration of middle managers. *Community, Work & Family, 11*(4). doi: 10.1080/13668800802361831

Pearlson, K. E., & Saunders, C. S. (2006). *Managing and using information systems: A strategic approach* (3rd ed.). New Jersey, NJ: Wiley & Sons.

Peppard, J., Ward, J., & Daniel, E. (2007). Managing the realization of business benefits for IT investments. *MIS Quarterly, 6*(1), 1–11. Retrieved from http://www.misrc.umn.edu/publications/misqe

Peterson, R. (2004). Crafting information technology governance. *Information Systems Management, 21*(4), 7–22.

Phillips, J. T. (2001). XML for content and e-commerce. *Information Management Journal, 35*(2), 54.

Pinto, J. K. (1986). *Project implementation: A determination of its critical success factors, moderators, and their relative importance across the project life cycle.* Unpublished PhD, University of Pittsburgh, United States, Pennsylvania.

Pinto, J. K., & Kharbanda, O. P. (1996). How to fail in project management (without really trying). *Business Horizons, 39*(4), 45.

Pinto, J. K., & Mantel, S. J., Jr. (1990). The causes of project failure. *IEEE Transactions on Engineering Management, 37*(4), 269.

Pinto, J. K., & Prescott, J. E. (1988). Variations in critical success factors over the stages in the project life cycle. *Journal of Management, 14*(1), 5.

Pinto, J. K., & Prescott, J. E. (1990). Planning and tactical factors in the project implementation process. *Journal of Management Studies, 27*(3), 305–327.

Pinto, J. K., & Slevin, D. P. (1987). Critical factors in successful project implementation. *IEEE Transactions on Engineering Management, EM34*(1), 22.

Pinto, J. K., & Slevin, D. P. (1988). Project success: Definitions and measurement techniques. *Project Management Journal, 19*(1). Retrieved from http://www.pmi.org/

Pinto, J. K., & Slevin, D. P. (1992). Project implementation profile (PIP). *Mental Measurements Yearbook, 13.*

PMI (2013). *A guide to the project management body of knowledge* (5th ed.). Newton Square, PA: USA Project Management Institute.

Power, D. (2005). Determinants of business-to-business e-commerce implementation and performance: A structural model. *Supply Chain Management, 10*(2), 96.

Reich, B. H., & Benbasat, I. (2000). Factors that influence the social dimension of alignment between business and information technology objectives. *MIS Quarterly, 24*(1), 81.

Rosacker, K. M. (2005). *Managing information systems projects within state government: Factors critical for successful implementation.* Unpublished PhD, The University of Nebraska, Lincoln, United States, Nebraska.

Rosacker, K. M., & Olson, D. L. (2008). Public sector information system critical success factors. *Transforming Government: People, Process and Policy, 2*(1), 60.

Sambamurthy, V., & Zmud, R. W. (1999). Arrangements for information technology governance: A theory of multiple contingencies. *MIS Quarterly, 23,* 261–290.

Sarantis, D., Smithson, S., Charalabidis, Y., & Askounis, D. (2010). A critical assessment of project management methods with respect to electronic government implementation challenges. *System Practice Action Research, 23,* 301–321. doi: 10.1007/sl1213–009–9161–9.

Scholl, H. J. (2004). Involving salient stakeholders: Beyond the technocratic view on change. *Action Research, 2*(3), 277–304.

Schultz, R. L., Slevin, D. P., & Pinto, J. K. (1987). Strategy and tactics in a process model of project implementation. *Interfaces, 17*(3), 34–46.

Sonde, T. (2008). Is your ERP system still falling short? *Financial Executive, 24,* 52–55.

Steinfield, C. W., Markus, M. L., & Wigand, R. T. (2005). Exploring interorganizational systems at the industry level of analysis: Evidence from the US home mortgage industry. *Journal of Information Technology, 20*(4), 224.

Stevens, B. (2004). The ethics of the US business executive: A study of perceptions. *Journal of Business Ethics,* 163–171.

Sumner, M., Bock, D., & Giamartino, G. (2006). Exploring the linkage between the characteristics of IT project leaders and project success. *Information Systems Management, 23*(4), 43–49.

Turner, J. R., & Müller, R. (2005). The project manager's leadership style as a success factor on projects: A literature review. *Project Management Journal, 36*(2), 49.

Van den Berg, P. T., & Wilderom, C. P. M. (2004). Defining, measuring, and comparing organisational cultures. *Applied Psychology: An International Review, 53*(4), 570–582.

Vangen, S., & Huxham, C. (2003). Nurturing collaborative relations: Building trust in interorganizational collaboration. *Journal of Applied Behavioral Science, 39*(1), 5.

Walsh, K. R. (2003). Analyzing the application ASP concept: Technologies, economies, and strategies. *Association for Computing Machinery. Communications of the ACM, 46*(8), 103.

Wang, X., & Berman, E. (2001). Hypotheses about performance measurement in counties: Findings from a survey. *Journal of Public Administration Research and Theory, 11*(3), 403.

Ward, M. A. (2006). Information systems technologies: A public-private sector comparison. *Journal of Computer Information Systems, 46*(3), 50.

Weill, P., & Ross, J. (2005). A matrixed approach to designing IT governance. *MIT Sloan Management Review, 46*(2), 26–29.

Wen, H. J., & Stephen, C. S. (2006). Strategic information technology prioritization. *Journal of Computer Information Systems, 46*(4), 54.

Wigand, R. T., Steinfield, C. W., & Markus, M. L. (2005). Information technology standards choices and industry structure outcomes: The case of the U.S. home mortgage industry. *Journal of Management Information Systems, 22*(2), 165–191.

Yates, J. C., & Arne, P. H. (2004). Balancing the scales: Managing risks in IT projects. *The Computer & Internet Lawyer, 21*(8), 1–7.

INDEX

Printed and bound in the United States of America